Entrepreneurial President

The publisher gratefully acknowledges the generous support of the General Endowment Fund of the University of California Press Foundation.

Entrepreneurial President

Richard Atkinson and the
University of California, 1995–2003

———

Patricia A. Pelfrey

UNIVERSITY OF CALIFORNIA PRESS
Berkeley Los Angeles London

University of California Press, one of the most distinguished university presses in the United States, enriches lives around the world by advancing scholarship in the humanities, social sciences, and natural sciences. Its activities are supported by the UC Press Foundation and by philanthropic contributions from individuals and institutions. For more information, visit www.ucpress.edu.

University of California Press
Berkeley and Los Angeles, California

University of California Press, Ltd.
London, England

Library of Congress Cataloging-in-Publication Data

Pelfrey, Patricia A.
    Entrepreneurial President : Richard Atkinson and the University of California, 1995–2003 / Patricia A. Pelfrey.
        p.   cm.
    ISBN 978-0-520-27080-0 (hardback)
    1. Atkinson, Richard C.   2. University of California (System)—President—Biography.   3. University of California (System)—History.   4. University of California (System)—Management.   5. Nuclear energy—Research—Laboratories—Management.   I. Title.
    LD755.A87P45   2012
    378.0092—dc23
    [B]

                                            2011042080

Manufactured in the United States of America

20   19   18   17   16   15   14   13   12
10   9   8   7   6   5   4   3   2   1

In keeping with a commitment to support environmentally responsible and sustainable printing practices, UC Press has printed this book on Rolland Enviro100, a 100% post-consumer fiber paper that is FSC certified, deinked, processed chlorine-free, and manufactured with renewable biogas energy. It is acid-free and EcoLogo certified.

CONTENTS

Foreword by Karl S. Pister   *vii*

About This Book   *xiii*

1. The Evolution of a Crisis   *1*

2. The Education of a Chancellor   *15*

3. Who Runs the University?   *38*

4. Seventeenth President   *54*

5. A Problem in Search of a Solution   *69*

6. "A More Inclusive Definition of Merit"   *86*

7. Reinventing the Economy   *100*

8. An Idea and Its Consequences   *115*

9. History's Coils: The Nuclear Weapons Laboratories   *139*

10. Presidents and Chancellors   *156*

11. Epilogue: One University   *161*

Appendix 1. Regents' Resolutions SP-1, SP-2, and RE-28   *173*

Appendix 2. Atkinson Presidency Timeline   *177*

Appendix 3. University of California Indicators, 1995–2003   *186*

Notes   *189*

Select Bibliography   *209*

Index   *215*

FOREWORD

I was delighted to be asked by the author to prepare a foreword for her book—a story focused on milestone events in the history of the University of California coinciding with the tenure of its seventeenth president, Richard C. Atkinson. While this period represents only 6 percent of the University's history, its temporal place in the history of our nation and the state of California gives it particular significance. *Entrepreneurial President* is a story about a university in which I have spent virtually my entire adult life—as student, faculty member, and academic administrator—and about a man, colleague, and friend for whom I have unmatched respect and admiration. I entered Berkeley as a seventeen-year-old freshman in 1942. Nearly seven decades later, now a triple emeritus at Berkeley, the opportunity to read Patricia Pelfrey's book brought a special pleasure. I have had the opportunity to know and in a variety of different capacities to work or be associated with the last nine presidents of the University. It is from this perspective that I write this foreword.

While there is a major focus on the Atkinson presidency—the man himself, the people inside and outside the University with whom he was engaged, and the trials and tribulations he experienced and largely effectively dispatched—there is much more to be found in this book. Pelfrey discusses three major issues—the University's transition to the post–affirmative action age; the expansion of its research enterprise; the controversy over its management of the Los Alamos and Livermore National Laboratories—always placing them in the larger historical context in which the University evolved. And, for the University of California, there is no shortage of complexity in this context.

Within the University one must number Regents, faculty, staff, students, and academic administrators as well as alumni. Outside the University are elected officials at all levels, business leaders, and members of the general public. Each of these groups has a tendency to view the president and his actions from a less than broad perspective. Pelfrey's thirty-two years in the Office of the President—during which time she was challenged to work closely with five presidents of widely differing personalities and styles—afford both a level and a breadth of understanding of everyday life in the Office of the President (UCOP) that few if any possess.

The story begins with what might be called the initial conditions that defined a significant part of the evolution of policy and practice in the University through Atkinson's tenure: the Regents' adoption of Resolutions SP-1 and SP-2, ending the use of gender, racial, and ethnic preferences in admissions and employment. The oft-quoted remarks of President Daniel Coit Gilman at his inauguration define the issue that consumed the Regents for many months and remain equally challenging today: "It is the University of this State. It must be adapted to this people, to their public and private schools, to their peculiar geographic position, to the requirements of their new society and their undeveloped resources. . . . It is 'of the people and for the people.'" Striving to answer the question Who are the people? is a theme found throughout this book.

In January 1995 President Jack Peltason announced his intention to retire the following October. This set off a search process by the Regents marked by the withdrawal of the first choice amid a flurry of bad publicity and a contentious sequel of events surrounding adoption of the two anti–affirmative action resolutions. A divided Board of Regents and an unhappy faculty and student body greeted Richard Atkinson when he assumed the presidency on October 1, 1995. As a very young man Dick Atkinson was shaped by the liberal education he acquired at the University of Chicago in the styles of Robert Maynard Hutchins and Mortimer Adler. His graduate work in experimental psychology, strengthened by his passion for and knowledge of mathematics and statistics, led him to Stanford, where he met and was impressed by the dean of engineering, Fred Terman. Two subsequent appointments—as director of the National Science Foundation and as chancellor at UC San Diego—played an important role in defining the character of Atkinson's presidential style and his approach to dealing with the three issues that are the focus of this book.

Atkinson was a man of action who expected the same from his staff. Having known and worked closely with him over a period of three decades, I would add that the intellect of this "man of action" was off-scale among colleagues in the academic world. In conversations I frequently found him completing my sentences and urging me to go on with my business. The knowledge he acquired in fifteen years as chancellor at San Diego, coupled with his record of scholarship and his knowledge of the byzantine concept of shared governance in the University, assured his position with the faculty and his fellow chancellors.

The passage of resolutions SP-1 and SP-2 during the final months in office of Atkinson's predecessor placed the new president in command of a ship whose crew showed signs of mutiny and whose owners were divided, riding in storm-tossed waters of politics. Pelfrey carefully leads the reader through this perilous journey with remarkable understanding and attention to detail. As a ship's officer during this voyage, I can attest to the events and their significance. Although the change in admissions policy dictated by the passage of SP-1 was a matter of record, its effective date was unrealistic in terms of the University's admissions calendar. The president's decision, through a series of events, some accidental and some intentional, came close to ending his tenure at an early date. The author carefully documents the resulting tension over the issue of presidential authority with respect to the Board of Regents. This is done in the context of the additional dispute that placed many faculty members at odds with the board over the matter of shared governance, namely, the Academic Senate's delegated authority to recommend the conditions for admission. That the University survived this extremely destructive period in its history is a testament to the quality and commitment to its mission of the people who serve it.

One can view a student's educational preparation for entrance to a university as consisting of traversing a pathway to an admissions gate and then successfully passing through the gate. The Regents' action changed the passage criteria but left the pathway untouched. Pelfrey explores the efforts to mitigate the serious impact of their action on educationally disadvantaged students in California, including engagement of UC campuses with neighboring K–12 schools serving these students.

With regard to the gate to admission, for decades the SAT I and SAT II had been considered the gold standard for measuring the probability of success of entering students. Atkinson's scholarly work as a social scientist led him to question the validity of this claim. Here the author traces the many disparate constituencies that weighed in on his proposal to drop the SAT I as a requirement for admission to UC. That he was successful in gaining faculty approval for his plan (here he was uncharacteristically out in front of the faculty) and forcing the College Board to develop a different kind of SAT, SAT-R, is a notable tribute to his scholarship as well as his interpersonal and administrative skills.

The twenty-three years that marked Atkinson's active role in the University as chancellor and president carry a common thread that informed his understanding of and vision for its mission. It was spun from the earlier association with Fred Terman at Stanford, where he experienced the power of Terman's model of university-industry collaboration. During his directorship of the National Science Foundation, the powerful thinking of Vannevar Bush was instrumental in further shaping his views. He brought this perspective to UC San Diego as chancellor in 1980. In a short time he established UCSD CONNECT, a highly successful model for translating the results of research into commercial products. The author's description of this phase of his career reads like a handbook for aspiring new research university presidents. The zenith of this vision of collaboration was reached in Atkinson's compact with Governor Gray Davis to establish and gain capital funding for four UC-run California Institutes for Science and Innovation, whose purpose is to foster interdisciplinary and collaborative research with industry to enhance technology transfer and commercialization. Whether as chancellor or president, although a social scientist by education, Dick Atkinson thought and acted with the pragmatism of an engineer or scientist—a rare exception in the experience of this writer.

Although created by the University and "managed" by it at the request of the federal government until recent years, the two defense laboratories at Livermore and Los Alamos have brought both fame and a wide range of challenging problems, internal as well as external. Along with Nobel Prizes for a number of its scientists, disruptive protests at Livermore and at the Office of the President have occurred. I placed "managed" in quotation marks to emphasize the often-conflicting roles played by the UC Office of the President and the US Department of Energy in managing the affairs of the laboratories, not to mention the occasional shot over the bow from a member of Congress. Couple this with a recurring anxiety, often reaching hostility, on the part of a significant number of University faculty as to the appropriateness of the University's role in nuclear weapons design and development, and you have described the breadth of administrative headaches that UC presidents have experienced. The author explores the example of the notorious Wen Ho Lee case, in which the president of the University learned of the alleged security breaches and dismissal only a day or so before publication in the *New York Times*. A consequence of the Lee case was the termination of the sole-source contract to manage the laboratories and subsequent open competition. Today the University's role is limited to scientific management, and the future is uncertain.

Pelfrey concludes the book with an interesting historical account of the manner in which two presidents, Sproul and Kerr, understood the meaning of "one university," along with questions surrounding its contemporary meaning and importance in a prolonged era of failure of the state to provide a sufficient resource base for the successful operation of the University in pursuit of its mission. At the time of writing, this failure has reached a crisis level for the University. Pelfrey asks what new organizing idea if any could replace the one-university idea. It is likely to be an evolution of both the Sproul and the Kerr model, moving in the direction of greater, not less, campus autonomy in response to market forces as well as individual campus strengths and inclinations. Only time will tell what the "collection of ten research universities—a single but not a monolithic institution of ten campuses" will look like in the years to come.

Karl S. Pister
Chancellor Emeritus, UC Santa Cruz
Former Vice President—Educational Outreach, UC Office of the President
Dean and Roy W. Carlson Professor of Engineering Emeritus, UC Berkeley

ABOUT THIS BOOK

Although the idea for this book dates to my retirement from the University of California Office of the President in 2002, its real origin can be traced to spring 1970. I was a graduate student in the English department at Berkeley, looking for part-time work while I completed my Ph.D. on the English poet William Blake. The position I landed, at 10 percent time, was in the immediate office of UC President Charles J. Hitch, in those years located across the street from the Berkeley campus. I was handed a stack of books and articles the president was interested in but did not have time to read (an astonishing fact to me—a university job that left you with no time to read?). My assignment was to boil each down to no more than two pages. It was my introduction to Hitch, a quiet, reserved, cigar-smoking, ex–Oxford economist. Not that I saw much of him. It was only later, when I had left Blake behind and made a career of doing various kinds of writing and analysis for his successors—David S. Saxon, David P. Gardner, J. W. Peltason, and Richard Atkinson—that I had the chance to see up close what was required of the president of a public research university.

Every president and every administration offered plenty of opportunities to learn how judgments about compromise, consultation, politics, and—on more occasions than you might imagine—fundamental questions of value were intrinsic to the job. The Atkinson administration seemed to me especially rich in the last— issues involving questions of academic value whose resolution demanded the reconciliation of politics and principle in setting policy directions for the University. These years also seemed to suggest the culmination of some important trends in the University, among them changing attitudes toward affirmative action (whose transformation into a serious public conflict was predicted by President David

Gardner as far back as 1987), the growing enthusiasm for the entrepreneurial impulse, and the beginnings of a different view of the traditional role of the president. All of which attracted me to the challenge of writing this book.

I am not a detached observer of the people and events I describe. At the same time, my background has offered useful advantages: a familiarity with the organizational workings of the University, access to information and individuals I would not otherwise have had, and the opportunity to see how decisions are made and how issues evolve over a series of administrations. I hope these advantages will balance the inevitable limitations of my point of view.

Although this book contains considerable information about Richard Atkinson's education and professional life, it is neither a biography nor a comprehensive history of the Atkinson administration. Such a history would include events and topics that are not covered here, among them the founding of UC Merced, the University's first new campus in forty years, and the struggles of the University's five academic medical centers in the health care marketplace. Nor is it an attempt to reach a summary judgment about the place of the Atkinson presidency in the University's history; it is far too early for such an assessment.

My goal in this book is to lay out the landscape of the Atkinson years and to explain how the three main issues I discuss were seen at the time, how the president and other University leaders tried to deal with them, and why they remain important to the people of California. As Peter Schrag has written of California, if the emerging American society fails here, in the most optimistic and ambitious of states, it may not work anywhere else either.[1] Among public universities, UC has occupied a similar place in the national imagination as a paradigm of what is possible. "The twentieth century was a grand century for the cities of intellect," UC President Clark Kerr wrote in *The Uses of the University*. "The century, that golden century, is now past, never to be replicated."[2] Today's outlook for higher education, perhaps especially in California, is far from golden. If Kerr's prediction is right, and the University of California's extraordinary academic quality becomes a casualty of today's economic, political, and societal trends, the Atkinson administration, the last of the golden century, will mark the transition to an era of strikingly diminished expectations.

Kerr had a preternatural awareness of the perils inherent in serving at the top of a multicampus institution. This is one reason that I have used so many of his observations in this book—as a reminder of the risks and darker possibilities of leadership. Another is that Kerr was not only a masterful academic leader but also a president who outlived his presidency by more than three decades. He had ample opportunity to reflect on the complexities of the job, the intricacies of UC governance, and the University's prospects. He is therefore a voice to be heeded, especially in a book whose underlying theme is the role of the president in the University of California.

Working with five UC presidents for more than three decades persuaded me that university administration is a complex and sometimes undervalued art. It also convinced me that the effort to advance the cause of knowledge, even in a high-rise bureaucracy, is an admirable pursuit.

I am indebted to the many individuals who agreed to be interviewed and who gave me valuable information and insights about the issues I explore here. Everyone who read (and sometimes reread) draft chapters has my deep appreciation for careful criticism and excellent advice. My special thanks go to Bruce Darling, Saul Geiser, Pat Hayashi, Larry Hershman, James Holst, Wayne Kennedy, Jud King, Robert Kuckuck, Debora Obley, and Karl Pister. I benefited immeasurably from their extraordinary knowledge of the University of California and their generosity in sharing it with me. I also want to express my appreciation to my colleagues on the staff of the Office of the President. They have contributed a high and generally unheralded level of skill and dedication to the University and in many ways served as its institutional memory. During the writing of this book, Judy Peck of Records Management Services and Anne Shaw of the Office of the Secretary and Chief of Staff to the Regents were unfailingly patient and resourceful in handling my frequent requests for information and documentation relating to the Office of the President and the Board of Regents. And I am grateful to Judith Iglehart, whose 2007 doctoral dissertation on technology transfer at the University of California characterized Atkinson as "the entrepreneurial president" and thereby suggested the title for this book.[3]

My entire family—in particular, my brother, Bob, and nephews, David and Matthew—gave me wonderful encouragement and support. Darrilyn Peters and Paula Peters, generous and indispensable friends, helped me work my way around every obstacle. Betty Lou Bradshaw's fine critical judgment and insights into the challenge of organizing complex material improved this book in many ways.

Finally, my thanks and gratitude to the five University of California presidents with whom I worked during my time in the Office of the President and of course especially to President Emeritus Richard Atkinson. This book has been written with his cooperation and assistance, including his help in obtaining support from the Koret Foundation, which made it possible for me to carry out the necessary research for a work of this kind, involving more than sixty interviews and many visits to the archives of the Regents, the Office of the President, and the San Diego campus. Although Atkinson's insights, reactions, and critiques have been essential to this account—and especially in helping elucidate how he approached his presidency—the views expressed here are my responsibility. Any errors of omission or commission are my responsibility as well.

Patricia A. Pelfrey
Center for Studies in Higher Education
Berkeley, California

1

The Evolution of a Crisis

*For some reasons . . . it has been very difficult for the University commu-
nity to create, develop, and rally around a vision of the University for the
future—a vision that can be supported by all constituencies, faculty and staff,
students, Regents, State government and alumni.*

—UC PROVOST WALTER MASSEY, REMARKS TO THE REGENTS, JULY
21, 1995

THE END OF RACIAL PREFERENCES AT
THE UNIVERSITY OF CALIFORNIA

On July 20, 1995, the Board of Regents of the University of California rolled back
thirty years of history by abolishing the use of racial and ethnic preferences in
admissions and employment. The two resolutions approved by the board, SP-1 (on
admissions) and SP-2 (on employment and purchasing), passed by a narrow margin after a long and exhausting day of regental maneuvering and unsuccessful attempts at compromise. The vote itself was the culmination of eight divisive months
of discussion and debate about the merits of affirmative action. It was a decision
made against the advice of the president, the vice presidents, the systemwide Academic Senate, and the nine chancellors of the University. Given the glacial pace at
which universities change course, this was a reversal of extraordinary speed.

There were historical ironies in the Regents' action. The University of California had been among the first universities in the country to establish programs
to attract more minority and low-income students to its overwhelmingly white
student body. In the 1970s, when a white applicant, Allan Bakke, challenged an
affirmative action program at UC's Davis medical school, the University took the
case all the way to the US Supreme Court. The decision in *Regents of the University of California v. Bakke,* which held that race and ethnicity could be considered
as one factor among others in admission, set a new legal standard for the use of
preferences in American colleges and universities. UC's efforts over many years
to prepare and enroll talented minority students were undertaken at the urging
of both the Regents and the legislature, in recognition that California was on the

1

threshold of becoming the first mainland state to consist of a majority of minorities. With annual immigration in the hundreds of thousands from some sixty countries, California was already one of the most diverse societies on the planet. Its public university seemed the last place in which anyone would contemplate a sudden break with three decades of affirmative action.

Yet in fall 1994, when the topic of racial preferences first appeared on the Regents' agenda, circumstances were ripe for such a challenge. Politically, the state was in the midst of one of its periodic spasms of anti-immigrant sentiment; 1994's Proposition 187, one of several anti-immigrant initiatives, would have ended access to health care and public education for illegal immigrants, most of whom were Mexican. (The measure was overwhelmingly approved by the electorate—including nearly two-thirds of white voters—but later thrown out as unconstitutional by the courts.) The state's Republican governor, Pete Wilson, had just ridden to reelection on this wave of anti-immigrant feeling, exacerbated by a prolonged economic downturn. In the first three years of the 1990s, with the collapse of the defense and aerospace industries, the state lost nearly half a million jobs and its unemployment rate leaped to over 9 percent.[1] The public mood was sour. Californians who were pessimistic about the direction their state was heading outnumbered optimists by two to one.

All state-supported agencies were struggling through their fourth straight year of draconian budget cuts. For the University, the cumulative shortfall—the difference between what it would have gotten from the state in normal times and what it actually received—amounted to nearly a billion dollars, the equivalent of the entire state-funded budget for three of its nine campuses. Divisions were rife within the University community over the budget crisis; deciding how to share the pain was a difficult and contentious process. The lingering effects of a highly public controversy over the University's compensation policies and practices that began with the 1992 departure of the previous president, David P. Gardner, made it even worse. Some on the campuses blamed the Office of the President, the University's systemwide administration, for transforming a bad budget situation into a terrible one.

But perhaps the key institutional reality that ignited the debate over affirmative action was the intensifying competition for a place at UC. Admissions standards at UC are closer to those of elite private institutions like Stanford than to those of most public universities. Under the state's 1960 Master Plan for Higher Education, the University's students must be drawn from among the top 12.5 percent of California high school seniors. To become eligible for admission to UC, students must meet stringent requirements in subject matter, scholarship, and standardized examinations. Eligibility, as the idea was applied at UC, did two things at once: it spelled out the University's academic standards, and it promised every undergraduate student who met those standards a place at UC, though not necessarily at the campus or in the program of first choice. In the words of a faculty white paper, eligibility is both "a 'road map' to students aspiring to attend UC and, since the 1960s, a guarantee of admission to those who meet the threshold requirements."[2]

Until 1973, UC was able to accommodate all applicants in the top 12.5 percent. In that year, for the first time, the University's Berkeley campus had to turn away qualified freshmen. Over the next twenty years, admission to both Berkeley and UCLA became increasingly difficult even for exceedingly well qualified students; many were redirected to other UC campuses. And despite fee increases to help deal with budget reductions, UC was still one of the best bargains in American higher education. Changes in the price structure of private institutions meant that UC was a place in which students could receive an undergraduate education comparable to a university like Stanford for a fraction of the cost. Demand in both undergraduate and professional programs was outstripping the spaces available at campuses like UCLA and Berkeley. In 1994, UCLA received 25,300 applications for a fall 1995 freshman class of 3,700; Berkeley's numbers were similar. The college-age cohort in California, the largest since the baby boom generation of the 1960s, was about to hit, and UC was already beginning to feel the insistent push of rising demand. The University would have to accommodate student numbers comparable to those of the 1960s but at an even faster pace and in the midst of a fiscal drought. Since it considered only the most highly qualified for acceptance into its undergraduate programs, admission to UC was intensely competitive.

In the mid-1970s, the California legislature had adopted a policy calling on UC and the California State University (CSU) system to enroll an undergraduate student body that approximated the ethnic and racial composition of the state's public high schools. By the 1990s, a public collision between these two realities—UC's high-stakes, zero-sum admissions policy under the Master Plan and the legislative mandate to encompass an ethnically and racially diverse undergraduate student body—was increasingly likely. That is exactly what President Gardner told the Regents during a 1990 discussion of affirmative action:

> So, we talk about these policies . . . as though they somehow all hold together to everybody's satisfaction, when in fact, translated into practice, everybody is unhappy. . . . The groups that are . . . more eligible on academically objective criteria are unhappy because we're turning them away. Those who think the academically objective criteria are, in fact, discriminatory against them because of special problems and circumstances in their communities, think we ought to rely less on those and more on subjective criteria. Anyone who thinks they have the answer to this problem does not comprehend it. And those who comprehend it don't have an answer.[3]

It was a highly unstable environment in which the University of California was more than usually vulnerable to challenges from unhappy constituencies. Even so, the Regents' decision might never have happened were it not for Mr. and Mrs. Jerry Cook of San Diego.

In 1993, the Cooks launched a letter-writing campaign to legislators, University officials, and others about what they saw as the unfair advantage minority applicants enjoyed in UC's five medical schools. Their son, James, a white applicant who was also a Phi Beta Kappa graduate of UC San Diego, had been accepted at Harvard Medical School in 1992 but denied admission to UC's medical schools, including his first choice, UC San Diego. He reapplied in 1993 but was accepted only at UC Davis.

What made the Cooks different from other disgruntled families of rejected applicants was the energy and thoroughness with which they pursued information about the students who *did* get admitted. First, they gathered statistics about the students who were accepted at UC San Diego's medical school between 1987 and 1993. Later, they analyzed similar figures for UC Irvine and UCLA. These statistics, they claimed, demonstrated two telling facts about UC medical school admissions.

One was that minority students on average had the lowest grades and test scores of those accepted at UC medical schools. The Cooks translated these abstract numbers into visually compelling form by producing a chart, called a scatterplot, that showed the distribution of grades and test scores for those admitted. Most minority scores clustered at the bottom.

Further, the Cooks maintained, their figures showed that minority students' chances of being admitted were three times greater than those of nonminority students—a much larger disparity than one would expect if race and ethnicity were just one factor among others. As a result, according to the Cooks, the University discriminated against highly qualified whites and Asians, who were forced to go to expensive private and out-of-state institutions for their medical education.

The matter might have ended there, were it not for two things. First, through persistence and determination the Cooks won a sympathetic hearing for their views from several Regents, including Clair Burgener of San Diego and Ward Connerly of Sacramento, an African American businessman recently appointed to the board by Governor Wilson. Connerly later wrote that he first heard about the Cooks' complaints from Regent Burgener who, concerned that the couple might sue the University, asked Connerly to meet with them in his capacity as chair of the Regents' committee on finance.[4] Connerly did so in August 1994. The Cooks did not know that Connerly was of African American heritage until they met him in his office, and they immediately assumed he would have no interest in their cause. They were wrong. He was impressed both by their son's qualifications and by their statistics, including the scatterplot. "The last thing I wanted was to become embroiled in racial politics on the Board of Regents," Connerly wrote. "But . . . I said to them what I couldn't deny in my heart: 'This is wrong.'"[5]

Second, Governor Wilson was about to make a bid for the presidency in the 1996 national elections. His outspoken support for Proposition 187 during his 1994 gubernatorial reelection campaign had won him both a landslide victory in

California and national attention as a potential presidential candidate. Opposition to affirmative action was the centerpiece of his presidential agenda. The University of California was a promising target for a demonstration of this anti–affirmative action strategy; ending racial and ethnic preferences in California's leading public university would have a nationwide impact. As governor, Wilson not only appointed members to the UC Board of Regents (Connerly, an old friend, was one of his nominees), but was a member himself.

Regents Connerly and Burgener asked UC President Jack Peltason to put the Cooks' report and the issue of medical school admissions on the agenda for the board's next meeting in November 1994. At that meeting, UC officials did not dispute the Cooks' assertion that the grades and test scores of minority students admitted to UC's medical schools were generally lower than those of white and Asian applicants. It was the consistent disparity in these academic measures among racial and ethnic groups, after all, that made affirmative action necessary in the first place. Rather, as Peltason emphasized in his introductory remarks, every student accepted by a UC medical school was deemed academically qualified to become a physician. In admitting students, the University did what other selective universities did, which was to assemble a class that reflected different backgrounds, experiences, races, and interests.

Other speakers reminded the board of how slow the journey toward educational access had been for minorities who aspired to become physicians. In 1964, 97 percent of all medical students in the United States were non-Hispanic whites; in 1968, when the UC Davis medical school opened, its first class had no African Americans, no Latinos, and no Native Americans, at a time when 25 percent of California's population consisted of members of minority groups. It was only as medical schools began actively recruiting minority students in the 1970s that enrollments began to rise.

The Regents' deputy general counsel, Gary Morrison, discussed the legal ramifications of professional school admissions. He told the board he had reviewed the University's medical school admissions practices, and though he had a very few changes to recommend, generally they were legally sound and consistent with *Bakke*.

Dr. Michael Drake, associate dean of the UC San Francisco school of medicine, explained that in the ferociously competitive world of medical school admissions, grades and test scores were not the only factors that the University considered. Good physicians must excel at other things besides chemistry and anatomy. Admission to medical school was not simply a reward for having performed well in the classroom:

> To be sure, classroom performance above a certain level is required to indicate that the student can withstand the considerable scholastic challenge of a modern medical

education. But although there are levels of classroom performance that are so poor that they virtually guarantee failure, there is no level of performance so high that it guarantees an outstanding physician. We have to look deeper, at the people behind the scores.[6]

And the University, in looking at "the people behind the scores," did not end its scrutiny of prospective students with an assessment of individual merit. As a public institution, it took into account health care trends in California, physician manpower needs, and social policy. All the evidence, the University argued, suggested that minority physicians were far more likely than others to practice in medical specialties and geographic areas where the state's needs were greatest.

Dr. Drake told a story to illustrate his point that the University was not sacrificing excellence in pursuing diversity. Every year at UCSF, he told the Regents, members of the medical school graduating class select the classmate they believe most closely approximates the ideal physician. In each of the previous two years, the students chosen by their peers were members of minority groups.

UC's medical school admissions policies and procedures were, at bottom, a complex calculus that balanced academic merit and intangible qualities of mind and character with the professional workforce requirements of a highly diverse society. The need to strike this balance was why exceptionally qualified applicants like James Cook could be accepted at a private institution like Harvard and turned down at a public institution like UC.

Regent Connerly was unconvinced. He felt the presentation failed to answer the questions raised by the Cooks and to address the issue of whether, in employing racial preferences, the University was ignoring the rights of individuals of all races for access to higher education. "It is time to take off the training wheels," he said at the November 1994 meeting, referring to UC's admissions policies.[7]

Six weeks later, in early January 1995, he told the secretary of the Regents that he wanted the issue of affirmative action put on the agenda again. His interest now extended beyond the question of medical school admissions to the broader issue of affirmative action in the University at all levels.

Peltason immediately made a counteroffer: a series of presentations over the next six months that would inform the board about the nature and purpose of affirmative action, as it functioned not only in the admissions process, but also in employment, contracting, and purchasing. Peltason also told Connerly that he was initiating a review of the University's current practices in affirmative action and would report to the Regents on that review.

In presentations throughout the winter and into the spring, University officials hammered at themes that echoed the discussion in November. UC's academic standards for all entering students were high, and in fact eligibility requirements had been made more stringent five times over the previous twelve years.[8] Admissions policies and selection procedures were both rigorous and fair, subject to constant scrutiny by faculty and administrators to ensure their effectiveness and their relevance to the times. The most important point, made over and over again, was that these policies and practices sought to honor the Regents' 1988 policy on diversity at UC. This policy, which reflected resolutions adopted by the legislature, declared that each campus would seek to encompass "the broad diversity of cultural, racial, geographic, and socio-economic backgrounds characteristic of California." The admissions process at the University of California represented, as one speaker put it, "a balance of educational values and public policy."[9]

Some Regents were persuaded by the administration's case. Others were not, and some were suspicious that UC officials were not giving them all the facts about how the University actually administered its admissions programs. As the spring progressed, an increasingly worried Peltason began working behind the scenes on a compromise with the governor and Connerly. He persuaded them to postpone the item until the July Regents' meeting to avoid making the issue a topic of contention during the crucial spring discussions with the legislature about UC's budget. He then made the case that, even if Connerly and the governor were right about abolishing affirmative action, a public battle on the Board of Regents was in no one's interest. A proposed ballot initiative banning racial and ethnic preferences in California state agencies—later to become Proposition 209—was in the process of qualifying for the November 1996 ballot.[10] It would take at least until that date for the Academic Senate, which had authority over the conditions for admission, to work its way through the many complications involved in so drastic a change in admissions policy. Therefore, Peltason argued, the politically wiser course was to spare the University a nasty and divisive war over an issue that could ultimately be settled at the ballot box anyway. In the meantime, the administration and the Academic Senate would have time to prepare in case the citizens of California voted to end racial and ethnic preferences.

Besides heading off a national and institutional controversy, Peltason was trying to protect the UC budget. It was threatened from two directions—the Republican governor, who wanted to ban preferences, and the Democratic legislature, most of whose members wanted to preserve them. Both Connerly and the governor seemed willing to listen. In June, as Peltason left for a conference in Italy, he thought he had succeeded in defusing the issue.

But Connerly had devoted much time in the intervening months to talking with faculty, students, and UC admissions staff. These conversations convinced him that the University's admissions practices, professional and undergraduate alike, relied so heavily on race and ethnicity that they violated the law as laid down in the *Bakke* decision. As a result, UC was lowering its academic quality by enrolling minority students who did not meet the same standards expected of other applicants. UC was, he believed, an institution with "de facto racial quotas."

On June 1, Governor Wilson issued an executive order calling for "decisions in public employment and contracting . . . based upon merit" and the end of "race- and gender-based preferential programs." That same day, in an opinion piece in the *Los Angeles Times,* the governor wrote, "While I have repeatedly declared that California should celebrate its diversity, achievement of diversity cannot be justification for lowering qualifications or preferring race and gender to merit."

In a last-ditch effort, Peltason, accompanied by Regent John Davies, the governor's appointments secretary, made a final visit to the governor to explain in person the difficulty of ending affirmative action in admissions on the short timeline contemplated by him and Connerly. Peltason wanted to put his own item before the Regents, he went on, an alternative that would essentially say that the board would make no policy decision about preferences until the outcome of the November 1996 ballot was known. Given Wilson's superior advantage with the board, Peltason also asked to present his alternative item first. The governor refused. There would be no compromise.

The debate had never been over whether all qualified California undergraduates would be admitted to UC—under University policy, every state applicant who met the University's eligibility requirements was promised a place at one of the eight general campuses. In its 137-year history, the University had never turned away a California resident who met these standards. It was under no such obligation where graduate and professional students were concerned; the two processes were different, just as the aims of undergraduate and professional education were different. But these facts were ultimately submerged in the polemics of the debate, and the image of excellent white and Asian students pushed aside to make room for less qualified African American and Latino students was burned into the public imagination.

On July 5, Connerly made public his resolutions abolishing racial and ethnic preferences. In his letter to the Regents, he referred to some of the concerns that had been expressed by his colleagues on the board and others—that the timing was suspect, that more facts were needed before a decision of this magnitude could be made, and that action now would put the University out in front on a controversial and inflammatory issue. "The question that is before us," he stated, "is a rather simple one: should the University use race and ethnicity in the decision-making process?" And he continued:

> The fact that the University of California might be the first state constitutional governing board in the nation to take a policy position which eliminates race-based decision-making does not disturb me as long as our position results from a deliberative process, which we have certainly had, and as long as our position is the correct one, which I strongly believe it is, although many of us will differ on this point. UC

has never before been timid about being out-front, I don't know why we need to start being so now.[11]

On July 19, President Bill Clinton defended affirmative action in a speech delivered at the National Archives against the backdrop of the original Declaration of Independence.[12] The battle over affirmative action was no longer just a California issue but a national one. When the Regents met the next day, the three major television networks—NBC, ABC, and CBS, along with its *60 Minutes* news program—showed up to cover the proceedings and the inevitable protest demonstrations amid a crowd of more than a thousand people. Governor Wilson framed the Regents' debate early: the question before the board, he said, was at bottom a choice between fairness to individuals or racial division. He used Berkeley admissions as an example of UC's discriminatory practices and responded angrily when Berkeley Chancellor Chang-lin Tien tried to correct some of his assertions about how the campus's admissions process worked.

It did not help the administration's case that the reviews ordered by Peltason had uncovered some practices that went well beyond the limits set by *Bakke*. UC Irvine and UC Davis, for example, routinely admitted all underrepresented minority students who met UC's basic admissions requirements. UCLA and UC Berkeley gave individual assessments to applications from underrepresented minorities but not to those of white and Asian students. With characteristic candor, Peltason made these legal vulnerabilities public in a letter to the Regents before the July meeting and pledged to end them. But the administration had handed Connerly and the governor a powerful talking point in their quest to demonstrate that affirmative action as practiced at UC was riddled with abuse.

All the pent-up expectation, anxiety, and antagonism of the previous seven months hung in the air as legislators, public officials, and members of the public lined up to address the board. Former Speaker of the Assembly Willie Brown argued passionately that the timing of this vote rested solely on the governor's presidential ambitions. The Reverend Jesse Jackson held the room spellbound by beginning his speech in a whisper before rising to his usual sonorous cadences as he condemned the Regents' proposed action as a tragedy. He asked the audience to stand and join him in a prayer; about one-third did. At one point in the proceedings, a bomb threat emptied the room and sent the Regents and the crowd spilling out of the building and into a nearby parking lot, where Jackson and the governor huddled briefly, Regents caucused, and rumors flew. One rumor was that the chancellors would resign en masse if the board approved the Connerly resolutions. After a long delay, the police let everyone back into the building.

It was a marathon day of emotion and eloquence on both sides. But in the end, Governor Wilson had the votes, and when the issue finally came before the board sometime after 8:00 P.M., the outcome was not really in doubt. The Regents

FIGURE 1. Governor Wilson listens as the Reverend Jesse Jackson speaks on affirmative action at the July 1995 Regents' meeting. *Los Angeles Times,* July 21, 1995, p. 1. Photo credit: Associated Press.

approved SP-1 by a margin of 14 to 10, with one abstention. Jackson and a group of protesters in the overflowing meeting room marked the moment by singing the anthem of the civil rights movement, "We Shall Overcome." The Regents decamped to another conference room to enact SP-2, 15 to 10.[13]

Why did the administration fail? Some blamed its presentations to the Regents, charging that they were overly long, involved, and tedious. But the admissions policies and practices they were describing resisted easy summarization. Their complexity reflected the difficulty of balancing so many issues involving individual achievement, institutional goals, and social policy.

Some blamed the president for not keeping the resolutions off the regental agenda in the first place. In addition to the fact that he had no authority to do so—any Regent could schedule an item for the board's consideration—this view underestimated the political and institutional realities Peltason faced. He was a political scientist by profession, a warm and genial man who had spent many years learning the politics of higher education in Washington, D.C., and Sacramento. Before his eight years as chancellor at UC Irvine, he had spent seven years heading a national higher-education association, the American Council on Education. All of his experience reinforced his belief in compromise. His protracted behind-the-scenes negotiations with Connerly over SP-1 were an effort to find a middle way that would spare the University an institutional bloodletting. But Connerly had a powerful governor as an ally, and powerful governors are rarely open to compromise. David Gardner, a highly gifted strategist in dealing with the Board of Regents, had failed in 1985–86 to head off a regental decision to divest the University of its stock in South African businesses, favored by Governor George Deukmejian. The board Peltason inherited was just three years removed from the executive compensation debacle, which had reflected badly on the Office of the President. Peltason had little maneuvering room and a governor leading the opposition.

If there were shortcomings in the administration's approach to making the case for affirmative action, it might have been a failure to imagine the other side of the issue. The administration's defense of its policies was reasonable and often persuasive, but perhaps it did not sufficiently acknowledge that these policies involved a trade-off: racial and ethnic preferences, in UC's zero-sum admissions universe, inevitably left some groups, notably poor whites and Asians, at a disadvantage.

In reality, it would have been surprising if the University administration had been critical of its own stance on affirmative action. For three decades, most of what Regents, governors, and legislators wanted to know from the administration was when minority enrollment figures were going to improve at UC. Affirmative action had become as much a matter of faith as a matter of policy. What the Cooks began in 1993 was a radical questioning of two assumptions that had held together the thirty-year consensus on affirmative action—that race and ethnicity carried an indeterminate but not decisive weight in selecting those admitted to the University and that diversity brought educational benefits to all students. With their scatter-plot and their anecdotes about highly accomplished nonminority students forced to seek expensive medical education outside their own state, the Cooks upended these assumptions. The challenge they put to the University—were its admissions policies fundamentally fair?—shifted the grounds of the debate from the social benefits of affirmative action to its impact on individual lives. The vote on SP-1 and SP-2, for all its obviously political overtones, raises the intriguing question of whether successive Boards of Regents really understood the trade-offs involved in their own long-held policies on racial and ethnic preferences.

One thing is certain. The University was caught in the crossfire of California's complicated demographic politics, with a determined governor on the other side. It was not to be the last time.

THE REGENTS CHOOSE A PRESIDENT

As the affirmative action debate unwound throughout the winter and spring and into the summer, another critical institutional question was in the process of being answered. Who would be the next president of the University of California?

In January 1995, Jack Peltason announced his intention to retire the following October. He had guided the University through three crisis-ridden years. "We haven't fallen off the cliff," he told a *Los Angeles Times* reporter in June, "but we have used up the short-term fixes." In a long career in higher education, he said, he had never occupied a position in which so many constituencies wanted to be informed and consulted first. UC Provost Walter Massey, an early frontrunner for the presidency, had already withdrawn his name from consideration. This time, some members of the board believed, the University should look outside the UC system for a new president. Regent Roy Brophy, a Sacramento builder, headed the search committee.

Its first choice, President Gordon Gee of Ohio State University, unexpectedly withdrew on June 22, the day before the Regents were to approve his appointment. Gee cited his devotion to Ohio State and the extraordinary outpouring of support from the university's trustees, faculty, students, and alumni when word of his impending departure leaked out. Another factor might have been articles in a San Francisco newspaper criticizing Gee's 1990 decision, while head of the University of Colorado, to approve more than $85,000 in deferred-compensation bonuses for several administrators, including himself. Deferred compensation was a sensitive subject at the University of California. A deferred-compensation program for UC chancellors and other top officials, established during more prosperous times, had been one of the flashpoints for the 1992 political firestorm over executive compensation. Peltason had been forced to spend large amounts of time trimming and then defending the University's executive salary and benefits programs before the legislature and the public.

Coming just a few weeks after Gee's abrupt withdrawal, the board's decision to end racial preferences at UC was widely viewed as putting the last nail in the coffin of the presidential search. "Finding someone now, either inside or outside the university, will be that much more difficult," the *Sacramento Bee* editorialized on August 13. "But what would be nearly impossible is finding a first-rank candidate for a politically damaged institution and getting widespread board concurrence from the divided regents in the short time before Peltason is determined to leave."

Yet the Regents were in no mood to temporize. The search committee turned its attention to the nine UC chancellors, several of whom had already been rumored to be under consideration. One of them was the chancellor of the San Diego campus, Richard C. Atkinson. He had been a candidate in 1992 when the Regents chose

FIGURE 2. Richard Atkinson and his wife, Rita, at the August 1995 Regents' meeting, following his appointment as seventeenth president of the University. *San Francisco Chronicle,* August 19, 1995, no page. Photo credit: *San Francisco Chronicle* photo by Chris Stewart.

Peltason instead, perhaps influenced by a 1980s lawsuit filed against Atkinson by a female Harvard professor involving an extramarital affair dating to 1976. Atkinson settled the lawsuit out of court in 1986, saying he chose this course because he and his wife wanted to get on with their lives.[14] When the search committee talked to people familiar with Atkinson's record in San Diego, he was praised for his leadership in transforming the campus from a good to an excellent university during fifteen years as chancellor. His solid success as an administrator and his stature as a scholar—emphasized by the faculty members on the search committee—won over first the committee and then the board. On August 18, five days after the *Bee's* editorial, the Regents voted 19 to 1, with two abstentions, to name Atkinson president of the University, effective October 1, 1995.

In the aftermath of the affirmative action vote, it was clear where the fault lines lay within the University. There were divisions on the Board of Regents, unhappiness among faculty leaders over the board's July action, institutional strains from a four-year budget crisis, and potentially damaging questions about just how inclusive the University could or would be in the wake of its newfound status as the first major American university to abolish racial and ethnic preferences in admission. Whether the new president, or anyone else, could construct "a vision of the University for the future" that UC and its many communities would support was far from certain.

The Education of a Chancellor

Those were wonderful days that shaped my views about the nature of a great university and the concept of a liberal education. The University of Chicago may not have produced its share of Wall Street financiers or corporate lawyers, but it has produced more than its share of academics. . . . I spent part of my career in La Jolla, California, at the University of California, San Diego, helping build what has become a world-class institution. And in the building process, the image of the University of Chicago was always very much in my mind.

—RICHARD C. ATKINSON, 2003

Richard Atkinson became an undergraduate at the University of Chicago, as he put it, "by pure happenstance." He was a sophomore in high school in February 1944, the child of immigrant parents—an English father and a French mother— neither of whom had attended college. One Saturday he went to an older friend's house to play basketball. His friend had bigger plans, however—an appointment at the University of Chicago campus to take the entrance examination. Having nothing else in particular to do, Atkinson tagged along, hoping for a basketball game later in the day. A friendly University of Chicago proctor told him he should take the exam even if he did not plan to enroll; after all, he was already there. He did, and although his friend was not admitted, Atkinson was awarded a partial scholarship. He decided to give college a try for the summer session and return to high school in the fall if things did not work out.[1]

THE UNIVERSITY OF CHICAGO AND BEYOND

Tests, with all their implications for opportunity, success, and failure, were to play an important role in Atkinson's career. So was the University of Chicago. The institution Atkinson entered in summer 1944 had already played a key role in the development of the atomic bomb; in the postwar years, science was prospering more at the University of Chicago than at any other American university, except perhaps the Massachusetts Institute of Technology and the Berkeley campus of the

University of California. Yet Chicago was also passionately committed to liberal education, embodied in its vigorous president, Robert Maynard Hutchins, and its Great Books curriculum, presided over by Mortimer Adler. It was a place bursting with excitement and energy; few campuses in the United States could offer the same intoxicating blend of classical learning and intellectual stimulation. For Atkinson, the University of Chicago was a life-changing revelation.

During his third year, Atkinson rented a room in the home of the renowned sociologist David Riesman. Riesman often included him in parties, where he met some of the era's most distinguished social scientists. His fellow students included future *Washington Post* columnist David Broder, Nobel Laureate James Watson of DNA fame, and cultural conservative Allan Bloom, whose jeremiad on the decline of intellect in America, *The Closing of the American Mind,* became a 1980s bestseller. One of Atkinson's most vivid memories was of a class called Observation, Interpretation, and Integration, taught jointly by Hutchins and Adler. One day the class discussion turned to the nature of a liberal education. Atkinson argued that any educated person should know the calculus. This was a minority position in that highly humanistic environment, and the student who argued most fiercely against it was Allan Bloom.

At Chicago Atkinson developed the clear and unadorned style that came to characterize his later writing as a social scientist and administrator. He preferred nonfiction to novels—perhaps a reason his own writing is sparing in its use of metaphors. Stimulating as he found the discussions of Plato's *Republic* and Aristotle's political theories, Atkinson was especially drawn to mathematics. He had the good fortune to work as a research assistant to Nicolas Rashevsky, a physicist and Russian immigrant who had joined the University of Chicago faculty in the 1930s. Rashevsky was convinced that mathematics was a crucial but neglected tool for understanding a variety of complex phenomena, including biological and social processes. Physicists laid the foundation for spectacular discoveries by creating simplified models of light or ocean waves, he argued, and then drawing conclusions about them that could be tested. Biologists and physiologists could employ mathematical models of body processes like cell division or nerve activity to do the same thing.[2] Rashevsky began by theorizing about cells, the smallest units of an organism, but did not stop there. Eventually he applied his theory of "mathematical biophysics" to historical and sociological issues, among them the question of whether altruistic or selfish behavior yields more "satisfaction" to individuals— an emotional state Rashevsky believed could be quantified and measured. It was a perspective that would have endeared him to Jeremy Bentham, the eighteenth-century father of utilitarianism and inventor of a method for quantifying happiness that he called the "felicific calculus." As Atkinson told a University of Chicago audience in 2003:

I did endless computations for [Rashevsky] on equations that were basic to his theories. This predated digital computers, and the work was done on a hand-cranked calculator. We ran into real problems that we never quite solved, because the equations proved to be too disorderly. For the mathematicians among you, they were second-order-difference equations, and years later, they were to become part of what is now called "chaos theory." If only I had known then what I know today.[3]

For Atkinson, the exciting thing about Rashevsky's approach was not its applicability to the imponderables of sociology but its implications for American psychology. The field had been dominated for almost fifty years by the behaviorism of B. F. Skinner, J. B. Watson, and E. L. Thorndike. Behaviorism was grounded in the idea that the major questions of psychology could be answered by observing and describing how people act, not how they think or what they feel. Environmental factors were seen as within the purview of scientific psychology because they reinforced or inhibited particular behaviors. But thinking, imagining, choosing, intending—what went on behind the scenes—were considered off limits because they could not be directly observed, measured, and tested. It was a climate inhospitable to theorizing about the mind's apparently inaccessible inner landscape.

In 1948, the year Atkinson graduated from the University of Chicago, a conference at the California Institute of Technology threw down a challenge to the prevailing orthodoxies of behaviorism. The Hixon Symposium, named after the foundation that sponsored it, brought together such scientific luminaries as the mathematician John von Neumann, the physiologist Warren McCulloch, and the psychologist Karl Lashley, who argued in an incendiary speech that behaviorism's focus on stimulus and response had failed to address a central question in psychology: the internal organization of the nervous system that allows humans and animals to orchestrate their own behavior. Several of the themes discussed at the conference, among them thinking as information processing and the mind as analogous to a computer, became the starting point for an explosion of revolutionary, theoretically grounded, and enormously productive research.

The Hixon Symposium ultimately came to be seen as the symbol of the cognitive revolution in psychology.[4] Rashevsky's bold theorizing that mathematical models could be applied to psychological processes was part of this revolution—a radical and exciting step toward an entirely new approach to dealing with psychological phenomena. Atkinson's later research on learning, cognition, and memory was representative of the innovative ferment in the field of psychology that began in the postwar years. His student work for Rashevsky, limited as it was, gave him a glimpse of this world early in his education.

Although he flirted with the idea of graduate study in biology at Chicago when his undergraduate years were over, Atkinson ultimately chose a different direction.

A friend invited him to attend a lecture by William K. Estes, a psychology professor at Indiana University who was becoming known for his work in mathematical models of human learning. They stayed after the lecture to speak with Estes, who, it turned out, was looking for graduate students with mathematics training. Estes encouraged Atkinson to enroll at Indiana University with the offer of a graduate fellowship, which he did in fall 1950.

Reserved and unhurried in manner, Estes spoke so quietly that students had to sit on the edge of their chairs to hear him. It was worth the effort; he was a stimulating thinker and mentor and an early pioneer in the field of mathematical psychology. Estes had been one of B. F. Skinner's brightest and most promising students, working with the master on measuring emotional reactions in animals. But he was not a committed behaviorist, even as a graduate student, and by the late 1940s he was employing mathematical models in his efforts to study human learning. Atkinson worked with Estes as he pursued his Ph.D. degree in experimental psychology. In a seminar, he met a fellow graduate student named Rita Loyd. They got to know each other at the psychology lab, where on one occasion she helped him with an experiment running rats through a maze. From that less than romantic beginning, their relationship ripened into a long and productive marriage that soon included a daughter, Lynn.

Once his dissertation was finished, Atkinson's professional life was on hold until he fulfilled his two-year military obligation, a rite of passage in the years before the draft was abolished. He chose the US Army. In 1954 he and Rita left Indiana for Fort Ord, California. With his background in mathematics and statistics, Atkinson was assigned to a group called HumRRO—Human Resources Research Organization—that conducted many research projects for the army requiring extensive data analysis. The Fort Ord unit had about twenty civilian Ph.D.'s and a military contingent of eight enlisted men, all with Ph.D.'s, reporting to a colonel with a master's degree. Atkinson was sent to work at the nearby Naval Postgraduate School (NPS), which had one of the few digital computers available anywhere in the country apart from a few federal research laboratories or academic institutions like Harvard and the University of Illinois. NPS's largely civilian faculty engaged in military research and offered graduate courses in technical fields to young naval officers.

NPS was set amid the coastal splendor of the Monterey Peninsula overlooking the Pacific, but for the next few years Atkinson spent most of his time in the computer laboratory, working on such topics as simulations of gamelike combat scenarios and large-scale statistical analyses of the psychological factors that influence soldiers in combat. The assignment was a stroke of luck for him—an opportunity to immerse himself in the world of digital computers at an early stage in their development.[5]

THE STANFORD YEARS

One Saturday Atkinson drove to Palo Alto to visit Bill Estes, who was spending the 1955–56 academic year as a visiting fellow at Stanford University's Center for Advanced Study in the Behavioral Sciences. The Center sits high above the university, with a commanding view of the campus and the surrounding hills designed to engender thought and scholarly contemplation. On that sunny, tranquil morning, Atkinson's conversation with Estes was interrupted by a pounding at the door. In burst a young man Atkinson did not know who immediately started expounding on a mathematical problem he was wrestling with. Estes leaped to his feet, and the two began writing equations on the blackboard, arguing back and forth as chalk dust flew. The young man was Patrick Suppes, a Stanford professor of philosophy and logic with an interest in theories of decision making. Like Estes, he had a yearlong appointment at the Center. The two men hit it off and collaborated on research focused on mathematical models in the social sciences. It was a fortuitous meeting for Atkinson that led to his appointment at Stanford University in fall 1956 as a lecturer in applied mathematics and statistics and a research associate in the Department of Psychology.

Atkinson's career at Stanford lasted until 1980, interrupted only by a three-year stint at UCLA in the late 1950s and a five-year leave of absence at the National Science Foundation in the 1970s. It was an exciting time to be involved in mathematical psychology, which was beginning to find its wings, and an exhilarating time to be at Stanford. In the 1960s its famous provost, Fred Terman, was transforming Stanford from a good regional institution to a national presence through his "steeples of excellence" strategy. Terman was an active national figure in the engineering profession, the author of a popular textbook on radio engineering, and, for four years during World War II, the head of the MIT/Harvard Radio Research Laboratory, a government-sponsored project whose top secret work on radar was an important contribution to the war effort.[6] Terman had earned his doctorate at MIT, and it seemed to him that despite the quality of some of its academic areas, MIT was poorly managed; there was no organized effort to decide what it did best, or could become best at doing. As dean of engineering and later provost, Terman was convinced that Stanford should decide what its academic strengths were and concentrate on developing them, "focusing largely on carefully selecting faculty in carefully selected fields," according to a recent biographer.[7] The idea was not original with Terman, but he applied it with unwavering focus and tenacity. He was a skilled judge of fields outside his expertise and of the intellectual potential of young faculty in those fields. One of his strategies for attracting the caliber of faculty he wanted was to check the annual list of nominees to the National Academy of Sciences, which awarded membership to the top forty of roughly a hundred candidates. Those who just missed the cutoff were highly likely to be chosen in the future. Terman would target a few of them for recruitment to Stanford every year.[8]

The postwar era of federal support for university research was beginning to unfold, and with good planning there were opportunities for the social and behavioral sciences, especially for faculty interested in quantitative approaches. During the 1950s, Stanford conducted a number of assessments of the teaching and research performance within these departments. Psychology was the department of Fred Terman's father, Lewis Terman—one of the fathers of IQ testing—and it had long been among the university's strongest. It was one of the few social science departments that got high marks in the national assessments of the 1950s.[9] Fred Terman and his close associate, Albert H. Bowker, were prepared to take psychology to the next level.

Bowker, the first chair of Stanford's Department of Statistics, had founded the Applied Mathematics and Statistics Laboratory where Atkinson worked during his initial year.[10] He was a man of few words but many ideas about Stanford's academic trajectory. On his appointment as graduate dean in the late 1950s, and with Terman's enthusiastic support, Bowker joined forces with Suppes to develop Stanford's strength in quantitative approaches to the social sciences at a time when few other institutions were moving in that direction. Atkinson's recruitment from UCLA in 1961 was part of their plan for the psychology department; so was the recruitment of Estes a year later. Atkinson's background in mathematical modeling and his solid experimental training at Indiana made him an attractive candidate. Early on in his Stanford career, he became coauthor, with Ernest Hilgard, of one of the most successful textbooks in the field, *Introduction to Psychology*. Rita joined as coauthor in 1971.[11]

In the entrepreneurial Stanford of the 1960s, faculty were expected to search aggressively for research funding, and even secretarial help was not to be taken for granted. Atkinson liked the competitive atmosphere, the bright graduate students, and the sense that opportunities were there for those prepared to work for them. He embarked on a series of studies with Suppes, including a 1960 book, *Markov Learning Models for Multi-person Interactions*, which used extensive experimental data to analyze the application of learning theory to game situations.

But what gained them a national audience was their work in the fledgling field of computer-assisted instruction. In the early 1960s Suppes was the director of Stanford's Institute for Mathematical Studies in the Social Sciences, one of the first university centers in the United States devoted to the application of mathematical methods to the behavioral and social sciences. It was there that he and Atkinson tested ideas for using computers to improve on traditional classroom techniques by making teaching more flexible and more adapted to differences in students' ability and motivation. At the time, the US Office of Education was encouraging research on computer-assisted instruction, and IBM, interested in potential commercial applications, agreed to work with Atkinson and Suppes on what became its pioneering IBM 1500 System. The system, with eighteen student terminals, was installed in East Palo Alto's Brentwood Elementary School in fall 1966.

Brentwood was an overwhelmingly minority school in a very poor area, with students lagging a year or more behind national norms. What Atkinson and Suppes proposed to do was to test the role of computers in teaching beginning reading and arithmetic to first- and second-graders, using programs the two had created. The premise of the Brentwood project was that teachers were compelled to teach to the broad middle of the class, which left less time for students in the top and bottom quartiles. The thesis was that computers could address the needs of these students, fast and slow learners alike, by allowing them to progress at their own pace and in ways adapted to their individual learning styles. The Brentwood experiment was the product of four years of preparation aimed at applying the mathematical models of the learning process that Atkinson had been working on since his graduate student days at Indiana University.

After conquering some initial anxieties, most of the schoolchildren loved the experience. *Life* magazine called it "an educational revolution . . . being taught by electronic schoolmarms—machines that are making an eerie and promising impact at all levels of learning," in a story it ran on the Brentwood experiment in January 1967. "With this technology," Suppes added, "we may be able to give each kid the personal services of a tutor as well-informed and as responsible as Aristotle."[12] Atkinson was more measured. A year later, in an assessment of computer-assisted learning in *Science,* he described the remarkably rapid progress of computerized instruction as well as the problems—a combination of cost, technical issues, and the difficulty of evaluating the effectiveness of this new pedagogical tool without a deeper understanding of the learning process itself, a topic he was confident would attract outstanding future scientists.[13]

IBM eventually chose not to pursue the computerized learning market. Atkinson and Suppes decided they would give it a try. Together they founded Computer Curriculum Corporation; Suppes wrote the software program for arithmetic, Atkinson the one for elementary reading. The computer-based system they developed served as a prototype for the commercial development of computer-assisted instruction in the United States. Their company prospered and was later sold to Paramount Corporation in the early 1980s.

Atkinson's most fundamental contribution to psychology, the one that earned him election to the National Academy of Sciences in 1974, was his seminal work on the structure of human memory. Speculation about how memory works has a long lineage, going back in modern times to such nineteenth-century psychologists as Hermann Ebbinghaus in Germany and William James in the United States. James made a famous distinction between primary and secondary memory—roughly

FIGURE 3. Richard Atkinson and Patrick Suppes at the Institute
for Mathematical Studies in the Social Sciences, Stanford
University, 1967. *Life,* January 27, 1967, p. 75. Photo by Ralph Crane.

speaking, short-term and long-term memory—in his 1890 *Principles of Psychology.*
His intuitions about these inner processes were brilliant, but they were qualitative
descriptions based on introspection. Mathematical modeling offered an opportunity to supplement such verbal accounts with something more quantitative and
experimentally based. Atkinson was one of a handful of researchers who created
the field of mathematical modeling in psychology.

He and his colleagues started by constructing mathematical models of simple types of learning that could be studied in the laboratory. These models would then be used to make precise predictions that could be tested against the data. In 1964 Atkinson and one of his graduate students, Richard Shiffrin, began developing a more complex model that would explain the structure of memory and how it operates, especially how short-term and long-term memory interact with each other. The model they developed is described in a 1968 paper titled "Human Memory: A Proposed System and Its Control Processes," among the most cited articles in the history of the social sciences. It argues that the structures of memory are fixed, but its "control processes"—the way memories are handled—are various.

The Atkinson-Shiffrin model was a major advance in the field for several reasons. It was, first of all, a general theory of memory, a more ingenious and sophisticated explanation of its structure than the prevailing model, developed by N. C. Waugh and D. A. Norman. "It is as if Waugh and Norman proposed the elements of earth, air, fire, and water, and Atkinson and Shiffrin proposed the elements found in the periodic table—the latter notion being more complex and comprehensive and explaining a wider variety of phenomena," as one commentator put it.[14] The simplicity and elegance of the theory they proposed made the Atkinson-Shiffrin model the "modal model" of memory—widely accepted as the standard in the field. The control processes they described, such as rehearsal, coding, retrieving, and decision rules, are now standard in theories of memory as well. Their work has had a lasting influence on the direction of research in experimental psychology, including the neuroimagery research that has flourished in recent years.[15]

THE NATIONAL SCIENCE FOUNDATION

In spring 1975 Atkinson received an invitation that changed his career. Guyford Stever, director of the National Science Foundation (NSF), approached him about serving as deputy director. Rice University President Norm Hackerman, a good friend and chair of NSF's advisory body, the National Science Board, called him to second the idea. Atkinson was intrigued but reluctant to leave academia. Ultimately he agreed to a temporary appointment—an academic year plus two summers, or fifteen months—with the understanding that he would be on leave from Stanford. The timing was right, and he was ready for a break from research and teaching. His daughter was entering Brown University in Rhode Island in fall 1975, and the chance to spend a year on the East Coast was a further attraction for him and Rita.

He saw NSF as an opportunity to experience the world of national science policy. It also turned out to be a long exercise in crisis management. The mid-1970s were the era of Senator William Proxmire and his Golden Fleece Awards, presented with much public fanfare to government-sponsored projects the senator considered intellectually frivolous and fiscally wasteful. NSF grants were among his favorite targets. One was an NSF-funded project on the mating habits of the screw-worm fly; another was a social science project on theories of love. Newspapers from the *National Enquirer* to the *Chicago Tribune* jumped in, with the *Tribune* running a story on an NSF-supported study titled "A Theory of Necking Behavior." The study turned out to be something far less titillating than its title: an engineering project on the necking behavior of metals, not humans.[16]

Hostile grilling by congressional committees was routine. Atkinson rarely appeared before a committee on the Hill without first arming himself with a few examples of basic research that had yielded a new drug or a better mousetrap, many of them torn from the day's newspaper. The sex life of the screw-worm fly ultimately turned out to be a key step toward understanding the biology of pest control, but in the mid-1970s the constant torrent of ridicule was damaging to NSF and to government support for basic scientific research. Proxmire's attacks were symptomatic of a shift in political winds. In Atkinson's words:

> At this time considerable criticism was being directed towards science activities of all sorts. Ever since the publication of Rachel Carson's *Silent Spring* in the 1960s, there was a growing feeling abroad that the purity of science, as it had emerged from World War II, was not quite as pristine as it had seemed. This was immediately after the Vietnam War and there were sizable cuts in science budgets; money was hard to come by, and scientists whose grants were not funded were critical of peer review and in turn of NSF. Proxmire was tapping into this public unease about science, and Congress followed his lead.[17]

The critics of NSF's peer review portrayed it as a good-old-boy system in which university researchers gave high marks to their colleagues' grant proposals as a way to ensure a favorable assessment of their own. Two of NSF's most strident and determined opponents were Congressmen John Conlan of Arizona and Robert Bauman of Maryland. They kept up a steady drumbeat of criticism in Congress, especially against NSF's science education curricula, which in their view did not embody appropriate American values. These curricula, developed during the post-Sputnik era of generous federal investment in national school reform, were intended to reflect the best and latest thinking on classroom learning. By 1975 NSF had sponsored forty-three curricular projects in mathematics and the natural sciences and ten in the social sciences.[18]

An NSF-funded anthropology project, *Man: A Course of Study* (MACOS), gave Conlan and Bauman the opportunity they were looking for. Developed by the distinguished Harvard professor Jerome Bruner, among others, MACOS was intended to teach fifth- and sixth-grade students how values can differ from one society to another. The flashpoint was a MACOS film explaining cultural practices among the nomadic Eskimos living in the harsh environment above the Arctic

Circle. Among those practices were wife-sharing and abandoning old people to die when they could no longer withstand the rigors of long treks. The public hue and cry over this controversial material, and MACOS in general, generated threats to require congressional review of all fifteen thousand NSF grant applications. Director Stever promised a comprehensive review of the science education programs to address the criticisms.

Atkinson arrived at NSF on July 1, 1975, just after the review came out. Instead of defending the educational rationale for MACOS and similar curricular programs, the NSF report justified its business practices and the peer review process involved in funding the science curricula. The result was to entangle two distinct but equally controversial issues—NSF's pedagogical decisions about science curricula and its management decisions about how projects were evaluated and funded. Worse, the document sought to minimize or obscure some careless practices that had crept into NSF's grant procedures, a fact that Conlan and Bauman knew because of leaks from several NSF staffers who shared the congressmen's disapproval of MACOS. It all came to a head in January 1976, when a report by the General Accounting Office (GAO) gave NSF low marks for its poor business practices and haphazard auditing procedures in the science education area.

Atkinson was put in charge of mounting a response. He assembled a few trusted colleagues, and together they spent an entire weekend examining NSF's grant-awarding process for curriculum projects, working practically around the clock. What they found was not evidence for the defense but what appeared to be additional ammunition for their critics: the fiscal and peer review problems in science education not only existed, but were more widespread than the GAO report suggested.

The question was whether to try to keep this new and damaging information under wraps to protect NSF's reputation or to go public with the fresh evidence they had found and risk the consequences. The decision, made after several days of anguished debate, was to disclose everything and to commit to correcting the flaws in the agency's business practices and audit procedures. It was a novel approach for a government agency, one that surprised and disarmed NSF's opponents.

In addition to overhauling the business side, Atkinson began a systematic revision of the problematic aspects of NSF's peer review process. He ordered all project titles and abstracts edited, if necessary, to remove anything that might conceivably be sensationalized by the media. This act incurred the wrath of the academic community, especially the physics community, some of whose members made a visit to NSF to complain in person to the director.[19] Atkinson also commissioned an independent evaluation of the agency's grant procedures. The study, conducted by two brothers—Jonathan R. Cole of Columbia University and Stephen Cole of the State University of New York's Stony Brook campus—included a statistical analysis that validated the soundness and reliability of peer review throughout NSF. Although the critics had been right about some of NSF's management weaknesses, much of the warfare over peer review was a way of attacking the agency for supporting the teaching of evolution in the schools. The Coles's study, published in *Scientific American*, lent some objectivity and context to the issue.[20] NSF emerged from the crisis more or less intact if not unscathed.

In summer 1976, when Stever left NSF to become President Gerald Ford's science adviser, Atkinson was named acting director. Sometime later, the White House sent the name of its nominee for NSF director to the Senate for confirmation; it was not Atkinson. The cognizant Senate committee was the Subcommittee on Health and Scientific Research, chaired by Senator Ted Kennedy. He was not inclined to make a new appointment so late in Ford's presidential term and wanted Atkinson to stay on in the acting role at least until the next election. Atkinson had worked closely with Kennedy during his first year at NSF and had gotten to know the Kennedy family years before during a brief stint as an educational adviser to Bobby Kennedy during Bobby's ill-fated 1968 presidential campaign.

Kennedy delayed confirmation hearings for several months and then, when the administration finally complained, pointed out that the White House had failed to consult with the National Science Board regarding its nominee—a routine matter but one that was nevertheless required by the legislation establishing NSF. By that time, however, the clock had run out on the Ford administration. When Jimmy Carter took office, one of his first official acts was to nominate Atkinson for the directorship. The nomination sailed through Kennedy's committee.

NSF's four previous directors had come from the natural sciences, so the choice of a social scientist to head the agency was unusual. Atkinson told the story of encountering the prominent World War II physicist I. I. Rabi on a visit to New York soon after his appointment as head of NSF. "Congratulations," Rabi greeted him, "and what area of physics are you in?"[21]

Defending the value of basic research was a long-standing priority at NSF, but Atkinson also took steps to promote ties between industry and research universities. The huge infusion of federal funds into research universities following Sputnik had eclipsed the pre–World War II collaborative relationship between universities and private companies.[22] American universities were producing a rich array of potentially useful research, but innovations were not moving into the private sector as quickly or efficiently as the economy required. NSF's analysis of the technology transfer process led to an early draft of what became the 1980 Bayh-Dole Act. Bayh-Dole allowed universities to keep the patent rights to inventions resulting from any federally supported research they conducted, and the outcome was an upsurge of technology transfer from research universities to the private sector. NSF also examined other incentives for investing in research, such as tax credits and industry–university partnerships. These studies led the agency to establish a program of joint research projects between industry and universities. It sponsored an extramural research program, funding projects to study the relationship between investments in R&D and various types of economic growth.

Atkinson dismantled an early 1970s program called Research Applied to National Needs (RANN), established in 1971 to focus on identifying important societal problems and ways to solve them. RANN was different from the kind of basic science research NSF specialized in, and was never completely accepted by the National Science Board.[23] Atkinson's decision to end it was probably his most controversial act as director of NSF.[24] The primary reason was to expand funding for research in engineering, which had not been included in NSF's original mandate. Atkinson believed that engineering had long since transcended its trade school origins and become a full-fledged intellectual discipline fundamental to the future of scientific and technological advance. At the very end of his tenure, he persuaded the National Science Board to elevate engineering to a full directorate.

NSF's responsibilities for science were not just national, but international, and in his second year as director Atkinson found himself in the middle of a diplomatic imbroglio. President Richard Nixon's historic visit to China in 1972 had begun a thaw in relations between the two countries, but it was only after the 1976 death of China's long-term Communist dictator, Chairman Mao Zedong, that momentum for change began to take hold. In 1978 the Chinese government signaled its interest in an exchange of students, scholars, and scientists with the United States. The Carter White House, eager to open up the relationship with China, welcomed the idea and designated the US Information Agency as the American representative in the discussions. The reaction from Chinese officials was negative: they wanted the National Science Foundation.

They got their way. Atkinson traveled to Beijing with a delegation led by Frank Press, director of the Office of Science and Technology Policy and science adviser to the president. The members were housed in a lovely wooded compound used for foreign notables, where they heard that the Gang of Four—Mao's wife and several close associates, now out of political favor—was being held under house arrest in a nearby mansion. When the Americans met with Mao's successor, Deng Xiaoping, they were struck by the spittoons strategically placed around the room and even more by Deng's practiced aim when he used them. Later their Chinese hosts told them that this was the aristocratic Deng's way of "expressing camaraderie with Chinese peasants."

Atkinson's principal instruction from the Carter administration was to see that the exchange agreement was formalized in a memorandum of understanding signed by both governments. The American side was hoping for a large exchange program—an optimistic five hundred per side as a first step—and for a broader discussion that would explore possible joint ventures in science and technology. But Fang Yi, vice-premier of the state council and Atkinson's counterpart, was interested only in an exchange program, and an informal one at that—no memorandum of understanding. At first Fang Yi was elusive about numbers. One day, however, he abruptly shifted direction:

> Finally, Fang Yi became very assertive and asked how many students other countries have studying in the United States. A direct question that required a direct answer. I began with Iran which had about 25,000 students and worked down a list of six or seven countries. And then being somewhat mischievous, I concluded by noting that Taiwan had about 9,000 students. A tense moment followed, and then another direct question. "How many can China have?" I decided to press to the limit, and said possibly a thousand. Fang Yi shot back, "Why can't we have as many as other countries?" The American side was stunned, but secretly delighted. After that, talks moved quickly and we soon had the basis for an agreement. But the Chinese insisted that it had to be at an informal level, not a government-to-government agreement.[25]

That became the sticking point, still unresolved at the end of the visit. When a delegation arrived in Washington in January 1979 to finalize an agreement, it was clear the Chinese were still determined to avoid a formal exchange. They informed Frank Press and Atkinson that they had stopped off in Los Angeles and San Francisco along the way, and the leaders of several universities in those cities had told them an informal exchange, with no government involvement at all, would be not only possible but welcome. Press, who had heard nothing whatsoever about these visits, immediately replied he was of course aware of them and could assure the Chinese that there would be no exchanges without the American government's approval. Atkinson signed the memorandum of understanding on behalf of the United States, the first of its kind in the history of the two countries.

By 1980 the planned fifteen-month leave from Stanford had turned into five years at NSF. Atkinson had guided the agency through what the *Washington Post* called "a rebuilding from the ravages of the Nixon anti-science era," weathering attacks on its system of peer review and its administrative integrity.[26] NSF funding, which had been on the decline when he arrived, grew by nearly one-third between 1976 and 1980, when the NSF annual budget topped a billion dollars—although the ravenous inflation of the 1970s ate up some of those gains. Even Senator Proxmire came around in the end, telling Atkinson that he had won not only Proxmire's confidence but the confidence of Congress as well. NSF introduced him to Washington, the politics of science, and the experience of making things happen in a complex organization. Later Atkinson would remember NSF as one of the most exciting and challenging periods of his life. Yet in 1980 he was beginning to think about leaving the agency, and his thoughts were turning to the possibility of a university presidency.

CHANCELLOR OF UC SAN DIEGO

NSF directors are natural candidates for university leadership posts, and Atkinson had already been approached by several search committees, including Brown University's. Early in 1980 he was invited to interview for the presidency of the University of Southern California. The process turned out to be less than confidential. Details of the search were splashed all over the *Los Angeles Times,* including Atkinson's name and that of another candidate. The *Times* also reported that Atkinson had strong faculty support but that one of USC's trustees, a former CIA director, considered him potentially subversive because he had ties to the Kennedy family. Neither Atkinson nor the other candidate welcomed the unwanted publicity or the evidence that USC did not have its search in order. Both withdrew.

Soon after the USC incident, University of California President David S. Saxon came to see Atkinson at NSF. Saxon was a physicist by training, and Atkinson assumed the reason for the visit was the physics community's unhappiness with an NSF decision about funding for a proposed accelerator. Saxon had other things on his mind, however. He wanted Atkinson to interview for the chancellorship of UC's San Diego campus. With the USC experience still fresh, Atkinson hesitated. Saxon then asked if he would be willing to talk with the search committee if the list were pared down to three candidates and the interview kept completely confidential. Two weeks later, Atkinson flew to Los Angeles to meet with the committee. On the day of the interview, he ran into a friend, Bob Adams, in the lobby of the hotel where he was staying. Adams was the provost at the University of Chicago and, as they quickly discovered, a fellow candidate for the San Diego chancellorship. Atkinson went away impressed with the good taste of the search committee. Adams later became secretary of the Smithsonian Institution.[27]

San Diego had a number of attractions. It was widely regarded as the best of the American research universities established after World War II. Although a young institution, UCSD was already a force in the sciences, built as a general campus in the 1960s on the foundation of the world-renowned Scripps Institution of Oceanography (SIO). Scripps had been established as a marine research station in 1903 and became part of the University of California in 1912. It took off after World War II, buoyed by the rising tide of federal funds and the energy and ambition of Roger Revelle, who took its budget from $1.5 million to $12 million during his tenure as director from 1950 to 1964.[28] Revelle, one of the founding fathers of UC San Diego, envisioned it as a public version of the California Institute of Technology (Caltech), focusing primarily on graduate education in scientific and technical fields, capitalizing on the established excellence of SIO. The Regents ultimately decided otherwise and designated UC San Diego as a general campus in 1960, but even so its inaugural class consisted of fifteen graduate students in physics. Revelle's vision had a lasting influence on UCSD's image of itself. He believed there was a certain order in building a great university: first assemble a group of outstanding academics, then bring in graduate students, and only later add undergraduates. Distinguished universities, he told a Princeton University audience in 1958, had to be constructed "from the top down and not from the bottom up—and from the inside out, not the outside in."[29] UC San Diego fit that pattern, and from the beginning the campus pursued a strategy of recruiting distinguished senior faculty to staff its academic departments. So many of its founding faculty were lured from the University of Chicago that in the early days UCSD was jokingly referred to as the University of Chicago at San Diego. By 1980 the campus was a powerhouse in mathematics, chemistry, physics, and biology, as well as oceanography. And it was located on one of the most beautiful stretches of the California coast. Atkinson's daughter, Lynn, had spent a summer at SIO as a research assistant, and her parents were deeply impressed by La Jolla and San Diego when they visited her.

Atkinson had many sources of information about the campus, and not only because UCSD was a leading recipient of NSF funds. SIO Director Bill Nierenberg was on the National Science Board, the governing body for NSF; UCSD's chancellor at the time, Bill McElroy, was a former NSF director; and Bill McGill, who had been the third chancellor of UC San Diego and then president of Columbia University, was an old and close friend. The 1,200-acre campus, originally a Marine base, sat on a scenic bluff overlooking the Pacific and had the international prestige and academic traditions of the University of California behind it. Although the system was struggling through a major budgetary downturn, there was every reason to think UC's and UCSD's long-term prospects were bright. Atkinson's experience as a faculty member at UCLA gave him a sense of what the University of California and public higher education were about. Several members of the search committee later described him as having impeccable academic credentials, an engaging enthusiasm, and developed ideas about what was needed at San Diego. He arrived in Los Angeles carefully prepared.

The interview with the search committee was at noon. That evening, Saxon called and offered Atkinson the job. After a long phone conversation with Rita, he called Saxon back and said yes.

"As you know from our discussions," Saxon wrote him after the Regents had approved his appointment, "the campus has had some tough problems and the fallout from them will present you with correspondingly tough challenges, but I am confident of your ability to handle the situation. I know that you and I have a common view of the high quality of the campus and of the brilliant future before it."[30]

The first of the problems was the campus rift over the outgoing chancellor, Bill McElroy. McElroy was a distinguished biologist whose pioneering work in the bioluminescence of fireflies was a dazzling example of everything Atkinson had argued for at NSF about the long-term payoffs of basic research; his exploration of how fireflies emit light led to important advances in genetic research.[31] After eight years as chancellor, McElroy had been forced to resign in the wake of a no-confidence vote by the San Diego faculty. The campus was torn by an ongoing power struggle between the administrative and academic vice chancellors, com-pounded by the faculty's unhappiness with organizational changes McElroy had made that, in the faculty's view, were instituted without sufficient consultation with the campus faculty senate. Many people felt the root of the problem lay in McElroy's failure to exert leadership in his relations with the faculty. This situa-tion left the academic vice chancellor, not the chancellor, as the campus's chief academic spokesperson.

McElroy, who was having troubles in his personal life, tried to forestall the no-confidence vote by privately telling the campus's academic leaders that he would quietly resign. But they insisted on taking the formal and public vote anyway. It was a symptom of just how deep and persistent tensions were; even secretaries in the opposing camps were not talking to each other. The faculty eventually went to Saxon, who was pained and puzzled by the whole affair. He respected McElroy and tried to rescue his chancellorship, but the faculty's mutinous mood and the bitter-ness of the situation were clear. He had a private talk with McElroy, who resigned soon afterward.

In April 1980, at Atkinson's request, Saxon appointed a committee to review the administrative organization of the campus, focusing on the senior management positions reporting directly to the chancellor. It was intended as a first step toward rectifying some of the imbalances in power and responsibility that had precipi-tated the turmoil between the chancellor and the faculty. The committee, chaired by physics professor and campus faculty senate chair Bill Frazer, gave him several useful options to consider, but Atkinson did not stop with a revised organization chart. By the end of his first year, there were new faces in virtually every senior administrative post. He wanted to start from scratch.

McElroy's fate was a cautionary tale, and Atkinson's first priority was building trust with the faculty. A few weeks into his tenure, during a round of visits to cam-pus departments, he got into a debate with a member of the English faculty over the nature of a liberal education. The professor reminded him that the faculty had already gotten rid of one chancellor, and they could get rid of another.

The San Diego faculty was a self-confident body with a strong sense of its pre-rogatives and institutional identity. There is a story, dating to the early 1960s, about a visit to the young campus by President Clark Kerr. When he encouraged the UCSD faculty to strive for the academic standards set by Berkeley, he was told they had no desire to sink that low. Saxon, worried that Atkinson might not fully appreciate just how much power the faculty wielded, dispatched the chair of the systemwide Academic Senate, Berkeley engineering professor Karl Pister, to give him a quick tutorial in the way shared governance worked at the University of

California. Atkinson listened. His first message to the UCSD senate was about the remarkable quality of the faculty and his hope that it would be at least as good by the time he finished his tenure as it was when he arrived. Unlike McElroy, who attended campus faculty senate meetings only occasionally, Atkinson showed up regularly and prepared meticulously. He invited the chair of the senate to become a member of his administrative cabinet and established a faculty liaison position in his office to ensure that faculty viewpoints were well represented. While he had his share of differences with the campus senate leadership over the years, Atkinson always took the faculty seriously. It was not only a matter of self-interest but of institution building, capitalizing on UCSD's strong faculty-centered culture as an incentive to attract more outstanding scholars and scientists.

He found a campus organizational structure, administrative and academic, that was adequate in some areas, embryonic in others. The campus was strong in many of the physical and biological sciences, with approximately 45 percent of its faculty and more than 50 percent of its student body concentrated in science and engineering. It was far less developed in the humanities, the social sciences, and the arts. The campus had no academic deans and no endowed chairs; he instituted both. He recruited a series of senior faculty members to serve as academic vice chancellor.[32] To deal with faculty criticisms that too much power had been concentrated in the administrative vice chancellor, he split the post into two positions, one responsible for business and planning and the other for budget. For the key position of director—later vice chancellor—for planning and budget, he recruited V. Wayne Kennedy, who had been associate dean of the medical school. Atkinson took control of the budget, in his view an indispensable step for any CEO, and appointed a budget committee headed by Kennedy to make recommendations about resource allocations to colleges and departments. One of Kennedy's responsibilities was to make sure that everyone understood how and why funds were distributed. Another was to put together an enrollment plan. The administrative and business infrastructure they created lasted substantially unchanged for more than two decades.

There was much more to do, and he wasted no time getting started. Although located on a stunning site, the campus had little sense of place. Physical planning had been haphazard and funding scarce in the tough budget years of the late 1970s. Capital planning, almost nonexistent when Atkinson arrived, got under way. The campus established a design review board, and Atkinson personally oversaw every building that went up on campus. When it appeared some campus neighbors might object to plans for stadium-scale floodlights in an athletic field, he had them installed without notice. On occasion he named some of the campus streets without bothering to seek the customary approval from the president or the Board of Regents, neither of whom apparently noticed the oversight. The Price Center, designed as a gathering place for students, was built early in Atkinson's tenure. Students protested his decision to add private vendors to the on-campus food service, but memories of its controversial beginnings eventually faded. Any project that involved tree removal was fraught with peril. There was intense faculty resistance to a plan to eliminate some trees from an area outside the Geisel Library known as Library Walk. Students quickly took up the cause, attaching dramatic white crosses to the doomed trees and chaining themselves to the trunks. Along with a faculty member who joined them during a public demonstration, they had to be forcibly removed. Atkinson remembered the incident as one of the most unpleasant experiences of his chancellorship.

It was important to get the administrative and physical infrastructure in place so that he could turn his attention to his central task: moving the San Diego campus from its spectacular early start to the next level of quality. The first step was a campaign to have UC San Diego elected a member of the Association of American Universities. The membership of the AAU included the most distinguished research universities in the United States and Canada. Berkeley had been a founding member of the AAU in 1915, and UCLA had been admitted in 1972. UCLA's election was precedent breaking at the time because it made UC the only university system in the AAU with more than one campus as a member, and the odds that a third UC campus would be selected were unpromising. But persistence paid off. In 1982 UC San Diego succeeded in its bid for election.[33]

Atkinson's AAU campaign was obviously directed at boosting the campus's national reputation, but it also carried a message for the campus itself: UCSD's future did not lie in following the Caltech or MIT model, despite the dreams of some of the campus's early builders. It was a public research university, different from Berkeley and UCLA but with the same broad range of intellectual disciplines and the same commitment to educate undergraduates. Election to the AAU was public testimony to its readiness to compete in the same academic league as the two older campuses. For Atkinson, the important issue was focusing the campus's energies and aspirations in this direction.

The San Diego community presented a different kind of problem. UCSD's unusual top-down academic origins encouraged the idea among the faculty that its most important connections were national and international, not local; early on, the needs of the city of San Diego had not been a major consideration. UC San Diego had been a center of strident, sometimes violent student demonstrations during the Vietnam era of the 1960s and early 1970s. Some of the iconic figures of the era—student-revolutionary Angela Davis, for example, and faculty member Herbert Marcuse, the German-born neo-Marxist theorist and favorite philosopher of the New Left—were active at UCSD and impossible to ignore. The mainstream reaction in San Diego was predictable. McElroy's predecessor, Bill McGill, vividly describes living through the nightmare year of 1968 and dealing with radical students, angry Regents, and outraged San Diegans in his *Year of the Monkey*.

Among other things, he had to cope with the angry editors of the *San Diego Union,* who pummeled the campus regularly and once published an editorial titled "This Is an Order" demanding that Marcuse—"professor of Left Wing philosophy"—be instantly dismissed.[34]

Unhappy memories of the days of student flag burning and political protest lived on in that conservative navy town. McElroy, a friendly and outgoing Texan, had tried to bridge the gap by inviting the community in and appointing a board of overseers to stimulate fund-raising. But the distance between the campus and greater San Diego remained more than geographic.

An example was a visit Atkinson received from the chair of a San Diego committee working on the city's official celebration of the 1987 bicentennial of the US Constitution. At the end of the meeting, during which UCSD's plans for the celebration were discussed, the chair asked to speak with Atkinson privately. His forthrightness, she told him, encouraged her to bring up a subject she had been warned not to mention: would he be willing to make an exception to UCSD policy, dating back to the Vietnam era, and allow the American flag to be flown on campus during the bicentennial events? Atkinson took her to the window, pointed to the American flag flying outside his office, and explained that no such policy had ever existed. Later he had flags—US, state of California, UC, and UCSD—installed at major entrances to the campus.

It would be difficult to overstate the challenges of bringing together the liberal campus and the conservative town, but Atkinson began to build methodically on the progress McElroy had made. San Diego was in transition from an economy based on tourism, retirees, the US Navy, and banking. Atkinson's constant message in dozens of talks at places like the Rotary Club and chamber of commerce was that UCSD was the city's key asset in making the leap to the newer, high-technology economy that was being born before their eyes.

The quality of teaching at UCSD was high, but the one-year student retention rate was the worst in the UC system—77 percent—when he arrived in 1980. The range of majors was narrow. Psychology, for example, was heavily experimental, and students complained that after four years they graduated knowing more about rats and pigeons than about people. Atkinson, though an experimental psychologist himself, sympathized with the students and pushed for broadening the department's curriculum. He worked with the faculty to institute popular new majors, including cognitive science, ethnic studies, and communications.

Undergraduate student life centered on four—later six—colleges modeled on the Oxford and Cambridge example, each with its own general education requirements, housing, and dining halls. As was the case at UC Santa Cruz, which also aspired to the Oxbridge ideal, the English college system did not adapt readily to the California academic climate, with its history of organization into disciplinary departments. The colleges were the site of pitched battles over curriculum and control during the student revolution of the 1960s. As chancellor in the 1980s, Atkinson was pluralist in the national debate over curricula; he did not agree with his old classmate Allan Bloom that the classical, University of Chicago–style core curriculum was the right model for everyone. He considered the course of study offered in each of the UCSD colleges rigorous and conducive to what mattered most—intellectual growth. His preference, he said, was "the Aristotelian approach that stresses knowledge of many areas and deep experience in at least one. . . . What is ultimately going to matter to students when their college years are over is not the particular books they read or the specific curriculum they followed but the cognitive skills they acquired."[35]

Atkinson warned departments that growth in student numbers alone, without a parallel growth in academic strength, would not be rewarded. Not that enrollments were unimportant to him; they were a central issue, in fact, because of their link to the budget—the more students, the more money from the state; the more money from the state, the greater the opportunities to attract outstanding faculty. In 1979, a year before Atkinson came to UCSD, the Office of the President had issued a report warning that UC campuses should brace for anything from small to large declines in student enrollment during the 1980s, the post–baby boom decade.[36] For UCSD, which had the same budget woes as the older campuses but not their thousands of alumni donors and large base of money from the state, every possible funding avenue had to be explored. This set up a tug-of-war between the faculty, who tended to see enrollment as workload, and the administration, which saw it as precious income in a world of scarcity. Atkinson fought for higher numbers than those proposed by the faculty every year, and he usually won. He was helped by UCSD's academic quality and by rising tuition at places like the University of Southern California, Stanford, and other private institutions, which made UC campuses financially attractive to bright students.

The austere budgets of the early 1980s improved by mid-decade, but funding circumstances still required Atkinson and his administrative colleagues to be consistently inventive and innovative in ways small and large. They were constantly on the hunt for opportunities for community or business partners who could help them expand the campus's academic reach and excellence. Atkinson focused his energy and persuasiveness on recruiting faculty and raising funds; he proved highly successful at both.

His growing reputation in San Diego and beyond led the Regents to consider him for president on three occasions, first as a successor to David Saxon in 1983, then again in 1992 and 1995. The Regents chose other candidates in the first two searches. Several colleagues thought that the experience of being passed over in 1992 left him depressed and discouraged; he had been a highly successful chancellor, and much as he loved San Diego, he was ready for something more. Around this time he was offered the presidency of the New York Public Library and briefly

FIGURE 4. Chancellor Richard Atkinson, First Lady Hillary Clinton, and David P. Roosevelt at the dedication of Roosevelt College, UC San Diego, January 26, 1995. *San Diego Union-Tribune*, January 27, 1995, p. 1. Photo credit: *San Diego Union-Tribune*, photo by Laura Embry.

considered it. But he and Rita ultimately decided that their roots were too deep in La Jolla and in the University of California for such a move.

In the mid-1990s two-thirds of the university presidents in the United States had served five years or less. Atkinson had headed San Diego for fifteen. It had been long enough to realize his most important aims: guarding the distinction of the faculty and broadening the scope and excellence of UCSD's academic offerings. The National Research Council's 1995 report on academic program quality at American research universities ranked the scholarly and scientific caliber of UCSD's faculty tenth in the nation—higher than UCLA's and indeed higher than any public US university's except Berkeley. Two UCSD programs—neurosciences and oceanography, the university's founding discipline—were rated first in the country.[37] Its strengths in the arts and humanities were competitive with the best public and private institutions.

Atkinson's UCSD years had seen the establishment of a school of engineering, a graduate school in international relations and Pacific Rim studies, research centers in disciplines ranging from US-Mexican studies to molecular genetics to supercomputing. UCSD was home to the world's largest laboratory for testing structural resistance to earthquakes, a place the state of California looked to for advice following the 1989 Loma Prieta temblor. One of the few programmatic goals he did not achieve was a law school; despite his intense and persistent lobbying, two UC presidents opposed the idea.

Enrollment had doubled and the campus's annual economic impact on the local San Diego economy, $300 million in 1980, had risen to more than a billion dollars a year by 1995. UCSD's contributions to building the city's high-technology sector were so far-reaching that *Washington Post* publisher, Kathryn Graham, once described the economic rebirth of the San Diego region during the 1980s as "the Atkinson miracle."

Institutional transformations of this kind are never simply the work of a single leader. Yet it is clear that Atkinson's Terman-influenced view of research universities was naturally attuned to the aspiring and entrepreneurial character of the campus. He finished what McElroy had begun—expanding the campus's view of itself from a science-centered to a broad-based research university qualified to compete with any in the UC system and beyond. One of his longtime University colleagues described him as among the brightest and most focused of UC's nine chancellors, genuinely—not just rhetorically—willing to take risks and reward creativity.

Anyone observing the pattern of Atkinson's decisions and administrative practice at both NSF and San Diego would have noticed some consistent traits. He was often impulsive, quick to embrace new ideas, highly intellectual, but with a distinctly un-academic dislike of verbal dueling. From a distance, he was often seen as a low-key persuader and consensus builder. Those who knew him up close also saw the drive, the willingness to remove people he did not think up to the job, and the sense of institutional direction that was always at work even if it was not always obvious to the casual observer. His friend and predecessor Bill McGill summed it up: Atkinson's "managerial style is a restless flood of energy. He simply does not rest until he has constructed paths to all of his goals."[38]

Fifteen years at San Diego had shown him that a chancellor should have many goals, because no matter how hard you worked there were some you were not going to accomplish. He had led San Diego to a new and higher level of academic quality. And it had at last led him to something he wanted and felt he had earned: he was the seventeenth president of the University of California.

3

Who Runs the University?

Multicampus systems, such as the University of California, which now domi-
nate public institutions of higher education in the United States, all seem
to be in constant stages of adjustment. They are inherently very difficult to
govern.

—CLARK KERR, *THE GOLD AND THE BLUE*, VOL. 1

After ... years of struggle, we recognize that the university is governed
in a most intricate, artistic way, by complex interactions among its many
parts. ... We no longer ask the ultimate question: Who runs the University?

—ROGER HEYNS, UC BERKELEY CHANCELLOR, "BERKELEY: TODAY
AND TOMORROW," 1971

The institutional train wreck known as SP-1 handed the administration and the
Academic Senate a political dilemma of daunting proportions. As a matter of long-
standing tradition, the University of California was committed to high academic
standards for entering students, a commitment that made UC an anomaly among
public universities from early in its history. As a matter of politics, UC leaders understood that no public university could expect support from a legislature whose
constituencies were sparsely represented on its campuses. Affirmative action had
been an admittedly imperfect but increasingly successful tool for helping strike a
balance between those two realities. Now that tool was gone.

Between 1980 and 1990 the number of African American, Native American,
and Latino undergraduates on UC campuses more than doubled, from 9,000 to
21,000.[1] But the fundamental problem persisted: underrepresented minorities
qualified for UC at a much lower rate than whites and Asians. There seemed no alternative to racial and ethnic targeting in admissions; analyses had demonstrated
that in UC's zero-sum admissions process, using the broader criterion of economic status would not work because it would result in qualifying larger numbers
of white and Asian students. There was also the strange phenomenon called the
achievement gap. When University analyses looked at SAT scores for all California

high school graduates who took the college entrance exam in 1995, they found that at every income level, from the bottom to the top, African American and Latino students averaged lower scores than whites and Asians did. In fact, the average SAT score for African American students in the highest income category was less than that of whites and Asians in the lowest.[2] The persistent gulf between whites and Asians on the one hand and African American and Latinos on the other had been noted in national studies of student academic performance as well. It was borne out by a post–SP-1 experiment at the UCLA School of Law. In 1997 the law school changed its admissions policies and procedures to focus on income rather than race. Although the result was a substantial increase in the socioeconomic diversity of students, the faculty ultimately concluded that the approach did not yield sufficient racial and ethnic diversity.

The achievement gap was one of the reasons UC's student recruitment efforts generally had concentrated more on race than on income and why SP-1's removal of race and ethnicity from the admissions process was seen as such a blow to the goal of a truly diverse student body. Most minority leaders considered progress far too slow, and Latinos, California's fastest-growing minority group, were especially vocal and impatient for results. Latinos represented almost 40 percent of K–12 public school students, but they qualified for UC at a rate of about 4 percent—a striking disparity widely noted in the state's capital. "We want to see more brown faces at UC," Latino legislators told UC officials. "We don't care how you do it."

SP-1 intensified such demands. The president and the chancellors could argue, as they frequently did, that the genius of the Master Plan was that it offered a place at the educational table to just about anyone with the talent and ambition to succeed and that the California State University and the community colleges provided an excellent education. The evidence they pointed to was that students who transferred to UC from these institutions did at least as well as students who entered UC as freshmen. But for many members of minority groups, a University of California campus was the only place to be; no amount of Master Plan rationality could extinguish this aspiration. And UC had just adopted a policy that appeared to guarantee its doors would be closed to them.

ACADEMIC DISSONANCE

SP-1, in fact, sent divisive ripples through every constituency that mattered to the University. Legislators threatened to decimate UC's budget in retaliation for the board's action. The number of underrepresented minorities admitted to the University in the year after adoption of SP-1 dipped slightly systemwide, but there were big drops at highly selective Berkeley and UCLA. That was enough to make SP-1 the subject of vituperative committee hearings in Sacramento. Supporters of affirmative action regarded the Regents' decision as a political act that demanded a political response.

The opportunity to mend rather than end affirmative action at the University of California had been lost. There had been no formal review of SP-1 by the Academic Senate, no time to consider workable alternatives—if such alternatives existed— no chance to prepare the University community, the public, or elected officials for a sudden and radical break with thirty years of affirmative action.

Nor was there leisure to absorb the sense of shock and near-despair that gripped the administration following the Regents' vote. The chair of the Academic Senate, UC Davis law professor Dan Simmons, was soon under fire by a number of his faculty colleagues for what they saw as his failure to hold the line with the Regents on faculty prerogatives in setting admissions standards. By September 1995 a group known as the Faculty Committee to Rescind SP-1 and SP-2 (FCRSP) had gathered more than a thousand faculty signatures on a petition asking the Regents to reverse their July decision. FCRSP's request was generated less by the content of the resolutions than by faculty concerns about violations of shared governance.[3] During the next year, the divisional academic senates on all nine campuses passed resolutions condemning SP-1 and SP-2 and urging the Regents to repeal them.

The faculty were disturbed for two reasons, one substantive and one procedural. Changes in admissions policy or practices had historically originated with the faculty, who had long since been delegated responsibility for setting "the conditions for admission" in the Regents' Standing Order 105.2. SP-1 represented not only a drastic change in admissions policy through its provision abolishing consideration of race and ethnicity. In the UC admissions process, between 40 and 60 percent of undergraduate students were admitted solely on academic achievement—grades and test scores. SP-1 increased those proportions to 50 to 75 percent. This meant, of course, that the latitude of admissions officers to consider students' accomplishments beyond grades and test scores had shrunk. The authority of both the faculty and the administration, who worked closely on admissions matters, had been abridged without consultation or discussion.

The procedural question was more open to dispute. Although SP-1 had been discussed by faculty, administrators, students, and members of the board at five Regents' meetings over eight months, it had not undergone the kind of detailed and thorough scrutiny by the Academic Senate that such a major policy shift would typically receive. Many faculty believed the Regents had ignored their own Standing Orders in bypassing what one faculty member described as the "process of deliberative analysis" in formulating admissions policy.

Some faculty members were sufficiently exercised to take their case to the American Association of University Professors (AAUP), a national group representing the academic profession. In November 1995 the AAUP announced it was launching an investigation into the circumstances surrounding the passage of SP-1 to ascertain whether the Regents had violated the university's traditions of shared governance.[4]

The SP-1 debate and its aftermath also raised questions about the role of the faculty versus the role of the administration in admissions. Over the years admissions had become more and more an administrative matter as UC's enrollment grew, and full-time staff took over some of the jobs involved in the admissions process, such as informing students and schools about UC eligibility and helping with the review of applications. Most student affirmative action programs were established by campus or systemwide administrations, many with little direct faculty involvement. John Aubrey Douglass, a scholar of California higher education, argues that race and ethnicity were included as factors in admission largely at the initiative of the administration, not the faculty, in reaction to the national civil rights movement of the 1960s and pressure from the California legislature in the 1970s and beyond.[5] As discussions about governance proceeded in the months following the Regents' decision, the degree to which admissions had become an administrative as well as faculty responsibility became clear. The administration asserted that its role was supported by the Standing Orders of the Regents, a point that was to become a subject of contention between the faculty and the administration.

Finally, there were the faculty who thought the Regents were right in abolishing racial and ethnic preferences. Their exact number was unknown, and they had been largely silent during the years of affirmative action.

Between January and June 1995 Academic Senate Chair Dan Simmons had visited each of the nine campuses and raised the issue of affirmative action with the divisional senates. He heard no dissent from the University-wide Academic Senate's official position of support for preferences in admissions and employment. Every campus senate approved a statement endorsing the benefits of affirmative action.[6]

Now the faculty opposed to affirmative action were beginning to find a voice. They argued that support for the policy was far less common among UC faculty than anyone suspected but that a climate of political correctness had long discouraged any expressions of doubt. In December 1995 the California Association of Scholars commissioned a poll of one thousand voting members of the UC Academic Senate by the Roper Center for Public Opinion Research at the University of Connecticut. Fifty-two percent of respondents answered "yes" when asked in a telephone survey if they favored the use of race or sex as a criterion for admission to UC. But when given a choice between employing gender and racial preferences or promoting equal opportunity without regard to race, gender, or ethnicity, only 31 percent chose the first option, gender and racial preferences. Supporters of SP-1 pointed to the Roper poll as evidence that UC faculty in general were far more ambivalent about admissions preferences than the official resolutions of the Academic Senate and the pronouncements of its leaders suggested.

SP-1 opened fissures in yet another direction. It was potentially devastating to the University's public image among the very minority students UC was eager to attract. Criticism of the board's action ricocheted around the country in angry editorials, indignant reactions by minority group leaders, and public statements by higher education organizations and K–12 educators deploring an end of affirmative action at the nation's leading public university. Protests became a regular adjunct to meetings of the Regents. All the talk of a new and chilling atmosphere for minority students at UC raised the prospect that SP-1 might awaken slumbering student activism on campuses across California.

SP-1 put UC in the glare of a national spotlight that its president, chancellors, and faculty neither welcomed nor sought. The deluge of negative publicity was not only a constant reminder that UC was seen as an institution trapped in an intractable problem. It made finding reasoned solutions to that problem all the more difficult to achieve.

"A PECULIAR SET OF EVENTS"

There was an even more immediate challenge. Faculty and administrators who were familiar with the daily realities of admitting students knew that SP-1's implementation date would not work.

That date—January 1, 1997—had no relationship to the way UC admitted undergraduates. Students enrolling in fall 1997 would have to apply by November 1996. To prepare for these students, campus and systemwide admissions staff would need to complete a series of tasks by the previous spring, around March 1996. They would need to know what new criteria and selection guidelines had been developed in response to the ban on racial and ethnic preferences. Then they would have to prepare and disseminate this new information to prospective students and their parents and high school admissions counselors.

By December 1995 the first step had already been taken. SP-1 had called for a task force to rewrite UC's admissions requirements in light of the ban on preferences, and it had worked steadily through the fall, finishing up by the end of the year. Atkinson's first reaction was that the Academic Senate and the administration could get the word out in time to implement SP-1 for the entering undergraduate class of 1997. But the more he thought about it and the more he discussed what needed to be done with faculty and admissions people, the more convinced he became that this was an impossible deadline. The major difficulty was meeting the University's responsibilities to inform students about the new criteria within the tight constraints SP-1 imposed.

The question was what to do about it. Taking a formal proposal to the Regents postponing the implementation date was an unpalatable option; the ban continued to generate fierce debate.

By January 1996 Atkinson had come to a decision. He would not ask the board to amend SP-1. The heart of the Regents' resolution, he reasoned, was the requirement to end racial preferences; implementation was essentially an administrative matter. Further, the board's support for SP-1 was hardly unanimous. Ten Regents had voted against it and one had abstained; it had prevailed by just four votes. He was optimistic that most Regents would agree to a postponement once they understood the complications posed by the January 1997 date.

He would talk privately with a number of Regents, in particular those who supported SP-1, and explain the complexities of the admission process and the logistical problems of implementation. With their concurrence, he would then announce a new effective date—fall 1998—more consistent with the admissions cycle and the academic calendar.

Atkinson told the University's chancellors and a few colleagues in the Office of the President that he was pondering this step. At the January Regents' meeting he began consulting with individual Regents, among them Ward Connerly and the governor's close adviser, John Davies. The conversations seemed to go well, and Atkinson felt the consultations could be completed the next week. He assumed that Davies would let Governor Wilson know about the change he was proposing.

What happened next precipitated "a peculiar set of events," as Atkinson later described it. Around 11:30 on the last day of the Regents' meeting, the Berkeley chancellor, Chang-lin Tien, pulled Atkinson aside. He had just learned that an Office of the President administrator had sent an e-mail to admissions officers around the UC system telling them that SP-1's implementation date might be postponed. The Regents' meeting was about to conclude, leaving Atkinson with no time to announce or explain to the board his intentions regarding SP-1.

In any event, the timing was awkward. During the meeting, student Regent Edward Gomez had introduced a motion to rescind SP-1 and SP-2, and an alumni Regent, Judith Levin, had urged delaying implementation for a year. Gomez's proposal was postponed indefinitely, and Levin's never came to a vote. An announcement by the president about deferring implementation at that point could be mistaken for a deliberate tactical move in the board's battle over SP-1 and SP-2.

Word was out and could surface publicly at any moment, however, so communication with chancellors and the Regents was imperative. On his return to the office that afternoon—January 19, 1996—Atkinson wrote the chancellors, with a copy to the Board of Regents, informing them that SP-1's effective date was being moved from January 1, 1997, to fall 1998. "Given the length and phasing of the admissions process," he wrote, "SP-1 will take effect for students seeking admission to the fall 1998 entering class. . . . The implementation timetable described in this letter has been discussed with members of the Board of Regents."

Atkinson spent the following Monday, January 22, in San Diego at a meeting of the search committee to select his successor as UCSD chancellor. Regents Connerly and Davies were also at the meeting. Neither mentioned Atkinson's letter.

That evening Atkinson flew to Sacramento for some meetings the next day. An urgent message from Governor Wilson awaited him. The two men shared a midwestern background and a common history in San Diego, where Wilson was serving as mayor when Atkinson became UCSD chancellor in 1980; they also worked together after Wilson was elected to the US Senate in 1982. When they met in the governor's office on the morning of January 24, Atkinson was completely unprepared for what happened.

Wilson was outraged. The letter to the chancellors about SP-1 was a total surprise; he had been blindsided by the news. Atkinson explained the problem with the implementation date, the difficulties involved in reversing a decision he had already made public, and his conviction that the delay was essential to meeting UC's commitment to the young people of the state. The governor was adamant that the letter had to be withdrawn. He put the matter bluntly: take back the letter or risk being asked to resign.

The meeting ended with no clear resolution. Afterward, Atkinson issued a public statement emphasizing that his decision "represents no change in Regents' policy as enunciated in SP-1" and that he had met with the governor to assure him that SP-1 would be implemented "in an orderly fashion."

That evening Atkinson met with Connerly, Davies, and Sean Walsh, a member of the governor's staff, to discuss how to resolve the dispute. It was another angry and heated exchange. All three told Atkinson the governor would not accept the changes he had announced and that his job was on the line. When Atkinson insisted he could not step back from what he had done, he was asked to propose something they could take to Wilson as a compromise. His first offer was to make SP-1 effective for graduate admissions in fall 1997 instead of fall 1998. No, they replied, that will not satisfy the governor. Atkinson then proposed making SP-1 effective for undergraduates in the spring quarter of 1998. It would be a largely symbolic change from fall 1998 because the few students who enrolled in the spring were mostly junior transfer students. Walsh and the two Regents were dubious about whether the governor would accept this as a compromise but agreed to take it to him.

A day or two later, Connerly called Atkinson and asked him to send the governor a draft statement incorporating his suggestion that the effective date of SP-1 be changed to the spring quarter of 1998. The governor was out of town but would be in his office on the morning of Saturday, January 27, and could review the statement if it was there by noon. Atkinson agreed and sent the draft.

This was the last he heard of the matter until the following Monday at 6:00 A.M., when a UC colleague phoned him with the news that verbatim portions of his draft statement had appeared in that morning's *Los Angeles Times*. More bad news was to follow. Over the previous weekend, Connerly had left a telephone message at the UC president's official residence in Kensington, saying that the governor had a number of changes to the draft statement. The problem was that Atkinson was not living there. He was staying in an Oakland apartment near his office while repairs were being made to the Kensington house. He was still unaware of Connerly's message later that day when he issued the draft statement, unchanged, convinced that the *Times* story demanded an immediate response.

From this point, events unwound with bewildering speed. The issue became not only the implementation date but also the authority of the president versus the will of the Regents. Wilson was angrier than ever. And by this time the disagreement between the UC president and the governor was public, with Regents lining up on both sides. Connerly had asked General Counsel James Holst for a legal opinion on the president's authority to change the effective date of SP-1. Holst's reply was diplomatic. He construed SP-1 as applying to all admissions decisions made after January 1, 1997, as the resolution had stated. On the other hand, the president enjoys broad authority to interpret and implement the Regents' policy. Further, the Board of Regents has the right to change any plan with which it disagrees. "The issue now," Holst concluded, "is a matter of what is the best policy for the University"—a question that should be settled by the board, not the general counsel.[7]

Ten Regents, including Connerly and Davies, as well as Governor Wilson and Assembly Speaker Curt Pringle, demanded a special meeting of the Regents on January 31 to review the performance of the president. Some of their colleagues on the board deplored the move. The special meeting would, in the words of Regent Bill Bagley, "escalate the politics to the continuing harm of my great institution, the University of California." Several other Regents said they were surprised but not overly concerned by the president's action. A few praised his initiative in taking steps to implement SP-1 in ways consistent with UC's admissions calendar.

Nonetheless, a public collision between the president and the Regents seemed inevitable. It was headed off on January 29, however, when Atkinson wrote two conciliatory letters, one to the governor and one to the Board of Regents. Wilson's handwritten changes on the draft statement Atkinson had sent him had included wording to the effect that the president recognized his obligation to implement SP-1 and was committed to doing so. To put an end to the controversy, Atkinson offered to write the governor a letter incorporating these points.

In that letter he alluded to the misunderstandings of recent days and referred to the president's "legal duty" and "moral obligation" to carry out regental policy. He then wrote a separate letter to the board, acknowledging that he had "erred in not adequately consulting with the Regents before deciding to postpone implementation of SP-1" and explaining that the resolution would take effect for professional and graduate students in fall 1997. For undergraduates, it would be effective in the spring quarter of the 1997–98 academic year. This meant that the first full class covered by SP-1 would be that entering in fall 1998.

The special meeting was canceled. At their next regular meeting in February 1996, the Regents approved the timetable proposed by the president in his letter. In the headlong pace of events, few people noticed that while he had apologized for the miscues and miscommunications, the president had succeeded in holding his ground on the main issue. SP-1 would not be fully implemented until fall 1998, the date Atkinson had announced in the first place. And his presidency had escaped becoming the first public casualty of SP-1.

THE GOVERNANCE ISSUE

SP-1's effective date had been settled, but the governance crisis had not. UC President Emeritus Clark Kerr worried publicly about the symbolic implications of Atkinson's letter to the governor. Shared governance, he said, requires the president to work with all the University's constituencies—the faculty, the campuses, the Regents. For the president to say that he had a "legal duty" and a "moral obligation" to implement the policies adopted by the Regents was, for Kerr, to tip the scales too far in the direction of a single constituency, even if the board's legal authority for governing the University was indisputable.

Kerr's remark illustrated yet another of the governance consequences of SP-1. Shared governance is not just a question of legal power and delegations of authority, but of trust and goodwill among the faculty, the administration, and the board in addressing problems and issues facing the University. The circumstances of SP-1's adoption fractured this trust and disrupted the web of working relationships essential to running a large and complex institution. The president was at the center of this delicately balanced system and therefore a key person in restoring its equilibrium.

As a first step, in November 1995 Atkinson had asked Academic Senate Chair Arnold Leiman to begin a review of the Senate's organization and operations and its role in governing the University, a role that "is now highlighted again in the present discussions surrounding affirmative action."[8] In May 1996, with the AAUP report looming, the president made an effort to clarify the governance issue. He wrote to the Regents, with a copy to the AAUP, summarizing his views on how governance had operated in the passage of the two resolutions. He concluded that although the process leading up to adoption of SP-1 was "a significant departure from the way such decisions are traditionally made at the University," it did not rise to the level of a breach of shared governance. The Regents' action was within their authority; there had been ample opportunity for faculty and others to make their views known; and because affirmative action was a controversial issue on which consensus did not yet exist within the University community, it was not surprising that the events of the previous year had strained the University's governance mechanisms.

His letter included an opinion from the general counsel on the division of responsibility among the Regents, the faculty, and the administration in matters relating to admissions. The faculty, Holst wrote, were responsible for setting the "conditions of admission," understood to "refer only to the *academic* qualifications for admission." He concluded:

> Other admissions criteria, and the selection from among students who meet those criteria, are the responsibility of The Regents and the administration. This includes the role of race, ethnicity, and gender in selecting students from among those who meet the minimum academic qualifications as determined by the faculty.[9]

Holst emphasized that the administration had traditionally and appropriately consulted with the faculty in setting nonacademic admissions criteria and selecting from among qualified students. But his interpretation supported the president's argument that the board had acted within its authority.

Most faculty leaders were unhappy with this conclusion. They disputed the legal view that the faculty's role was only to determine the academic conditions for admission, which they saw as circumscribing their authority in a process in which the faculty perspective should be primary. The whole approach was, one faculty member said, like defining marriage only in terms of its legal obligations. His reaction reflected yet another twist in the controversy. It was turning out to be exceedingly difficult even to establish the basic terms in which the crisis in governance could be discussed.

In April 1996 the Berkeley division of the Academic Senate took the unprecedented step of approving a preliminary resolution that censured the Regents for violations of shared governance, failure to protect the University from political interference, and disregard of the vote by every campus academic senate calling on the board to rescind SP-1 and SP-2. The resolution would take effect only if approved by a majority of UC Berkeley senate members through a mail ballot scheduled for the fall. The ballot was never sent, however, in part because many faculty concluded that the University-wide Academic Senate's planned task force could address the issues they had raised. Another reason may have been a public statement that Atkinson, alarmed about the censure possibility, delivered at the October 1996 meeting of the board. In that statement, he acknowledged the faculty's unhappiness, telling the Regents that he had heard from many who were disturbed by the damage the vote on SP-1 and SP-2 had done to the University's system of shared governance. He had assured these faculty members that the Regents had articulated their full support for shared governance "in both public remarks and private statements." He concluded by voicing his own:

Our system of shared authority and responsibility among Regents, administration, and faculty is the single most important reason for the University of California's greatness, and it is just as essential to our success today as it has been for more than three-quarters of a century. I would not be president of this university if I did not believe the Regents join me in that conviction.[10]

THREE THEORIES

One reason for the continuing dissonance over the Regents' action, of course, was that the parties were acting on different assumptions not only about what had happened but also about what could and should have happened. At least three theories have emerged to explain why SP-1 and SP-2 passed and in the process created a governance crisis.

The first, articulated even before the board's decision, is that the vote was a clear and simple political intrusion into the University's autonomy. The governor, with Connerly's cooperation, made the University an unwilling partner in his presidential campaign by using the power of his office to compel those Republican members of the board who needed persuading to vote his way.

The second is that the administration and the faculty leadership badly misread the reactions and intentions of the board during the months leading up to the July 1995 vote. The administration, in this view, failed to recognize that its strategy of demonstrating how affirmative action operated was having the opposite of its intended effect. The more some Regents learned about what was actually involved in racial and ethnic preferences, the more their support for them wavered. A corollary is that if only the administration had offered a different version of affirmative action acceptable to a majority of the Regents, they might have agreed to mend rather than end it. As it was, the theory goes, the administration's failure to respond with a workable alternative left the board with no option except to abolish affirmative action altogether.

The third explanation maintains that SP-1 could have been avoided if only the faculty leadership had insisted on its right to review Connerly's proposal before the board took action on it. This theory assumes that a vigorous assertion of the faculty's role in admissions issues would have had a uniquely powerful effect, or at least one striking enough to persuade a majority of the Regents to postpone their vote for the weeks or months it would take for the Academic Senate to complete its review.

All three theories are speculative, since we cannot be certain about the motivation of individuals or how a scenario in which SP-1 and SP-2 were not approved would play out. Few people, for example, would dispute that political motives played a part in passage of the resolutions. The question is whether they were the only motives operating in those who voted for them. We do not know with any certainty whether these Regents responded to their conscience or to political pressure, but we do know that the makeup of the Regents had become more politically conservative over the administrations of two Republican governors, who nominated members of the board. Being a Republican does not necessarily mean being against affirmative action, of course; two Republican Regents, Bill Bagley and Roy Brophy, favored the University's programs. President Peltason said he went into the SP-1 controversy with the view—an "informal assessment"—that roughly a third of the board enthusiastically supported affirmative action, a third opposed it as unfair, and the remaining third agreed that it was unfair but did not feel strongly enough to challenge the president, the chancellors, and their fellow Regents who believed in the value of preferences in admissions. It was this third group of Regents that Connerly successfully mobilized.[11]

Peltason argues further that even if the governor's presidential campaign was the reason he supported the resolutions, that fact by itself does not constitute an infringement of the University's autonomy. As president of the Board of Regents, the governor had the right to support or oppose any UC policy he chose, and if his intent was to please the voters, that, in Peltason's view, did not change his right to act as he did. Just as Governor Deukmejian used the power and influence of his office almost a decade earlier to achieve UC divestment from South African businesses, a cause he believed in, so Wilson acted in pursuit of his own political beliefs and constituencies.

And if Peltason was right in his assessment that roughly two-thirds of the board was to one degree or another opposed to the use of preferences, the remarkable thing is how many Regents voted to retain them. Even if some did so mainly to spare the University the burden of being at the forefront of a divisive national issue, they had at least been convinced that abolishing affirmative action was less important than protecting the University and its reputation. The theory that the administration misread the board may in part be true, but it does not explain the closeness of the vote.

What alternative form of affirmative action might the administration and the faculty have presented to the Regents? They could have committed to a date at which UC would no longer use preferences in admissions, on the basis that even supporters of affirmative action saw it as a temporary measure. But such a proposal would have run into several major hurdles: the governor's 1994–95 presidential campaign timetable; Connerly's conviction that the University should not delay in doing what he considered right, regardless of the consequences; and the near-impossibility of forging agreement on a specific date when preferences would no longer be necessary.

Or the administration could have offered to rely on outreach programs, UC's long-standing efforts to improve the academic preparation of minority students in California's K–12 public schools. Outreach programs employed a variety of strategies, among them professional development for teachers, special classes to help minority students, and direct working relationships between UC and public schools. The University was already hard at work in this direction, with hundreds of outreach programs. But in the administration's view, outreach represented a long-term solution to a problem that, for reasons of both politics and principle, demanded a much more immediate answer. Outreach was just one of the University's means of enrolling more underrepresented students, not a substitute for consideration of race and ethnicity in the admissions process.

Even if the administration had decided to suggest a change, it would have faced two formidable obstacles. One was the zero-sum character of its upper-one-eighth admission pool under the Master Plan, which in a time of expanding enrollments meant that qualifying for UC was getting more difficult. Another was the stubborn fact that substituting economic disadvantage for ethnic and racial preferences was unlikely to increase the proportion of minority students on UC campuses.

And if the Academic Senate leadership had decided to make a strong assertion of its rights to compel the Regents to delay SP-1, it would have had to act quickly. Connerly's resolution was released on July 5, two weeks before the meeting at which it was considered. No one knew in advance which way the regental vote would go. The faculty senate had already gone on record as opposing any move by the Regents to ban affirmative action. A public challenge to the board's authority on governance grounds would risk alienating Regents who had not made up their minds or who were inclined to vote against SP-1. And while some Regents later deplored the passage of SP-1, few—if any—believed the board lacked authority to do what it did. A show of force by the academic leadership would have placed the administration in the untenable position of mediating a public fight between the faculty and the Regents. Or it might have created a temptation for the Regents to demonstrate conclusively that they, not the faculty, were in charge. In either case, the result might well have been a far worse rupture in the shared governance system than the one that actually occurred.

Regent Connerly had shown himself a skillful strategist, and never more so than in his timing of the release of his resolutions. The Regents as a whole and the UC community learned the details of his proposals a bare two weeks before the board voted on them. This was early enough to deflect complaints that he had given no warning of his intentions but late enough to make it difficult to sort out all the implications of the two proposals and organize and mount a rebuttal.

Did the Regents violate shared governance? The answer is probably a qualified no. Connerly had talked only of abolishing affirmative action, a question of broad policy appropriate for regental determination. But his resolution went beyond policy to prescribe an alternative admissions procedure that the faculty could legitimately claim they should have been consulted about. In the chaotic weeks between release of his resolution and the vote, there was no time to grapple with the many-layered substantive and procedural aspects of SP-1.

RIGHTS AND RESPONSIBILITIES

Connerly had written a letter soon after his appointment to the board that, in retrospect, sheds some light on his perspective on governance and his actions regarding SP-1 and SP-2. In December 1993, almost a year before the affirmative action issue arose, he commented on the role of the administration in a letter to his colleagues on the board:

> It is important for us to remember . . . that in an academic setting, the role of the administration is a rather unique one, in many respects. While the administration is the authorized agent of the Regents, the administration is also one of several constituencies which seeks to influence our decision-making. It would be naïve for us not to recognize that the administration of any deliberative body will have its own agenda, from time-to-time, and will be manipulating (I don't mean this in a negative sense) the Board to achieve the outcome desired by the administration. . . . I have no problem with that. In fact, I expect and want it to happen.
>
> It is important, however, that the governing body set standards of accountability for the administration. . . . If we accept the view that the administration is a "constituent" member of the University family, like the faculty, the students, the alumni, and others, then it becomes easier for us to accept the notion of accountability.[12]

President Peltason responded in part:

> The Board of Regents is not an impartial judicial hearing body, a legislative committee, or a court of law. . . . Although there are circumstances and issues in which the Board solicits a wide variety of comments and hears from a number of different constituencies, the Board is not there to balance among competing claims and pick and choose which it will support.
>
> The Board of Regents is the *governing* body of a great university, an incredibly complex multicampus university. The administration—and this is also true of the Academic Senate—is not just one of many constituencies, but is the Board of Regents' *chosen and publicly designated agent* in whom it has vested confidence and to whom it has delegated responsibility to manage the University. . . . Although I think you did not intend it, your comments could be interpreted as saying that the Board considers recommendations from the President and the Chancellors as merely one among several competing recommendations from various constituencies. For the Board to send such a signal would radically undermine the authority of its officers and make it extraordinarily difficult for them to bring tough or controversial recommendations. Such a method of governing would not work in the best of times.[13]

It was nothing new for a Regent or Regents to disagree with a position taken by the president or the faculty. It was new for a Regent to state as a principle that the administration was just one constituency among others and that its recommendations carried no more weight than those advanced by any other segment of the University community. In practice, the Connerly position would put the president permanently on the defensive in his relationship with the board, weakening his authority while leaving his responsibilities undiminished.

Most Regents probably did not share his view, but some did seem to share his skepticism about the administration's commitment to implementing SP-1. For months and even years after its adoption, a number of Regents, Connerly in particular, spoke openly of their doubts about the administration's good faith willingness to carry out SP-1. Connerly referred often and publicly to his suspicion that admissions officers and other UC officials were dragging their feet on implementation or actively searching for detours around the ban on preferences.

The problem that consistently arose in wrestling with the governance crisis was that shared governance had succeeded in large part by *not* talking about the relative rights and authority of the Regents, the faculty, and the administration. Roger Heyns, a UC Berkeley chancellor who knew something about conflict in academic institutions, was right in pointing out that the issue of who runs the university is a dangerous question to ask. The campaign to end affirmative action raised this question in its starkest form.

The events surrounding SP-1 illustrated the influence a single and determined Regent can have. Regardless of the merits of the issue, repeal of affirmative action was accomplished by taking a major policy question beyond the closed circle of normal regental discussion and decision making into the glare of public and media attention. The University is a public institution and should expect public scrutiny. But to make a controversial and unresolved issue the focus of public and political debate is to risk submerging its complexities and short-circuiting opportunities to work through disagreements within the UC community itself. SP-1 set a precedent for public regental advocacy disruptive to the orderly functioning of the board—and of the University.

SP-1's ban on racial preferences was rendered moot by voter approval of a 1996 ballot measure, Proposition 209, which ended affirmative action in all California public entities; Ward Connerly led the campaign for its passage.[14] A challenge to the law by the American Civil Liberties Union (ACLU) was denied by the Ninth Circuit Court of Appeals the following year, and the ACLU's subsequent appeal to the US Supreme Court failed.[15] What if Proposition 209 had gone down to defeat at the polls? Had this been the outcome, Atkinson considered it inconceivable, especially in light of the close vote on SP-1 and SP-2, that the Board of Regents would have chosen to continue on the anti–affirmative action course set by their July 1995 resolutions.

The passage of SP-1 made Atkinson the first University of California president in two decades to face the conflict between the Master Plan's goal of broad

educational access and UC's high admissions standards without the tool of affirmative action. In the months after SP-1's adoption, it became increasingly clear
that the measure was a new kind of Gordian knot, impossible to cut through with
a single stroke, whose coils reached deep into politics, governance, and competing
conceptions of academic merit. Unraveling SP-1, strand by laborious strand, was
to be a central task of the Atkinson administration. Even in 1995 it was obvious this
would be the work of years.

Seventeenth President

[Both chancellors and presidents] are surrounded with potential adversaries but only the president has no rooting section—only potential assailants, except for the members of his or her own personal staff and, possibly, the regents. . . . At all times, the urgent issue was: how much could I accomplish and how well in whatever time was available?

—CLARK KERR, *THE GOLD AND THE BLUE*, VOL. 1

The presidency of the UC system is a task of extraordinary complexity. Located at the nexus of the often conflicting expectations of the regents, the faculty, the students, the alumni, the staff, the governor, the legislature, and the general public (including many special interest groups), the president is also the "manager" of a ten billion dollar per year enterprise. The president is the one person whose mandate is the welfare of the university as a whole, beyond the aggregate of its components.

—[UC SANTA CRUZ CHANCELLOR EMERITUS] ROBERT SINSHEIMER,
THE STRANDS OF A LIFE

This job is like dancing on lily pads. Sooner or later you sink.

—FORMER UNIVERSITY OF CALIFORNIA PRESIDENT

FROM CHANCELLOR TO PRESIDENT

The office Atkinson walked into on his first day as president was near the top of a twenty-eight-story semicircular building with a commanding view of the Oakland hills. Commissioned by the industrialist Henry J. Kaiser and completed in 1960, the Kaiser Center's sleek modernism and innovative design epitomized the company's far-flung commercial empire and, along with it, the confident optimism of midcentury America. It was the largest building west of the Rockies in the year it rose on the shores of Oakland's Lake Merritt, clad in a facade of aluminum and glass. Kaiser had shrewdly foreseen the many potential uses of aluminum in the postwar American economy, and his insight paid off handsomely. On his instructions, as many as possible of his namesake building's 900,000 square feet were fashioned from products sold by Kaiser industries—especially the mega-profitable aluminum. The result was aesthetically striking. The Kaiser Center's slim, curved, gleaming silhouette, reflected in the waters of the lake in a famous photograph by Ansel Adams, moved the architect Pierluigi Serraino to remark that the building looked as if it had been "dropped from the moon."[1]

The Kaiser Center's expansive energy had a certain educational parallel in the California Master Plan for Higher Education, another creative design of 1960. But otherwise the building did not evoke academic associations. The Office of the President had moved there from Berkeley in 1989 for reasons both practical and symbolic—to consolidate its 1,500 employees in one place and to underscore the systemwide headquarters' separate identity from the Berkeley campus. Critics saw the Kaiser Center as too elegant and too corporate for a public university. Some within the UC community regarded it as an architectural expression of how the campuses viewed the Office of the President—an expensive bureaucratic road-block to their goals and desires.

When Atkinson was appointed, UC Davis Chancellor Larry Vanderhoef wrote him a letter of friendly advice that summarized this perception succinctly. The Office of the President was too big, too costly, too slow, too focused on operations, too insensitive to campus needs. The solution he proposed was to slash middle management—highly intelligent people, he wrote, whose industry served only to hobble the decision-making process—and to turn over several major UCOP activities to the campuses.[2] Just two days before Atkinson's selection, in a gloomy editorial about the questions the University's new president would face, the *Sacramento Bee* seemed to agree: "How much of the bloated bureaucracy, in its plush Oakland high-rise, could be eliminated?"[3]

Some of the tension between the campuses and the Office of the President was endemic to any large academic organization. Some was the result of UC's special history. Unlike many multicampus systems in the United States, which are organized around a collection of existing, often very different institutions, the University of California started in 1868 with one campus, Berkeley, and expanded outward into ten research universities. In the early years of UC's existence, the University *was* Berkeley, administrative authority was concentrated in the Board of Regents, and the president's power was essentially limited to academic issues. Only in the twentieth century did the Regents begin to share their authority, first with the president and the faculty and much later with the chancellors. The process was neither smooth nor swift. It gave rise to more or less permanent frictions between those who feared excessive campus independence would erode the unity of the University and those who resented excessive bureaucratic controls from the Office of the President.

In October 1995 the issue of how UC was governed, and in particular the role of the Office of the President, reached a new level of intensity. The Board of Regents and the Office of the President had been operating in crisis mode for more than three years. The faculty was unhappy about what it saw as excessive administrative pay and regental encroachment on its authority in the decision to adopt SP-1. Between the executive compensation controversy beginning in 1992 and the affirmative action fight in July 1995, a demoralizing parade of mini-scandals on the campuses and in UCOP had stoked the fires of internal recrimination and fault-finding, particularly with the Office of the President. These "untoward events," as one vice president called them, popped up so regularly for a while that they required almost daily meetings, absorbing large amounts of administrative energy and attention. The result was to raise serious questions about the University's administrative organization as well as its internal audit and business practices. How could the University face its external crises—its tarnished public image and its sinking budgets—if it could not get its own house in order? "In my opinion, the University system is in a hell of a mess," a veteran chancellor emeritus wrote Atkinson in September 1995, and recommended the appointment of a group of wise elders to assess the University's prospects and organization. In the waning days of the Peltason administration, a blue-ribbon commission to "conduct the broadest inquiry into the organization and administration of the University of California" had been considered briefly.[4] Some Regents liked the idea of a review, but they were more focused on the weaknesses in UCOP's business side exposed by recent events. During his first week in office, Atkinson wrote the Regents that he would look into commissioning a study of the Office of the President by a task force of business leaders.

The task force met once or twice, but that was as far as it got. In part, the president had more immediate worries on his mind. In part, he had his own ideas about what needed changing.

Atkinson's opinions about the Office of the President resembled those of other chancellors—that it exerted too much control and issued too many directives. As the head of one of the younger campuses, he was keenly aware of the power of the older ones and familiar with the convoluted internal politics of the University. Although a critic of some aspects of UCOP's operations, he felt that the University of California, as a system, did not need reorganizing. It needed to get its priorities in order, and he had some ideas about what they were.

ADMINISTRATIVE AGENDAS

Atkinson's first task was to establish his relationship with three major internal constituencies, the faculty, the chancellors, and the twenty-six-member Board of Regents. His scholarly reputation was a natural advantage with the Academic Senate, and he felt completely at home in UC's faculty culture. The chancellors posed a more sensitive issue. Making the leap from fellow chancellor to president involved a certain inescapable awkwardness, given that several of his chancellorial colleagues had been his rivals for the job. For the most part, it was an uncomfortable but temporary challenge. Whatever feelings the chancellors harbored about his selection, Atkinson was well known to them and had earned their respect for his accomplishments at San Diego.

The highest hurdle was the Regents. Chancellors are a step removed from the board; their principal responsibility at board meetings is presenting and defending their campus's proposals, and although Regents and chancellors occasionally ally with each other, these alliances typically revolve around specific campus projects or initiatives. The president works directly with the Regents, especially the chair, on every major question facing the University. His responsibility for setting the agenda makes him a powerful influence on the substance and timing of issues that come before the Regents. On the other hand, the success or failure of any president is determined in large part by whether the board supports him and his goals. As Kerr knew, Regents are indispensable allies and dangerous antagonists. Regental confidence, once lost, is difficult to retrieve.

Few Regents would have questioned Atkinson's academic stature or his administrative abilities. But he had been a compromise candidate selected by a divided board, some of whose members had been partisans of other chancellors. Some Regents had hesitated over choosing a president whose personal life had been written about in the press, even if the lawsuit was long in the past. At UCSD he was a familiar figure in the endless round of meetings, ceremonies, dinners, and civic occasions that are routine fixtures in the life of a chief campus officer. Among the Regents Atkinson was a much less visible presence. He sometimes sent a vice chancellor to represent him at Regents' meetings and rarely attended the Regents' dinners that took place at every meeting. His aloofness from these events was unusual in someone with presidential ambitions, and it did not go unnoticed. However successful he had been as a chancellor, as a president he had something to prove.

David Gardner tells a story in his memoirs about his first Regents' meeting, a contentious affair marked by bickering and bad feeling. He decided on the spot to tell the Regents that he had two choices about how to spend his time: he could referee Regental squabbling, or he could concentrate on doing the job the board hired him to fill. His successor, Jack Peltason, used his first Regents' meeting to make it clear that, while he served at the board's pleasure, he was not willing to have twenty-six bosses telling him what to do.

The defining event for Atkinson came later, four months into his administration: the explosion over the implementation date of SP-1. Although the media focused on the theatrics of the situation, behind the scenes most Regents soon came to understand that what happened was at bottom a case of mixed signals and miscommunications, not a challenge to their authority. Atkinson endured some bruising twists and turns along the way, including the governor's public threat to have him fired. But by the time the incident was over, he had passed the first crucial test of his presidency.

That episode revealed something about the kind of president he was going to be. David Saxon's leading tendency was to reason his way to decisions; David Gardner's, to plan any significant step with meticulous care; Jack Peltason's, to nurture cordial relationships and seek reasonable compromise. Atkinson's was to rely largely on his instincts and an exceptional intelligence. He was neither an administrative planner nor a long-term strategist. His style tended more toward inventive extemporizing and watching for the possibilities on the horizon that would get him closer to his goals. He paid less attention to occasional losses than to having the right people heading in what he considered the right general direction.

His research on leadership during his years as a cognitive psychologist convinced him that attempts at scientific analyses of the subject were no more enlightening than the anecdotal evidence invoked in MBA programs and executive seminars. His day-to-day experience as an administrator suggested that delay and indecisiveness at the top can become a destructive virus in an academic organization. "In a university environment," Atkinson once wrote, "there is a tendency to check with every constituency several times, often without being precise about the possible alternatives from which one must choose a course of action. Formulate the options clearly and then push for agreement."[5]

Atkinson's political astuteness was often at war with this drive to bring issues to a resolution. He did not always choose to employ his political skills, sometimes for reasons of principle but sometimes in moments of impatience or exasperation. He disliked long meetings, hated red tape, and had a great deal of trouble tolerating delay. Saxon thought the reason for Atkinson's restiveness during lengthy policy discussions was that he was ahead of everyone else in the room. In any case, Atkinson's headlong pace was well known to those who worked with him. Once, at San Diego, he asked his secretary why it was taking her so long to place a series of phone calls. "I'm dialing as fast as I can," she answered, to which he replied, "Dial faster!"

In Oakland the new president soon became a familiar figure to everyone, regardless of place in the hierarchy, who was working on a project that interested him. Surprised staff members would look up to find him at their elbow, curious to know how they were coming along on something he was waiting for. He believed competition sharpened performance, and if you did not move speedily enough on an assignment from him, you might discover he had moved it down the hall to someone else. Everyone soon learned that he did not tolerate long-winded disquisitions on any subject. Working for him was a perpetual exercise in learning to be concise.

Vice presidents sometimes found it unsettling that their staff knew more than they did on urgent topics the president wanted to resolve quickly. It was part of Atkinson's penchant for blowing up the boxes on organization charts, which he had been doing at NSF and San Diego long before Arnold Schwarzenegger made it a political battle cry. He was constitutionally curious and open to all kinds of ideas, no matter who proposed them or how extreme they might appear. It was symptomatic of a management style that did not make for an orderly day. On the other hand, one of his strengths as an executive was a temperamental affinity for the often crisis-ridden and disorderly nature of administrative life. The Office of the President, despite its staid bureaucratic facade, sat at the center of a huge decentralized university and was rife with constant pressures from all directions— Regents, legislators, chancellors, faculty, students, the public, the sheer unpredictability of events. He found a certain amount of chaos stimulating, and when things got too comfortable, he was apt to create a little disequilibrium of his own.

The single strongest influence on his administrative perspective was his early professional experience with Stanford's intensely competitive culture under Fred Terman—for grants, prestige, and institutional influence. The Terman approach was a practical and highly focused way of leveraging resources and abilities in good and bad times alike, one that he had seen tested at Stanford and later employed himself at UC San Diego. Atkinson operated on the conviction that nothing is more important to organizations than encouraging talent and that talent is best encouraged by giving it the widest possible scope, without overly specific prescriptions about outcomes. He had no micro-managing tendencies. At NSF and UC San Diego he had focused his energies on a few major priorities, and once in Oakland he left the day-to-day running of the Office of the President to the vice presidents and the campuses to the chancellors. Chancellors and vice presidents could seek help or advice if they wanted it, but as long as things were going smoothly, they did not hear from him. Anyone who lost his confidence, however, could expect to hear from him early and often.

The immediate challenge was to manage his relationship with a board that had unpleasant memories of the executive compensation controversy and was still at odds over the vote on SP-1. Depending on the Regent and the issue, there were always critics: Ward Connerly, on any proposal that he thought threatened to violate the ban on racial and ethnic preferences; Frank Clark, on hospital-related questions; Velma Montoya, on executive pay; Glenn Campbell, on a range of topics. By the end of his tumultuous first year, however, relations with the Regents settled into a predictable if not always harmonious pattern. He made a habit of alerting key Regents when large issues loomed and having vice presidents talk routinely with members of the board to keep informed about what the Regents were thinking. An indirect measure of his success was a series of regental decisions in the mid-1990s to delegate more authority to the president. This was the result of the

Regents' desire to streamline the agenda to spend more time on substantive issues, but they would never have expanded the authority of a president they did not trust.

GOALS

With his long experience in the UC system, Atkinson understood that anything he wanted to achieve must be done within the University's culture of shared governance, marked by highly collaborative and consultative decision making. What he wanted to accomplish as president involved three overarching issues. The first was threading his way through the complex maze of post–SP-1 admissions. The furor over SP-1's implementation date paled in comparison to the political and educational repercussions that would follow if the resolution choked off the admission of significant numbers of minority students to UC.

The second issue was the University's budget. Like most other public institutions in the United States, the University of California had taken staggering hits to its budget in the late 1980s and early 1990s. UC coped by reducing its workforce by five thousand employees, freezing salaries—in 1993, for the first time since 1933, they were actually cut—and raising tuition. By 1995 its budget from the state was roughly $900 million less than it would have been if the state had funded normal cost increases over the previous four years.[6] The bleak fiscal outlook had begun to improve the previous year with a compact hammered out between the University and the governor that put a floor under UC's budget and allowed some enrollment growth and improvement in faculty salaries. But no one expected that UC would recoup its losses from the early 1990s, or even that its state-funded budgets, which had sunk by some 20 percent, would improve much in the next few years. Warding off more damage was essential.

The third issue was the imperative of growth created by Tidal Wave II. The California State Department of Finance's demographic data showed that the number of high school graduates was on the cusp of a decade-long climb. According to UC's analyses, these figures meant that the University should be prepared to enroll an additional 63,000 students, an increase of 43 percent. The California Postsecondary Education Commission's studies echoed the University's projection that enrollments would rise from 147,000 in 1998–99 to 210,000 in 2010–11.[7] Educating these undergraduates would require replacing 4,000 faculty expected to leave or retire during this period and adding 3,000 new faculty, for a total of 7,000.

Tidal Wave II was the first big expansion of college age students since Clark Kerr's presidency in the 1960s, but it was larger than Tidal Wave I and would last longer. In the Kerr era, UC absorbed 6,000 additional students annually for seven years, opening three new campuses in the process. Now UC would be accommodating approximately 5,600 additional students annually over twelve years, with only one new campus. The Regents had just selected a site, UC Merced, but moving it from concept to construction would be a massive undertaking. Academic quality could be at risk if enrollment growth throughout the University were not carefully and thoughtfully handled.

Atkinson set to work defining an agenda for his administration, which he distilled into a list of nine goals:

- Maintain faculty quality;
- Ensure diversity at UC;
- Expand UC's partnership with the K–12 schools;
- Reinforce public perception of UC's role in research and encourage new forms of cooperation with industry;
- Maintain the vitality and quality of education at UC;
- Maintain UC's world leadership in the application of digital technology to learning and instruction;
- Expand UC's role in extended education;
- Restructure business practices and distribute authority to the campuses so that they are as entrepreneurial as possible, yet with the clear proviso that authority is exercised according to systemwide policy, with the Office of the President playing an oversight role to ensure accountability;
- Strengthen UC's ties with the public, its elected representatives in Washington and Sacramento, and its one million alumni.

The obstacles were clear: the state's fiscal crisis; the crisis of funding and performance in California's public schools; the negative reaction among many legislators and members of the public to the affirmative action battle; public perceptions that the faculty pursued research and neglected undergraduate education. In this unpromising environment, the University gained an asset in an October 1995 report by the National Research Council on the quality of American graduate programs. The NRC survey was a reputational study, which meant that the academic departments it covered were assessed for the caliber of their faculty and programs by other academics. Reputational surveys have limitations, among them the risk of favoring long-established universities. They can also be difficult to carry out because some departments include a proliferating number of subspecialties, not all of which may be equally strong.[8] Nonetheless, there are good reasons why the NRC was considered the best and most reliable assessment of faculty and program quality in the United States. The 1995 study assessed 3,634 programs in forty-one fields at 274 universities, reflecting the judgments of nearly eight thousand faculty members about which Ph.D. programs ranked highest in the nation for their performance in preparing scholars and scientists. Berkeley's outstanding ratings were no surprise; it had more programs ranked among the top ten in their field than any other university. But a bias toward established programs does not explain the stellar marks given to young campuses like UC San Diego, whose faculty quality was rated tenth in the nation and which had just under half of its twenty-nine doctoral programs ranked in the top ten of their disciplines. As a system, UC's rankings were unmatched anywhere: more than half of the 229 UC programs assessed by the NRC were in the top twenty in their field in terms of faculty quality; more than a third—78 of 229—were rated among the top ten. A study of American research universities published two years after the NRC evaluations also noted the remarkable performance of the smaller campuses: "The eye-catching additions to the [top] ranks in our classification of research universities, however, are the UC campuses at Santa Barbara, Riverside, and Santa Cruz. The speed with which these institutions rose from modest beginnings is astonishing." The authors emphasized UC's unusual one-university concept—its common salary scale, criteria for promotion and tenure, high standards for graduate programs, and a systemwide academic senate—as an important factor in the rise of a system of campuses marked by unusual quality.[9] The award of three Nobel Prizes to UC faculty in October 1995 came just in time to underscore the NRC results.

The NRC study was a gift to the new administration. It gave UC officials ammunition for making the case to the governor and the legislature that UC was a wise investment for the state. It proved that the University had managed to elude damage to its academic quality despite the huge fiscal losses of the early 1990s—a strong vote of confidence in UC's future at a moment when confidence was needed.

A second and far greater gift was soon to follow. The California economy was about to recover from its long nosedive of the early 1990s. At the beginning of 1996, the state's economy began to pick up speed, and by the end of the year economic growth in California surpassed that of the nation as a whole for the first time since 1989.[10] Almost 350,000 jobs were created during the twelve months of 1996, many of them in California's high-technology sector. The dot-com boom had begun, and one of the state's greatest public beneficiaries of that economic explosion would be the University of California. Just before Atkinson took office, the University and Governor Wilson reached agreement on a compact intended to halt the budgetary freefall of the previous five years. A succession of compacts—later called partnerships—ratified by Governors Wilson and Davis promised the University a minimum level of funding in exchange for specific actions UC would be held accountable for performing, such as meeting agreed-upon faculty teaching loads and improving graduation rates. In each of the first five years of the Atkinson administration the state's contribution exceeded the compact agreement by a significant margin.[11]

In fall 1995, however, all this was in the future. The most pressing issue on Atkinson's mind was organizing his administration to deal with the budget challenge. "I plan to take an active role in the budget development, resource allocation, and budget implementation processes," he wrote the Regents in his first official communication to the board, a letter dated October 3, 1995. He announced that the UCOP budget office, which had been under the provost and academic vice president, would report directly to him. He took over as chair of the Executive Budget Committee, which oversaw the eighteen-month process of planning, coordinating, presenting, and defending UC's proposed annual operating and capital budgets to the Regents, the governor, and the legislature.

His next step was to institute two major changes in how the Office of the President allocated funds to the campuses. The first had to do with overhead or indirect costs—reimbursement from federal or other grants for the administrative costs of conducting research. It was an issue stretching back at least to the mid-1970s and the administration of David Saxon. The argument was over how to distribute these reimbursements among nine campuses that varied greatly in the amount of research they conducted. The practice was to share some of the total with less research-intensive campuses, which meant, of course, that campuses with more contracts and grants forfeited indirect cost funds they would otherwise have gotten. Unsurprisingly, faculty at these campuses—especially UC San Francisco and UC San Diego—were unhappy with the arrangement. Saxon compromised by altering the distribution formula somewhat; under his successor, David Gardner, campuses got an increasingly larger proportion of the funds they generated—a return of about 65 percent or 70 percent on their indirect cost reimbursements. Chancellor Atkinson thought they should be getting a return as close as possible to 100 percent.

President Atkinson could make it happen, and he did. After subtracting enough to cover several long-established commitments, 94 percent of indirect costs flowed back to the campuses that generated them. The new formula made little difference to the campuses in the middle of the research spectrum, like UC Davis, or at the top, like UC Berkeley and UCLA, because they would get approximately the same amount as under the old formula. It added up to a huge increase for the most research-intensive campuses in the system, UC San Francisco and UC San Diego. UC Santa Barbara, UC Riverside, UC Santa Cruz, and UC Irvine, on the other hand, lost considerable sums of money they would have had under the old policy. Atkinson's position was that this problem could be dealt with by giving special consideration to specific funding needs at the affected campuses and that any disadvantage was offset by the new incentives for campuses to work harder to obtain contracts and grants.

The second budgetary change dealt with allocating enrollment funds. UC's budget from the state of California is distributed to the individual campuses by the Office of the President. UCOP had long followed the practice of giving each campus enrollment funding based on how many undergraduate and graduate students it had—more for graduate students, less for undergraduates, reflecting the overall greater costs of graduate education. Atkinson began having second thoughts about this policy when the University struck a new and advantageous deal with the state that meant a more generous per-student allocation of funds. He reasoned that since the state of California gave UC a certain number of dollars for every student it enrolled without worrying about whether those students were graduate or undergraduate, the Office of the President should do the same. This strategy had a number of advantages. If UCOP had continued the practice of giving each campus more money for every graduate student enrolled, it would have been necessary to cut the funds to Berkeley and UCLA, which were not anticipating major graduate growth, in order to support those campuses that wanted to expand their graduate programs—principally Davis, Irvine, and San Diego. Atkinson told the chancellors bluntly that he was adamantly opposed to any funding arrangement that could threaten the academic quality of Berkeley and UCLA. The new approach not only headed off this potential problem; it also helped mute campus complaints about UCOP funding decisions because every campus would be treated the same, aside from giving additional financial aid funds to those enrolling large numbers of needy students. Further, revising the policy made UC's practices in allocating enrollment money the same as those used at the California State University, which simplified dealings with the state Department of Finance.

Perhaps most important, Atkinson wanted to sever the relationship between graduate and undergraduate funding because he thought this policy encouraged two undesirable results. It was a formula-driven approach that hampered campus flexibility without giving enough help to smaller, younger campuses that were striving to increase their graduate enrollments. Further, he felt the academic marketplace, not only internal considerations like graduate-undergraduate ratios, should be the main determinant of the nature and size of UC's graduate programs. He wanted bloc grants that the campuses could use for graduates or undergraduates, depending on each campus's history, circumstances, and opportunities.

It was, in Atkinson's view, simple, transparent, and fair. It was not universally popular. The new policy did not erase the historical advantage enjoyed by Berkeley and UCLA, which had much larger base budgets than any other campus. Some of the smaller campuses complained that removing the funding differential for graduate students ultimately discouraged rather than encouraged growth in graduate enrollments. Nonetheless, it can be argued that the new policy gave all campuses more equal access to resources when this was urgent—during the Tidal Wave II years of burgeoning undergraduate enrollments. At UC Santa Cruz, for example, undergraduate enrollments mushroomed by 50 percent in the late 1990s and early 2000s.

The price Atkinson paid for greater campus equity (indirect cost reimbursement) and more chancellorial flexibility (enrollment allocations) was the loss of some of the president's ability to control campuses and chancellors through the power of the purse. The Office of the President had long reserved a certain amount of indirect cost reimbursements that the president could use for new initiatives or special situations and that the chancellors could use—with the president's approval—for new initiatives or special situations of their own. These Opportunity Funds, as they were called, were now flowing directly to the campuses. It did not make much difference during the high tide of UC budgets during most of the Atkinson administration, but in more recent years it has set limits on what the Office of the President can do for the smaller campuses, including the new campus at Merced.

THE USES OF PROSPERITY

California's returning economic strength transformed the University's overriding budget issue from surviving the worst to making the best use of prosperity. Although Republican Governor Pete Wilson was generally supportive of the University, it was not until Gray Davis was elected governor in 1998 that UC's budgets began to take off. As Wilson's Democratic lieutenant governor, Davis had found himself with little to do, and he intended to make up for lost time once he won the governorship. Davis and Atkinson had met in San Diego years before, when Davis was Governor Jerry Brown's chief of staff, and they worked well together. Education, especially K–12 education, led Davis's agenda, but he understood the importance of higher education to California's high-tech economy and the special place of the University in promoting innovation.

Returning prosperity made some of UC's intransigent problems suddenly manageable. The most important was achieving the goal that led Atkinson's list: making faculty salaries competitive again, for the first time since the late 1980s. This was critical in light of the heavy recruiting necessary to deal with Tidal Wave II. Around the middle of Atkinson's tenure, chancellors' salaries, which had fallen well behind the marketplace, were raised as well. Research budgets, slashed in the early 1990s, came roaring back. Despite the budget balancing under way in Congress during the mid- to late 1990s, federal agencies were doing relatively well in terms of appropriations for research. UC's largest source of federal funds, the National Institutes of Health, was receiving annual increases between 6 and 7 percent, the National Science Foundation around 4 percent. Nonetheless, state support was indispensable, not least because it was the seed money that made UC faculty competitive for federal and private moneys. UC could argue that the state's investment paid off: in 1996–97, the University spent 1.2 billion federal and private dollars on research—six times the funding contributed by Sacramento.[12] During the Atkinson administration, the state bolstered UC's base budget for research by $80 million, creating and supporting new initiatives in medicine, agriculture, biotechnology, supercomputing, and industry-university partnerships, to name just a few.

There were problems that even strong budgets could not solve. California politics had already shaped UC policy in the form of SP-1 and SP-2, and it was to intrude again on two major issues.

UC salaries and benefits were politically wired topics always on the verge of detonating in the legislature. The sheer size and variety of the University's workforce made it politically vulnerable: UC employed more than one hundred thousand people working in a huge array of jobs and classifications—academic and nonacademic, part-time and full-time, lecturers and tenured faculty, executives and staff, doctors, nurses, firemen, police, union and nonunion.

Gay and lesbian groups had long been lobbying for domestic partner benefits. In 1997 the issue boiled over. The question was whether the University should begin offering health benefits for same-sex domestic partners of its faculty and staff. The Academic Senate had officially expressed its support for same-sex domestic partner benefits every year since 1991, and the idea was popular within the UC community. In 1997 the chair of the Academic Senate (and faculty representative to the Board of Regents) was Duncan Mellichamp, an outspoken and determined chemical engineer from UC Santa Barbara. He made domestic partner health benefits his special cause and became an advocate for putting the issue on the Regents' agenda.

Some of Atkinson's advisers urged delay. UC spent $400 million annually on health benefits for its faculty and staff, a figure that would increase by $2 million to $5.5 million if benefits were extended to same-sex domestic partners. There was also a legal question: could UC offer benefits exclusively to same-sex domestic partners without discriminating against opposite-sex domestic partners? At first Atkinson was inclined to agree about postponement, especially in light of the obvious political tensions involved. But it was important to the faculty, and in the end he was persuaded that the issue was a matter of equity.

Everyone knew that a vote on health benefits for couples who lived outside the bounds of traditional marriage meant another public fight on the Board of Regents. The odds approached virtual certainty, in fact, because Governor Wilson still harbored presidential ambitions and was committed to ensuring this would not happen in his state. Wilson as mayor of San Diego from 1971 to 1982 had been a moderate and pro-choice Republican; Wilson as governor and presidential candidate in the 1990s had become a defender of much of the conservative right's social agenda. Despite attempts to defuse the issue by having the Regents instruct Atkinson to make the decision using his presidential authority, the governor insisted on a vote at the board's November 1997 meeting.

Every projection showed the proposal losing by a small margin. The cause looked even more likely to fail when the governor filled three vacancies on the Board of Regents in the days leading up to the meeting, two of them on the morning of the vote itself. Wilson arrived at UCLA's Sunset Commons for his first Regents' meeting since the July 1995 vote on SP-1 amid crowds of demonstrators, with news helicopters buzzing overhead. His argument to the board was threefold: the University, as a public trust, was obligated to uphold the institution of marriage; the recommendation would set an expensive precedent for other public entities; and, in any case, offering benefits to same-sex domestic partners but not to unmarried heterosexual couples violated antidiscrimination laws. On the advice of General Counsel Holst, the wording of the president's recommendation had been amended to avert a legal challenge from opposite-sex domestic partners. The governor responded with a letter from an acting assistant professor of law at Boalt Hall arguing that the amended recommendation would still be illegal under the California Labor Code. The professor was John Yoo, later to become famous as a member of George W. Bush's Justice Department and the author of a series of legal memoranda justifying torture.

Another objection to the domestic partner proposal came from Regent Velma Montoya, who asserted that it was illogical to extend benefits to retired domestic partners if, as the administration claimed, an important purpose was to keep the University competitive for the best faculty, staff, and graduate students. Her amendment to restrict domestic partner benefits to active employees failed, 14 to 12. When the board then proceeded to vote on the president's original proposal to offer domestic partner benefits, Montoya abstained.

And then the unexpected happened: the measure barely squeaked by with a vote of 13 to 12. It was unclear whether, in the heat of the moment, Montoya failed to realize that her abstention would deliver a ringing defeat to the governor. A frustrated Wilson slammed his pencil down with such force it jackknifed off the Regents' table and landed on the floor. Governors rarely lose on regental votes, and this loss made headlines. "UC Regents Defy Wilson, OK Gay Partner Benefits," the *Los Angeles Times* intoned on November 22, adding that the "measure passe[d] on 13–12 vote even though governor hastily appoint[ed] two to the board Friday in an all-out effort to stop passage."

The domestic partners benefits debate could have been a repeat of the affirmative action debacle of July 1995. But this time the issue was narrower, and several of the Wilson-appointed Regents deserted him, including Ward Connerly, who said that the values of equality, individual liberty, and the pursuit of happiness were so important that they transcended the institution of marriage.

A little over a year later, Atkinson and the University faced a different challenge from another political quarter. With Gray Davis's election as governor in November 1998 the Democrats were firmly in control of both the executive and legislative branches of California government. Strong union support had been important to Davis's electoral success. In the mid-1990s public employee unions had undertaken a vigorous national drive to expand collective bargaining. In California, a prime union target for action was the University of California. When teaching assistants (TAs) were ruled eligible for collective bargaining, the United Auto Workers (UAW)—the union covering TAs—decided to make a major push. UC's position, supported by the Academic Senate and the campus administrations, had long been that TAs were students first and employees second and that unionization could erode the academic character of teaching assistantships by transforming a system of faculty-student mentoring into an employer-employee relationship. In November 1998 TAs throughout the UC system announced their intention to strike if the University did not agree to collective bargaining.

The California Labor Federation, the state's largest union association, joined with other labor organizations and legislators to bring heavy pressure to bear on UC. It culminated in a stormy meeting between Atkinson and his collective bargaining staff and several legislators, including the colorful and outspoken San Francisco Democrat John Burton, who threatened to slash the University's budget if UC did not support TA unionization.

Not long before, Atkinson had happened to meet Art Pulaski, secretary-treasurer of the California Labor Federation, during a long plane flight. The two hit it off immediately and were soon deep in discussions about labor relations issues at UC. Pulaski's argument was that the University's attitude toward the unions had been adversarial from the beginning of collective bargaining at UC and the California State University in 1979, a hostility reflected most recently in its position on the TA issue. He began calling Atkinson during UAW-UC negotiations, and Atkinson gave him a sympathetic hearing. Some UC officials argued for challenging TA unionization on the grounds that it was inconsistent with the provisions of the Higher Education Employer-Employee Relations Act, the 1979 legislation governing UC's and CSU's interactions with their employees and employee representatives. With a Democratic governor and legislature united on the other side of the issue, political realism argued otherwise. Atkinson had been impressed by Pulaski's case for the advantages of a more conciliatory stance toward employee unions and was unconvinced that unionization would prove irreparably damaging to the academic nature of teaching assistantships. Ultimately he made the decision—controversial within UC—to end the University's opposition. In spring 1999 TAs across the system voted to bargain collectively. UC's size and stature made it a victory of national proportions for the unions.

But Atkinson's biggest challenge that year did not involve California's unions but California's schools. The catalyst was SP-1.

5

A Problem in Search of a Solution

In the end, the story of California's public sector over the past generation is a chronicle of a place that has been living on, and drawing down, its accumulated social capital. After California's huge investment in public services and public infrastructure during the 1950s and 1960s—estimated to have averaged a staggering 22 percent of all total state spending between 1950 and its peak in 1967—the state began a long slide of neglect.

—PETER SCHRAG, *PARADISE LOST*, 1998

What happened after the Outreach Task Force report was a confluence of leadership, money, and vision—support in the public schools, the state government, and the highest levels of the University. But the underside of that whole wonderful moment, the one thing we didn't recognize, was that when you are given that much money and that much responsibility you are going to become a target.

—ROBERT POLKINGHORN, FORMER ASSISTANT VICE PRESIDENT— EDUCATIONAL OUTREACH, 2008

During the brief hiatus between Atkinson's selection and the beginning of his tenure, he received a letter signed by the University's nine academic vice chancellors about "the crisis that now engulfs the K–12 system." California's public schools lingered near the bottom of the fifty states by virtually every measure, from class size to teacher education. The state of California had no real plan to address the problems of the schools, the vice chancellors wrote, and neither did the University of California. The number of faculty focused on K–12 in its departments and schools of education did not top one hundred. Only presidential leadership, they concluded, could make the plight of the schools a UC priority and persuade business and government, both state and local, to act.[1]

There was nothing really new about the vice chancellors' plea, not even its urgent, even desperate, tone. California's schools had been trapped in a prolonged downward spiral since the 1960s, buried under the tax revolt, the state's apparently unquenchable attractiveness to new citizens from around the world, and the inability of state government to deal with both realities at the same time. In 1964–65 California was fifth among the states in per-pupil spending and half of its overwhelmingly white high school graduates were headed for college, compared to one-third nationally.[2] In 1990 and again in 1992 the National Assessment of Educational Progress found that California schoolchildren scored among the lowest of the states in eighth-grade mathematics and fourth-grade reading. By the mid-1990s the state had sunk to fortieth in expenditures per pupil and forty-fifth in the number of computers per student. Half of the state's mathematics teachers had no training in mathematics or in how to teach it. The proportion of public high school graduates going on to UC or the California State University was not rising but declining; in 1995 it had fallen by 20 percent.

The state's huge network of public schools, organized into one thousand school districts with nearly six million students, served a young population that was 42 percent white, 36 percent Latino, 9 percent Asian and Pacific Islander, 8.5 percent African American, and less than 1 percent Native American. One-fifth had limited proficiency in English; a growing number came from poor immigrant families. In its annual report on California schools for 1994–95, researchers from Policy Analysis for California Education (PACE) pointed out the disparity between the ethnic and racial makeup of California's schoolchildren and its voters. While the school population was diverse and rapidly becoming more diverse, voters in the November 1994 election were "more white, more wealthy, more conservative, and better educated than the general California population."[3] The suggestion that an aging white electorate was reluctant to support a school system devoted increasingly to Latino, Asian, and African American children was undercut by the fact that in 1988 this same electorate had approved Proposition 98, which required that 40 percent of the state budget be set aside for support of the K–12 schools and the community colleges. Even Proposition 98, however, had failed to stem the deterioration of the nation's largest school system. There were excellent public schools and school districts in California, but the enterprise as a whole was in near-disastrous condition.

The idea that any single institution could make a genuine difference required a greater leap of faith than most educational leaders were ready to take. As it happened, however, the vice chancellors found an unexpected ally in SP-1. As part of the maneuvering over the resolution on that historic day in July 1995, Ward Connerly and his supporters on the Board of Regents agreed to add a call for expanding the University's outreach to students from disadvantaged groups. Section 1 mandated the creation of a task force that would "develop proposals for new directions and increased funding . . . to increase the eligibility rate" of students who had suffered economic or social disadvantage. The task force, whose membership would embrace representatives from UC, the business community, students, other segments of education, and "organizations currently engaged in academic 'outreach,'" was directed to submit its report to the Regents within six months of its establishment. In fact, the Outreach Task Force report did not see the light of day until July 1997, just in time for the second anniversary of SP-1.

SP-1 had the effect of concentrating UC's attention on schools with a new sense of purpose. Now that the Regents had removed consideration of race and ethnicity from the admissions process, admitting more African American, Latino, and Native American students rested on improving their academic training before they applied to UC. This was exactly what the Outreach Task Force was expected to do: produce a strategic and comprehensive plan for accomplishing this and a workable proposal for how to fund it.

UC had three decades of experience with outreach and eight hundred programs, largely if not entirely organized and run on the campuses.[4] The broad scope of SP-1's outreach mandate, however, would require the University to rethink its responsibilities in a university-wide and indeed statewide context.

There were few precedents for an organizational and fiscal challenge of this order. UC had a proven record in large, cooperative projects requiring interdisciplinary focus and sophisticated logistics. But the most successful, like the Manhattan Project, involved clearly defined scientific or technical problems that were likely to yield to intense and concentrated effort. Outreach was not like that: the time frame for schooling was decades and the results difficult to quantify with any precision. Change on the scale required would be costly and difficult to accomplish in California's vast school system. As far back as 1968, UC President Charles Hitch had envisioned a leadership role for UC in reforming the K–12 schools, as part of an ambitious initiative to address the plight of California's cities. The urban crisis program, the centerpiece of his first year as president, included a call for large new investments in teacher training, student outreach, and educational research to improve elementary and secondary schools throughout California. The dream was grand in scale but short-lived. Although many within the University supported the idea, efforts to persuade the legislature to pay for it were unsuccessful; funding was sparse from the beginning and soon dried up entirely. Hitch later ruefully described the urban crisis experience as "something like going on a tiger hunt with a popgun."[5]

This was the possibility that troubled Atkinson the most. If thirty years of preferential admissions and eight hundred outreach programs had not produced significant gains in minority eligibility, how could outreach on its own possibly do the job? When the Regents shut the door on using the admissions process to admit more minority students, they opened another door into a universe of problems over which UC had little control: poverty, discrimination, academically marginal schools, and underqualified teachers. The University and K–12 schools were separated by huge organizational differences. UC faculty members were partners with the administration and the Regents and exercised a central and powerful influence on any major decision affecting the welfare of the institution. They enjoyed considerable autonomy in terms of how and what they taught the best students in the state. K–12 teachers were employees in a highly distributed bureaucratic system, with few opportunities to define the scope of their proliferating responsibilities for marginally prepared students, diminishing control over curricula, and limited prospects for advancement. The K–12 students UC was most interested in were in the upper middle of the spectrum—students who were on the edge of qualifying for college and who with a little help and encouragement could make it over the University's academic hurdles. These were not the students that teachers and principals were inclined to worry about. Their educational future was glowing, compared to that of their many classmates who had managed to progress through the school system without acquiring a secure grasp of how to read or do basic arithmetic. In 1990s California, success meant getting large numbers of K–12 students to pass minimum-standard statewide tests, not qualifying them for Berkeley or Caltech.

Atkinson's attitudes toward schooling were strongly influenced by his early work on computer-assisted instruction in the Palo Alto schools. The experience gave him a sense of just how wide and challenging the learning differences among schoolchildren could be. He saw the California public school system, in social science terms, as bimodal in its output; that is, it turned out some of the best-prepared students in the world and many of the worst. The paths of these two kinds of students began to diverge early and, as he knew from his years of research into how children learn, were deeply rooted in the family; children whose parents read to them at an early age, for example, tended to do far better in school than children whose parents did not. California needed to protect and nurture the talent of those superbly prepared students at the top even as it removed the obstacles that held other children back. The policy challenge was keeping an eye on both ends of the spectrum, making sure that the gifted prospered but also that the struggling had the opportunities to succeed.

Within the University itself, there were few institutional incentives for faculty to involve themselves in the hands-on, practical problems of schooling. Many faculty, while troubled by the state of the K–12 schools, did not consider them a UC responsibility. Yet the only way outreach could succeed would be by acquiring the legitimacy and credibility that faculty involvement conferred—a highly uncertain prospect in UC's research-oriented culture.

SP-1's ringing endorsement of outreach was an opportunity to begin repairing some of the damage the resolution had inflicted on the University's reputation among talented minority students. Nonetheless, the outreach mandate, however defined, involved large risks for the University. The Outreach Task Force could fail to come together on a single plan and splinter into warring groups. It could come up with a reasonable plan that would nevertheless founder on regental or legislative opposition. The Regents had committed the University to a major public experiment in increasing UC eligibility, raising expectations that could well turn out to be impossible to fulfill. Yet the only alternative was to proceed.

ASSEMBLING THE OUTREACH TASK FORCE

It was agreed early on that the task force would have two cochairs, one from within the University and another from the business community. Atkinson asked the provost and senior vice president for academic affairs, C. Judson King, to serve as the UC cochair. Jud King was a longtime Berkeley faculty member and chemical engineer who was drawn to administrative work early in his career by a deep-seated curiosity about UC's intricate administrative machinery and the dynamics of getting things done in a large university. In addition to his considerable knowledge of the institution, he was patient and low-key, with a gift for remaining precise and reasonable even in discussions of hotly contested topics.

The external cochair—Richard Clarke, retired chief executive officer and chairman of the board of the Pacific Gas and Electric Company—was an enthusiastic Old Blue, an alumnus of UC Berkeley's school of law and its school of business. Although a supporter of SP-1 and later of Proposition 209, he was neither ideological nor doctrinaire. Clarke was well known and well connected in the Bay Area business community, among which a diverse and highly educated workforce was viewed as an important competitiveness issue. He understood the political thicket he was about to enter, and he had the stature and self-confidence to deal with the Regents as an equal.

The task force convened for its first meeting in February 1996 with thirty-five members and very little prospect of reaching unanimity on a plan of action. Its membership was drawn from constituencies with a stake in outreach—among them the University itself, the business community, the California State University and the community colleges, the K–12 public schools, the California Postsecondary Education Commission (CPEC), and the California Department of Education. A majority of the representatives were affirmative action advocates who had opposed SP-1; many were still angry about the Regents' action. Some of the K–12 people were suspicious of UC's commitment to stay involved with outreach once the political pressure to do so receded. A small minority, mostly Regents who had voted for SP-1, were determined to see that the task force did not venture a single step beyond the boundaries imposed by SP-1. Clarke and King worried that this lopsided division of opinion and emotion would deadlock the task force's deliberations. From the beginning, they took pains to focus attention not on the members' differences but on their common ground.

But what *was* the common ground? SP-1 had clearly forbidden race-attentive admissions policies, but did it also prohibit racial and ethnic targeting in outreach efforts? That was not entirely clear. In January 1996, even before appointments to the task force had been completed, Atkinson sought an opinion on this point from General Counsel James Holst. Holst concluded that SP-1 allowed race-attentive approaches in outreach programs as long as other kinds of disadvantaged students—principally economically disadvantaged whites and Asians—could also participate if they wished. However, he went on, the Regents' decision to appoint a task force to explore "new directions and increased funding" for outreach strongly suggested that "SP-1 should be understood to provide for expansion and support of outreach efforts for socio-economically disadvantaged students and to await the recommendations of the Outreach Task Force with respect to the extent to which race-attentive outreach should be used, its effectiveness generally, efficacy and the extent and timing of changes to current programs."[6]

This gave the task force ample room to define the precise meaning and scope of UC's future outreach efforts. The question hovering over this interpretation, however, was whether Regent Connerly would ask the Regents to revisit SP-1 to make it explicit that racial and ethnic targeting in outreach and financial aid was forbidden. Atkinson decided to raise the issue directly, arguing to Connerly that the University should have some leeway in adapting to the reversal of thirty years of race-attentive policies. In a letter dated March 5, Connerly agreed. He added:

> In deciding not to place this issue before my colleagues [on the Board of Regents], I am hopeful that the University will voluntarily discontinue any outreach programs or financial assistance that smacks of being exclusionary. Although the immediate response will be that we are not operating exclusionary programs, that response does not square with an oft-stated argument made by many in defense of race-based outreach; namely, to expand outreach to all disadvantaged students, regardless of race or such considerations, would "dilute" the programs. In my view, an absence of adequate resources is not a sufficient rationale to practice policies of exclusion.[7]

Within the Outreach Task Force, the anti–SP-1 majority argued for continuing the traditional outreach orientation to underrepresented minority students (African Americans, Latinos, and Native Americans), citing a 1988 UC policy on undergraduate admissions that called for "a student body . . . that encompasses the broad diversity of cultural, racial, geographic, and socio-economic backgrounds characteristic of California."[8] The pro–SP-1 minority quoted the 1995 Regents' resolution back at them: "The University of California shall not use race, religion, sex, color, ethnicity or national origin as criteria for admission . . . [and] this policy will achieve a UC population that reflects this state's diversity through the preparation and empowerment of all students in this state to succeed rather than through a system of artificial preferences."[9]

Clarke and King were searching for a conceptual starting point, a basic premise that would bridge these political and policy differences. The task force began with an examination of the University's eight hundred existing outreach pro-grams. From its beginnings in the activist 1960s, UC outreach had taken a rich and ever-changing variety of forms: systemwide and campus initiatives, staff-run and faculty-run efforts, UC programs and cooperative programs undertaken with other public or private universities and colleges. No one had given much thought to organizing this array of activities into some larger organizational framework, campus or systemwide; there did not seem to be any particular need. In fact the highly decentralized character of most outreach programs was entirely consistent with the University's cultural preference for leaving such initiatives to individual creativity and local campus control. Little formal evaluation had been done of most outreach programs, at UC or elsewhere, and few systematic data existed about results. That would require tracking student progress over a number of years, an expensive process that seemed less important than getting services to schools and students. Much of the available evidence was therefore anecdotal or incomplete.[10]

The task force commissioned research from independent consultants and in-vited expert testimony on public education, UC eligibility, surveys of successful state and national outreach programs, and a host of other topics. It heard from members of the public, school superintendents, teachers, parents, and students. The effort yielded a mountain of data, analysis, and expert opinion but little ap-parent agreement. Some wanted to use class rather than race to target low-income students from all backgrounds. But earlier UC studies had demonstrated that this approach would not work, at least in terms of yielding more minority students, because the low-income category included so many Californians of every race and ethnicity. How far the task force could and should go toward race-attentive outreach became a major sticking point, miring the discussion in recurring intel-lectual clashes over the pros and cons of affirmative action. The early meetings in particular had an adversarial tone; both sides seemed reluctant to embrace any step that would allow the other to claim a victory.

King and his staff—especially Dennis Galligani, assistant vice president for stu-dent academic services—were working feverishly behind the scenes to come up with a proposal that could serve as the centerpiece of the task force report. As the weeks ticked by, there were times when the whole project seemed frustrating and futile. The task force was being asked to conjure up new and untried ideas about outreach that would bring more minority students to UC's campuses while reso-lutely ignoring the reality of race—a strange assignment that, if it could be done at all, left a crucial question unanswered: who was going to pay for it?

When the breakthrough finally came, it turned on a fundamental demographic fact about California's schools. UC analyses showed that 79 percent of the students in California's academically poorest schools were African American, Latino, and Native American. The proposal King and Galligani put before the task force called this phenomenon "educational disadvantage" and defined it broadly as enrollment in the bottom quintile of California schools (each quintile consisted of about 150 schools).[11] By almost any social or educational measure, the differences between the top and bottom 20 percent were striking: the best schools were likely to be suburban, with students who did well on the SAT, whose family income was more than $60,000 a year, and whose fathers had attained at least a high school diploma. In contrast, students in the lowest 20 percent were much more likely to be enrolled in urban and rural schools, to be members of families that received Aid to Families with Dependent Children, to have difficulty with spoken or written English, and to score poorly on the SAT. Their fathers were much less likely to have a high school diploma (36 percent, compared to 90 percent of students' fathers in the top school quintile). The students enrolled in California's lowest-ranked schools were the least represented students on UC campuses.

King and Galligani proposed that UC ground its outreach strategy in this demographic reality of California's schools—that the more struggling and impoverished the school, the more likely its students would be African American, Latino, or Native American. At the same time, such schools included whites and Asians who would also benefit from UC outreach. UC and its campuses would go directly into the state's lowest-performing schools and, working in partnership with teachers, principals, and the surrounding community, begin the work of transforming them from the ground up.

It was a disarmingly simple idea that, as most members immediately recognized, gave them the foothold they had been looking for. After months of squabbling and dissension, the Outreach Task Force had at last found something on which to agree. And in the process, it had finally escaped the iron bands of SP-1.

THE SCHOOLS AS THE INSTRUMENT AND THE PATH

The school performance concept differed from the older, largely student-centered outreach in two crucial respects. It did not require an exclusive (and now illegal) focus on race, the big stumbling block in the Outreach Task Force's discussions. It scaled down the overwhelming size of California's K–12 system into smaller and more manageable units—geographic regions in which individual campuses would work with partner schools. The task force envisioned that these partnerships would eventually include approximately fifty high schools, one hundred middle schools, and three hundred elementary schools around the state.

Most of what UC had been doing in outreach was directed at students, not at schools, in order to reach underrepresented minority students directly. But school improvement had a history in the Office of the President, dating to the presidency of David Gardner in the mid-1980s. Gardner had headed the Reagan-era commission that issued *A Nation at Risk,* a national report that described the academic performance of the U.S. public school system as so poor that had it been imposed on the American people by a foreign power, it might have been considered an act of war.[12] Soon after he became UC president in 1983, Gardner commissioned two reports, one on UC's role in improving schools and student preparation, the other on the mission of the University's schools and departments of education to help K–12 schools prepare students for higher education. Both reports struck the same note: the University had an important role in training better teachers and creating better schools.[13] One outcome was an office of university–school education, charged with sharing relevant UC research findings and innovations with teachers and principals—a kind of educational extension service. The task force report took this idea and redefined it into a unified plan for school–university partnerships embracing education from elementary schools through community colleges. Now UC was committing itself to something it had never attempted before: a comprehensive school-improvement enterprise that would train teachers, rework curricula, inform students about college admission requirements, and in general work with teachers, principals, and superintendents to raise academic achievement in the state's most beleaguered and underfunded schools. These schools had fewer experienced teachers than the average school and a much higher rate of turnover among all school personnel, from superintendents to students. They also suffered from what one University official called "initiative fatigue," the result of more than a decade of overlapping and uncoordinated federal, state, and local attempts to improve their academic performance.

In hindsight, it seems clear that the task force ultimately focused on the schools for its principal strategy because there was nowhere else to turn. "If outreach programs might be compared to a raft on a sinking ship," one of the task force–commissioned reports observed, "the argument is that the University can only accomplish its goal of enrolling and graduating increased numbers of well-prepared disadvantaged students if it does not focus exclusively on offering life rafts but also helps to save the ship. Hence a variety of programs which do not provide direct student services are now part of the discussion of strategies for increasing the eligibility and competitiveness of underrepresented students."[14] The Outreach Task Force report used a different metaphor to make the same point: "It is through the schools (and with schools as the instrument and the path) that UC can have the most powerful influence in equalizing educational opportunities."[15]

"The schools as the instrument and the path" was the organizing theme of the Outreach Task Force report, its most ambitious idea and its most important innovation. Putting the schools at the center gave the Office of the President a plan of action and the campuses a clear sense of direction. Every campus already had a special relationship with a local school or schools and a variety of programs to encourage more minority students to prepare for college. These would become the foundation on which the task force's new and ambitious strategy would build. This foundation would also include the active involvement of school principals and district superintendents, a characteristic of many of the most successful school-improvement programs. To cast the net as widely as possible, the task force sent a draft of the report to every principal and superintendent in California.

Once consensus had solidified around the school partnership idea, the rest of Clarke and King's proposal quickly fell into place. It laid out three strategies in addition to school partnerships: academic programs for students at all levels, from the primary grades to the community colleges, to motivate and prepare students to qualify for UC; informational programs to let students, counselors, and families know about UC's admissions requirements early enough to make a difference (a direct response to a RAND report finding that many minority students found UC unwelcoming); and UC faculty research on the fundamental causes of educational disparities among groups and ways to evaluate the effectiveness of its outreach programs to students, teachers, and schools.

UC had three major University-wide programs that centered on students. The largest, the Early Academic Outreach Program (EAOP), was administered by the Office of the President and dated to the 1970s. Its principal focus was informing and encouraging students from the middle grades on to take the right courses and acquire the right skills to gain admission to UC. EAOP had long been aimed at junior high school students, but the task force recommended extending it to the community colleges, which enrolled close to 80 percent of the state's college-age minority students.

UC's two other major outreach programs, MESA and Puente, looked like especially promising vehicles for attracting more community college transfer students to UC. MESA—Mathematics, Engineering, Science Achievement—launched at Berkeley in 1970 by an engineering professor, began as a small collaborative initiative with teachers from nearby Oakland Technical High School, specifically geared to helping disadvantaged students learn enough basic math and science to make biology or chemical engineering a realistic career aspiration. Its initial support was seed money contributed by a few oil companies. MESA did not remain small or local for long, however. With infusions of state funding, the MESA program went from strength to strength, multiplying on campuses throughout California and ultimately at schools and universities around the country. MESA's combination of student academic preparation; cooperation among UC, the schools, CSU, and community colleges; and promotion of community engagement was a template for outreach programs far beyond the boundaries of science, engineering, and mathematics. The Puente Program, which initially concentrated on attracting more Latino transfer students to four-year colleges, had also evolved from modest origins into a national model of how successful student-centered, interinstitutional efforts could be. Both MESA and Puente were ripe for expansion under the University's new outreach initiative.

King and Clarke outlined the Outreach Task Force report to the Regents at their meeting in July 1997, in a presentation that also included testimony from UC San Diego professor Cecil Lytle, representing several dissenting members of the task force who had submitted a minority report.[16] Most Regents found the task force's four-point strategy compelling, however. Regent Meredith Khachigian praised the report and urged her fellow board members to make a personal commitment to implementing its recommendations as quickly as possible. The majority report was approved.

In January 1998 Atkinson announced that Santa Cruz Chancellor Emeritus Karl Pister would work with Jud King and the chancellors on launching the new outreach enterprise. Like King, Pister had strong roots in the University and the Berkeley campus. He once estimated that over his long career he had held twenty-four different titles, among them engineering professor, department chair, chair of the University-wide Academic Senate, dean of engineering, and chancellor at UC Santa Cruz. During the debate over SP-1, Pister was one of the chancellors who signed a public statement urging the Regents not to abandon affirmative action. He held deep convictions about the role of education in achieving social justice and the University's responsibilities as a land grant institution dedicated to public service. For too long, he believed, UC's institutional energies had been focused almost exclusively on the gate—the formal academic requirements for admission. Now it needed to concentrate its resources and resourcefulness on the pathway, which for Pister meant not just the schools but also the community and the family. Within the University, he was convinced that faculty commitment to outreach was the only way to make it part of UC's core missions. Atkinson and King agreed. Pister's appointment was intended to send the message that outreach was a faculty concern, not simply an administrative one.

OUTREACH TAKES OFF

The first and most pressing question about outreach was money. The task force estimated that its plans would cost approximately $60 million annually, derived from the state of California, partner institutions, private foundations, business and industry, and the federal government.[17] This figure was more than twice the amount the University was already spending on its outreach activities, and no one considered it easy to achieve. UC's 1997–98 budget request asked the state for a modest augmentation of $5 million to implement the task force's recommendations, promising to submit a plan for attracting funding from a variety of sources over the next several years. Privately, UC budget officials thought UC would be lucky to persuade the state to add anything to the $32 million for outreach included in Governor Wilson's last budget—a final conciliatory gesture by the departing governor, some said, for his role in the passage of SP-1.

As it turned out, the state of California more than doubled its investment in outreach, to $76 million in 1998. And that was just the beginning. In November 1998 Gray Davis won a landslide victory in the gubernatorial race, and he intended to use his electoral mandate to transform education in California, especially in the public schools. Atkinson was a member of Davis's Education Transition Group, responsible for shaping his education agenda. The 1999 Public School Accountability Act, passed in a special session of the legislature convened by Davis, mandated a number of school reforms, including standardized testing throughout California to measure student progress toward curricular standards set by the state. Money was pouring into the state treasury, thanks to California's economic recovery, which in turn dramatically expanded the schools' allocation under the Proposition 98 mandate. Davis asked his secretary of education, Gary Hart, to formulate a comprehensive plan for implementing his school reform proposals, which he had vowed to put into place by the start of the new fiscal year on July 1. More than anyone else, it was Hart—a member of the Outreach Task Force—who successfully harnessed the University of California to Davis's school reform movement.

Hart had been elected to the state senate in 1974 and chaired the California Senate Education Committee for twelve years. One of his accomplishments had been his sponsorship of a 1988 bill creating the California Subject Matter Projects (CSMPs), a major source of high-quality professional development for teachers run jointly by UC, CSU, and independent universities. The CSMPs had started life in 1973 as the Bay Area Writing Project, a UC Berkeley School of Education program designed to improve the teaching of writing in elementary and high schools. Within a decade, the program had become the National Writing Project (NWP), serving seventy thousand teachers in 118 sites in the United States, Europe, and Asia. The NWP model was to identify master teachers and bring them together with less experienced teachers for intensive five-week summer sessions. Its phenomenal success led to its application to other disciplines as the California Subject Matter Projects. When he left the legislature in 1994, Hart created CSU's Institute for Education Reform at Sacramento State University. He visited both CSU and UC campuses to look at teacher education and came away with the impression that UC's programs, few as they were compared to CSU's, were of higher quality.

Based on his experience working with schools and children at Stanford, Atkinson told Governor Davis that his program for reform should include summer institutes for K–3 teachers to improve the teaching of reading, the indispensable foundation for all future learning. Hart began to wonder about using the CSMPs to run these institutes. Would it be possible, he asked, for UC and CSU to train six thousand beginning teachers? The state would pay $1,000 per teacher, and another $1,000 would go to every teacher who successfully completed the program, for a total of $12 million the first year. It was a dazzling sum, far more than had ever been invested in anything like this, and Governor Davis wanted UC to lead the statewide effort. The first Reading Professional Development Institutes, codirected in summer 1999 by master teachers from elementary schools and faculty from UC, CSU, and private institutions, built on what had been learned through the highly successful CSMPs, using its reading program as a model. Hart immediately began envisioning a second year of reading institutes, this time with a much larger enrollment: California Mathematics Institutes for teachers in grades four to six; institutes for high school teachers of algebra and English; and English Language Development Professional Institutes to help teachers learn how to teach English and math to students who were not native speakers. The total allocated for these programs in the governor's 2000–2001 budget was $70 million.

Atkinson's worries about creating impossible expectations began to recede. Outreach was taking off beyond his and the task force's most optimistic dreams. For most of the next few years—1999 to 2001—the University's biggest challenge was keeping up. Once the passion for school reform took hold in Sacramento, it became an irresistible force, gaining momentum by the day. Public groups like the California Commission on Children and Families and private organizations like the Bank of America Foundation, eager to be a part of school reform, contributed money, moral support, and publicity. Sailing on this wave of legislative and public enthusiasm, UC expanded or established not only campus–school partnerships but also after-school programs (some of them computer-based), teacher training, curriculum development, even a charter middle and high school at UC San Diego for low-income students who would be the first in their families to graduate from college. Many of these initiatives involved CSU, the community colleges, and local groups interested in education.

UCOP assumed an enrollment of 14,000 teachers in the Reading Professional Development Institutes in 2000, their second year. No sooner had the announcement gone out than nearly 24,000 teachers signed up. The University and its outreach partners took them all. The English Language Learning Institutes enrolled 10,000 teachers in 2000; the various California Subject Matter Projects, 25,000. In all, 70,000 California teachers in more than four hundred institutes were trained in teaching the foundational skills of language, reading, and mathematics.

Hart wanted even more: institutes to train principals to lead their schools into the new era of high standards. "No single person at a school is more important to student achievement than the school principal," he declared, and UC was to sponsor the institutes on its own—specifically, the graduate schools of education at Berkeley and UCLA. It was only in part a tribute to UC's quality. Hart intended to force UC into a more direct role in school reform and in the preparation of school administrators. UC's schools of education saw their mission as research, not training K–12 personnel. Hart thought otherwise, and lawmakers underscored the point for him by passing legislation that gave UC base funding but also required the University to raise private funds for scholarships to train two hundred principals a year. Berkeley and UCLA were not enthusiastic about the assignment or the process Hart proposed for establishing the program. It was a clear intrusion on UC's autonomy, if a relatively benign form of the genre, and the target number was probably more than the education market in California could absorb. UC eventually struck a deal for a more realistic goal.

THE RISE AND FALL OF OUTREACH

Skeptics could argue that the Davis school reform program, for all its whirlwind of activity, was palliative at best in light of the schools' massive ills. Yet for a few exciting years, from 1998 to 2001, California's decades-long inertia seemed to have shattered under the pressure of the Davis administration's resolve to do something at last about the public schools. The University of California was a key institutional leader in making it happen, thanks to the fortuitous combination of the University's response to SP-1 and the new governor's education agenda.

The first sign of a reversal of fortune was Hart's resignation as education secretary in March 2000. His meteoric tenure had lasted less than a year, but during that brief time he had served as the driving force behind Davis's vision of school reform and proven himself indispensable to making the case for outreach. With his departure, the University lost one of its most effective advocates.

At the same time, the University's outreach efforts were coming under increasingly critical scrutiny by the legislature, which was divided over whether the bulk of the funding should go to programs for students or for school partnerships. Exactly how many additional UC-qualified underrepresented minority students were all those outreach dollars producing? Lieutenant Governor and ex officio Regent Cruz Bustamante pressed UC administrators publicly about this issue at a number of Regents' meetings. During an outreach report to the Board of Regents in May 2000, Karl Pister said that UC could present statistical evidence of progress, but that was not enough for some members of the legislature; they demanded something far more difficult to establish, proof of a direct relationship between investment and outcome. Vice President for Budget Larry Hershman added that the California Assembly was insisting on regular evaluations of UC outreach programs, rejecting UC's explanations that such assessments were meaningful only if they took place over a period of years, not months. These were not the answers Bustamante wanted to hear. Future-oriented efforts are all well and good, he insisted, but in the meantime the state was losing a generation of students. Pister had heard all this before, having spent many difficult hours in Sacramento explaining to legislators that preparing students for college starts as early as kindergarten, so expectations of instant increases in minority admissions were simply unrealistic. Bustamante's cross-examination was the last straw. It was Pister's last

Regents' meeting as vice president for outreach. He left immediately after his presentation, without waiting for the customary Regents' resolution thanking him for his service.

Many legislators thought UC had not done enough to diversify itself on every level, from administrators to faculty to students, and they were predisposed to be skeptical of anything that sounded like delay. At their peak, UC programs were reaching 300,000 students, the campuses were partnering with 256 low-performing schools, and 70,000 teachers were taking part in the California Professional Development Institutes and Subject Matter Projects. UC and its partners were reaching into low-performing schools as early as the elementary grades, more teachers in those schools were getting the professional training they needed, more of their students were doing better in academic subjects, and more students were being accepted at UC and other colleges and universities. The bright clear line connecting funding and results remained impossible to draw, however, at least as quickly and definitively as legislative critics wanted. Manuel Gómez, Pister's successor, compared the legislative impatience for results to uprooting a tree to measure its growth. While the University was focusing its energies on making more disadvantaged students eligible for UC, the legislature was looking beyond eligibility to enrollment, insisting that progress meant more minority students on UC campuses, not more minority students eligible for UC campuses. It was said that the legislature gave UC money in July and wanted a report by September.

There were other critics: CSU, for example, which had been bypassed in favor of the University; the California Department of Education; and the county offices of education, which felt they had the infrastructure and the presence across the state to handle school improvement themselves. It was not exactly clear, in fact, who was in charge of the public schools—the state Board of Education, the superintendent of public instruction, the secretary of education? The political undercurrents among the state's educational hierarchy were confusing and treacherous. Complaints about how outreach money was spent did not come only from the legislature.

The accountability problem was in part a function of the University of California's decentralized organization and culture, in which each campus, by long tradition, created outreach efforts and school partnerships that reflected its particular history, strengths, and proclivities. Precise comparative evaluations across the UC system were difficult to make. Richard Clarke, who came to outreach with a corporate perspective, found this aspect of UC organization baffling.

But probably the toughest aspect of the accountability issue was the breakneck pace of the school reform movement and the rollercoaster-like trajectory of outreach funding. State and UC outreach funds combined, which had soared to almost $100 million in 1999 and reached a crescendo of $184 million in 2000 (over

$300 million including federal, foundation, and private funds), dropped to $177 million in 2001 and collapsed into freefall the following year, hitting a low of $37 million by 2003. In the beginning, the scramble to keep even with the demands of two urgent agendas—UC's and the governor's—made it impossible to ensure the quality of every program or initiative. In the end, just as outreach was beginning to take hold, the money vanished as suddenly as it had appeared. The dot-com boom was over. So was the hope that the most comprehensive K–12 partnership in the University of California's history would continue in a form anything like the first few exuberant years.

LESSONS

The Outreach Task Force report had set five-year goals for school partnerships, student academic outreach, and informational outreach. The past and the future of outreach were the subject of a report commissioned by Atkinson and released in 2003, his last year as president. Chaired by Les Biller, former chief operating officer of Wells Fargo Bank, the Strategic Review Panel on UC Educational Outreach concluded that UC's efforts had already achieved many of the goals set by the Outreach Task Force, even though its self-imposed five-year deadline was still more than a year away.[18] More Latino and African American students were enrolled at UC in 2003 than in 1996, the year Proposition 209 became law. The proportion of underrepresented minority freshmen admitted to UC had increased by 15 percent, from 15.5 percent in 1998—the year SP-1 took effect—to 17.8 percent in 2002, with a similar increase in the proportion of minority transfers from the community colleges. More than a third of the Latino and African American students admitted in the fall 2001 class were graduates of a UC partnership high school or had participated in a UC outreach program.[19] In a number of the low-performing schools UC worked with, student counseling was stronger, parents more involved with their children's education. The subject matter projects and teaching institutes made thousands of California teachers better at their craft and many thousands of California students better prepared for college as a result. The Principal Leadership Institutes, which continue today, are one of the few programmatic contributions by a California research university to the practice rather than the theory of schooling.

At the same time, UC's outreach programs had not altered the statewide pattern of student achievement—nor, as the panel sensibly observed, could they be expected to. The organizational and cultural differences between UC and the schools turned out to be formidable obstacles; so did the multiplicity of actors in school reform, from superintendents to colleges and universities to governors. "Two of the greatest barriers to improving effectiveness [of outreach programs]," the report went on to say, "are the misalignment of accountability structures and goals of the University and K–12, and the poor coordination of efforts among all outreach stakeholders."[20] Outreach Vice President Manuel Gómez thought there were too many goals and too many programs, a situation that strained the University's organizational capacities beyond their limits: "What we needed—but never had the opportunity to do, given the demands on UC—was to select a relatively small set of programs that would allow us to bring a laser-like focus on a set of goals that UC could sustain over a long period of time."[21] Outreach has not evolved into what so many within UC hoped it would be—a core mission of the University under permanent faculty leadership. Still, many of those who led the outreach effort are convinced that the University was on the right track, especially with its school partnerships, and could have made a real difference in student achievement in California if state money had not evaporated.

Atkinson was right to be apprehensive about the political risks to the University. When the funding stopped and UC was forced to cut its programs and school partnerships, K–12 skepticism about UC's commitment seemed justified. The University was faced with a term-limited legislature unwilling or unable to understand the enormity of the challenge and the complexities of measuring progress. At bottom, the outreach experiment was cut short by the political and economic swings that seem endemic to California. The obstacles on the pathway to higher education, the accumulated weight of poverty, racism, a broken school system, and societal indifference, remain for too many California students.

At the beginning of it all, during the Outreach Task Force's early deliberations, Gómez saw the goal of its work as a quest for new language that would empower UC to come to grips with its responsibilities for access in the post–affirmative action world. "Educational disadvantage," a concept that included race and economic status but also sought to incorporate the part played by low-performing schools and struggling communities, was a first cut at rewriting the lexicon of affirmative action to fit the University's new political and institutional realities. The outreach action plan itself was a rough draft of a new University of California, racially neutral and magically diverse. Although the odds of succeeding the first time were never high, the process of working through the massive institutional changes set in motion by the battle over affirmative action had begun.

"A More Inclusive Definition
of Merit"

The Regents have considerable freedom to avoid public discussion of contro-
versial issues, and to delay taking action on issues that are politically sensi-
tive. Often, though not always, time drains the passion out of an issue, and
allows it to be . . . resolved quietly and administratively, rather than noisily
and politically.

—MARTIN TROW, MARCH 1997

To meet its responsibilities to a diverse and knowledge-based society, the Uni-
versity of California must choose the state's highest-performing students in
ways that are inclusive and fair. More, they must be demonstrably inclusive
and fair.

—PRESIDENT RICHARD C. ATKINSON, JULY 2001

SP-1, which had hung like a storm cloud over every Regents' meeting for nearly
six years, was rescinded by the Regents in May 2001. Its demise was as steeped in
political drama as its birth.

The political complexion of the board was changing. In early 2001 there were
five vacancies on the Board of Regents that Governor Gray Davis would soon be
filling with Democratic nominees. Atkinson's sense of the situation was that after
six years the board was weary of the public criticism and internal divisions created
by its July 1995 resolutions and that many Regents had come around to the idea
of repealing them.[1] Ideally, this move would be led by a Regent, perhaps SP-1's
most committed nemesis, Bill Bagley, who missed few opportunities to remind
the board of the negative consequences of its action. Failing that, Atkinson was
prepared to introduce a resolution himself at the strategically right moment.

He had come to this conclusion because SP-1 remained a stubbornly symbolic
and distracting issue. It could not be resolved "quietly and administratively" because it had been enacted by the highest authority in the University, the Regents

themselves. Nor had the passage of time dimmed SP-1's ability to mobilize fierce opposition. The Coalition to Defend Affirmative Action by Any Means Necessary—a student group organized to oppose the Regents' 1995 ban on affirmative action—mounted protests at every Regents' meeting, undeterred by arrests for disrupting the board's discussions. Sometimes the near-hypnotic chanting outside the room where the Regents met—"The people united will never be divided"—was accompanied by taunts and threats directed at the Regents in general and Regent Connerly in particular. The protests helped keep alive the gloomy post–SP-1 prognostications that diversity faced a dismal future at the University of California. The Latino Caucus, now the largest in the legislature, made ending SP-1 a major goal.

The shared-governance implications of SP-1, still unresolved, continued to fester. SP-1's Section 5 circumscribed the faculty's ability to consider anything other than grades and test scores by raising the percentage of undergraduates who must be admitted "solely on the basis of academic achievement" from the traditional 40 to 60 percent to 50 to 75 percent. Even those who acknowledged the board's authority to ban affirmative action were likely to view Section 5 as a regental infringement of the faculty's delegated responsibility for admissions. In February 2001 Atkinson had put a proposal before the Academic Senate, called comprehensive review, that would eliminate this two-tier system entirely. For the moment, however, the two-tier system, along with Section 5's revision of it, was firmly in place.

Several years earlier, during one of many discussions about UC's outreach initiatives, Regent Bagley observed that the "taint" of having voted for SP-1 might make direct regental participation in UC's outreach activities "counterproductive." Why not rescind both SP-1 and SP-2, he urged, especially since Proposition 209 was the applicable law? Board chair John Davies responded that "it is difficult for the Board to go forward when its members continue to look to the past."[2] But the past continued to control events. Just to raise the possibility of repeal was to risk reopening the unhealed wounds of 1995.

In the weeks leading up to the March 2001 Regents' meeting, however, it was becoming clear to the administration that UC could be at the brink of another disaster. Lieutenant Governor and Regent Bustamante announced that he and student Regent Justin Fong would spearhead a drive to rescind the 1995 resolutions at that meeting. When the topic nonetheless failed to appear on the board's March agenda, the several thousand people who had shown up in the expectation of a vote scrapping SP-1 voiced their disappointment by booing both Regents.

Despite the misfire, their publicly stated intent to put repeal before the board raised a troubling prospect. The May meeting, Fong's last as student Regent, would also be his last opportunity to put the question of rescinding the two resolutions on the agenda. What if support for rescission fell short, and the Regents voted to reaffirm two of the most controversial resolutions in the history of the board?

Senior Vice President Bruce Darling began estimating votes. His calculations, based on discussions with individual Regents, were that a motion to rescind SP-1 would lose, perhaps by only a few votes, perhaps more, because some Regents were undecided about which way to go. Atkinson was skeptical about the numbers, but he agreed with Darling's suggestion that there was a better strategy than simply calling the question and scheduling a vote. Under any scenario, Connerly's support was crucial to success. The Regents who had voted in favor of SP-1 and SP-2 would vote for its repeal only if Connerly were on board.[3]

With Atkinson's concurrence, Darling spoke to Regent Judith Hopkinson, who supported repeal, about the idea of crafting a compromise resolution along these lines. Hopkinson was enthusiastic. Connerly had his doubts about the entire enterprise and made it clear he would not agree to anything that smacked of rolling back the two measures. With this understanding, he was willing to work with them to see if some kind of mutually acceptable solution were possible.

Despite his skepticism, Connerly had found Darling's case for attempting a compromise resolution persuasive. It ran like this: the ban on affirmative action would remain intact, given the reality of Proposition 209; rescission now would avoid a possible recurrence of conflict among the Regents as the governor's appointees, likely to favor repeal of SP-1 and SP-2, would soon constitute a majority of the board. A serious point of friction with the faculty would vanish. UC would restore its battered public image among California's rapidly growing minority population. Not least, the board would at last be unified after its long and rancorous division over a polarizing issue. Darling then outlined a set of elements that could serve as a starting point for a resolution that might win the consent of a majority of the board:

· a statement that the Regents had adhered to the requirements of Proposition 209 and would continue to do so;
· a reaffirmation of UC's long-standing commitment to enroll a diverse student body;
· an expression of the University's intention to support outreach and to improve the K–12 education and therefore the college-going opportunities of California's children;
· a commitment to increasing student transfer from the community colleges, which enrolled 80 percent of the minority students in California higher education; and
· an acknowledgment of the Academic Senate's full authority over admissions.

The first four provisions assured Connerly and opponents of affirmative action that the statewide ban on racial and ethnic preferences would remain unchallenged. The last one addressed the faculty's strong objection to what they saw as regental intrusion into long-held faculty terrain.

With a first draft of the resolution in hand, Darling began describing it to individual Regents. Language was crucial, down to fine shades of meaning. Connerly, for example, at first insisted that the resolutions be "replaced" rather than "rescinded," although he later agreed to "supersede" instead. He also wanted a statement to the effect that some students admitted after SP-1 took pride in knowing that they had gotten into UC solely through their own academic achievements— an inflammatory assertion to supporters of affirmative action. It took eight weeks of writing, rewriting, and compromise to create the version scheduled for a vote at the May 2001 Regents' meeting, known as RE-28 because of its order on the board's agenda. It was a razor-thin balance of opposing views.

Waiting out the slow, incremental process of building consensus around the resolution had not been easy for Atkinson, whose style ran more to immediate action. Further, he suspected that the compromise resolution on the May agenda sacrificed too much to Connerly's position and might end by pleasing no one and provoking a new round of political strife.

This was exactly how things appeared to stand on May 15, twenty-four hours before the vote on repeal. A *Sacramento Bee* article quoted Connerly as saying that he himself had written RE-28, after being asked by a group of Regents to draft a resolution "that would resolve the issue [i.e., the continuing conflict over SP-1 and SP-2]."[4] His claim to sole authorship may have been intended simply as a reassuring signal to his supporters that there would be no retreat on the affirmative action ban. It infuriated Democrats in the legislature, however, whose anger over Connerly's role in ending racial and ethnic preferences at UC still burned. No Democratic legislator would trust any resolution from the father of SP-1 and SP-2. There were threats to inflict retributive damage on the University's budget if the board adopted RE-28.

The resolution was now in serious jeopardy. Atkinson immediately began thinking about introducing a separate and more strongly worded resolution of his own. Darling convinced him that the better strategy was to revise RE-28 yet again. In the version they proceeded to hammer out, SP-1 was "rescinded," not "superseded." The assertion that some minority students took pride in their admission to UC without the aid of racial preferences was gone. A new clause noted that the Academic Senate's reassessment of UC admissions policies, among them the use of the SAT I and the adoption of comprehensive review, was under way and would be completed by the end of 2001. This was a reminder that decisions were pending that could open the way to a UC admissions process less focused on quantitative measures of student ability. Finally—a change of great importance—the resolution now reaffirmed directly and unambiguously the Academic Senate's authority to determine the University's admissions standards.

Connerly did not like all the revised language, particularly the use of the word *rescind* and the deletion of the clause about minority students. But he recognized

FIGURE 5. Regents Ward Connerly (*right*) and Robert Morrison (*middle*) during the discussion of the rescission of SP-1 at the May 2001 Regents' meeting. *Los Angeles Times,* May 17, 2001, p. B-1. Photo credit: Associated Press.

how drastically the *Sacramento Bee*'s article had diminished the odds of passing the resolution. Darling's calls to individual Regents informing them about the latest incarnation of RE-28 went on long into the evening.

The impasse was not broken yet. The fate of RE-28 had become entangled with the Latino Caucus's goal of removing the SAT I examination as a requirement for admission and hastening the approval of comprehensive review, which would broaden the criteria on which students were evaluated. In exchange for his support of RE-28, Regent Bustamante wanted the resolution to include a clear commitment that whatever admissions changes the faculty recommended to the Regents would become effective in fall 2002.

The timing was not a problem; the governance implications were. Academic Senate Chair Michael Cowan was confident the Senate's review would be finished by the end of 2001, in time to cover the class admitted in 2002. But the Regents could not commit to a specific implementation date for any admissions changes without infringing on the authority of the Academic Senate. It was the short-circuiting of Senate review that had angered the faculty in the passage of SP-1. The compromise, worked out with Cowan's consent, was a letter from the president to Regents Bustamante and Bob Hertzberg (also speaker of the assembly)

FIGURE 6. A Riverside student celebrates the Regents' decision to rescind SP-1. *Los Angeles Times*, May 17, 2001, p. B-1. Photo credit: Associated Press.

confirming a fall 2002 implementation date for comprehensive review—but only if the Academic Senate recommended it and the Regents approved it.[5]

As protesters gathered at UC San Francisco the next morning, May 16, the fragile compromise nearly shattered. Atkinson and Darling were asked to attend a hastily called private meeting just before the board was scheduled to assemble. Regents Bustamante, Hertzberg, and Fong, joined by ten Democratic legislators, wanted to discuss RE-28. They had done their own editing of the resolution. The version they produced would put the Regents on record as promising three things: the elimination of the SAT I without any further faculty review; the adoption of the comprehensive review policy, also without faculty consultation; and—presumably with SP-1 in mind—a guarantee that the Board of Regents would no longer play a role in setting admissions policy for the University. In effect, they were asking the board to abrogate its own authority to govern the University of California, an authority guaranteed to the Regents in the California Constitution of 1879. It was an impossible demand, as Atkinson and Darling told them, and even to propose it would doom any prospect of passing RE-28.

Even with Governor Davis's endorsement, approval was no sure thing. The first vote taken by the Regents was a procedural one that waived the usual committee consideration of RE-28 so that it could be brought directly to the full board. Many Regents, whatever their position, were angry at the bare-knuckles politics leading up to the morning of May 16. During the discussion, several voiced their disapproval of the legislators' punitive behavior and inappropriate fiscal threats—the Board of Regents, Connerly pointed out, "is one of only two bodies that the people of California have safeguarded in their constitution." Nonetheless, consistent with a statesmanlike willingness to compromise, he seconded Regent Hopkinson's motion to approve RE-28. With that, everyone knew it was over. Amid cheers and applause, each Regent cast a vote. Regent Odessa Johnson prefaced hers by announcing that she was wearing black for the funeral of SP-1 and SP-2 and that she was voting for the future of the students of the University of California.

The president had been convinced up to the very last moment that any resolution with the word *rescind* in it would never survive the opposition of SP-1 and SP-2 supporters remaining on the board. When RE-28 passed unanimously, a photograph taken at the time captures Atkinson, arms thrown wide in amazement and relief, looking heavenward as if thanking some higher power.

ADMISSIONS IMPLICATIONS OF SP-1

A positive outcome of SP-1 was the impetus it gave to moving UC toward a wider and deeper definition of merit in evaluating students for undergraduate admission. This may seem paradoxical in light of the fact that the resolution contemplated more reliance on grades and test scores, not less, as reflected in its controversial Section 5. But SP-1's insistence on quantitative measures was not seamless. Section 4 called upon the president and the Academic Senate to develop "supplemental criteria":

> In developing such criteria, which shall provide reasonable assurances that the applicant will successfully complete his or her course of study, consideration shall be given to individuals who, despite having suffered disadvantage economically or in terms of their social environment (such as an abusive or otherwise dysfunctional home or a neighborhood of unwholesome or antisocial influences), have nonetheless demonstrated sufficient character and determination in overcoming obstacles to warrant confidence that the applicant can pursue a course of study to successful completion, provided that any student admitted under this section must be academically eligible for admission.

This section opened a crack through which such "opportunity to learn" factors might legitimately enter into admissions decisions. It also opened larger questions. Is learning entirely or even mostly a matter of innate intelligence or talent? It was obvious that the more affluent the family, the better the educational opportunities available to the student; if the public schools were below par, private schools were a realistic option. If a poor student in an academically impoverished school district managed to make good grades nonetheless, what did that say about her desire to learn and steadfastness in the face of difficulties, even if her test scores were lower than those of other competitors?

The task force appointed by President Jack Peltason in summer 1995 to make the University's undergraduate admissions policy consistent with SP-1 had thought about these questions. Its recommendations for the future pointed in two directions: toward a broader review of student characteristics and promise and toward developing admissions criteria that were also flexible enough to give students the opportunity to demonstrate the full range of their talent and achievement. "Readily and presently available indicators," the task force said in its December 1995 report, "such as GPA and test scores, by themselves cannot provide a comprehensive assessment of the cognitive ability, intelligence, and achievement of an individual, nor do they assess adequately the candidate's potential for growth."[6]

University policy, pre–SP-1, had termed grades and test scores "academic" criteria and such factors as economic or educational disadvantage "supplemental" criteria. The task force noted the lesser value the word *supplemental* implied. "This . . . may have led to the mistaken assumption that students who are selected on the basis of academic plus 'supplementary criteria' are less academically qualified than other admitted students, when, in fact, these students do meet all academic criteria for eligibility to UC."[7] What if some version of what had been designated supplemental criteria were incorporated in new paths to admission that were consistent with SP-1? These ideas—comprehensive criteria and comprehensive consideration of every student's achievement and promise—were the foundation of the faculty and administration's policy response to SP-1. They were the starting point of the search for an admissions process that gave appropriate weight not only to grades and test scores but also to context and character.

BOARS AND THE PRESIDENT

The Academic Senate committee with primary responsibility for admissions issues was BOARS, the Board of Admissions and Relations with Schools. After approval of SP-1, BOARS began a wide-ranging series of discussions about ways to promote student diversity within the boundaries laid down by the resolution. Characteristically, Atkinson did not wait for the University's admissions machinery to grind its way to a new policy. He began searching for ideas and proposals, anything that might conceivably offer an avenue to keep underrepresented minority students coming to UC campuses. The California legislature was not waiting either. Senator Teresa Hughes floated a proposal calling on UC to abandon its practice of admitting undergraduates from the upper 12.5 percent of California high school graduates statewide. Under her plan, UC would make eligible for admission any student ranked in the upper 12.5 percent of *each* California high school.

This had been one of the tentative proposals of the faculty–administration Task Force on Undergraduate Admissions Criteria. Jud King asked his staff to run some numbers. The analyses simulated the outcome in terms of both student diversity and academic quality under three scenarios: Assemblywoman Hughes's 12.5 percent, 6 percent, and 4 percent. Atkinson preferred the 4 percent number as striking the best balance. It would not increase the University's racial and ethnic diversity dramatically, but it would protect UC's high admissions standards and expand its geographic diversity by bringing in more students from rural schools and schools that had historically sent few students to UC campuses. Propelled by a growing sense of urgency, in late 1997 Atkinson began talking publicly and enthusiastically about the 4 percent possibility. Around the same time, the idea got a push from an analysis done by the California Postsecondary Education Commission.

CPEC had just completed its latest eligibility study, conducted regularly to measure whether UC and CSU were admitting students in their required proportions of 12.5 and 33.3 percent of the state's public high school graduates. The 1997 CPEC study, published in January 1998, showed UC's undergraduate admissions rate was 11.1 percent of California high school graduates, 1.4 percent below the University's Master Plan obligation of 12.5 percent. Director of Admissions Research Saul Geiser immediately began simulations, which showed that adding the top 4 percent from each high school to the 11.1 percent of students already eligible under the traditional statewide criteria would return the overall pool to almost exactly 12.5 percent of all California high school graduates, as the Master Plan required. This "happy and fortuitous result," as Geiser described it in a January 1998 e-mail to Jud King, was due to the overlap between the top 4 percent and 11.1 percent pools. His simulations revealed that most of the top 4 percent of students in the upper tier of California high schools were already attending UC, which meant that the new policy would primarily draw top students in lower-performing schools. These results opened the door to Atkinson's version of the various proposals using class rank in individual high schools as a way to qualify students for UC, because students admitted in this fashion would not displace any students who were already eligible. Thus the divisive zero-sum politics that had characterized the earlier affirmative action debate could be avoided.

The University called it Eligibility in the Local Context—ELC—but it was not a substitute for the traditional 12.5 percent statewide path, as Assemblywoman Hughes had proposed. ELC became a new path to admission, and its rationale was squarely in line with the idea that UC should broaden opportunities for students to demonstrate their readiness for college. It differed from a similar percentage plan adopted at the University of Texas, the Top Ten Percent Program, in two ways. ELC stipulated that UC, not individual high schools, would review students' transcripts to determine whether they ranked in the upper 4 percent of their class. And it expected ELC students to complete the same high school course requirements every prospective UC student was required to take.

When ELC was launched in 2001, UC assumed that most of the students who qualified for UC under the program would be eligible *only* through ELC. This turned out not to be the case. All but a handful of ELC students also qualified under the existing 12.5 percent statewide academic criteria. Puzzled at first, UC admissions officials soon determined that this unexpected pattern was largely the product of ELC's success. When the program was introduced, Atkinson sent a letter to every California high school junior who was eligible—some thirteen thousand students—with his congratulations and encouragement to apply. For many students in schools that traditionally sent most of their graduates to CSU or a community college, if they attended college at all, UC was not on their radar. Atkinson's letter changed that. Some were now motivated to complete UC-required coursework during their senior year. Others had already taken the required coursework but did not realize it until Atkinson's letter arrived; many of these students went on to complete the UC application process and become eligible under statewide criteria. Nor was the change confined to students. In some cases, ELC motivated parents and schools as well. An example was Pittsburg High, a San Francisco Bay Area school whose principal had decided not to participate in the program—too much work, he said—until parents complained to the local school board. UC extended its ELC deadline to accommodate Pittsburg High's students. In the first year alone, ELC attracted two thousand new applicants to UC. Over half were underrepresented minority students.

COMPREHENSIVE REVIEW

ELC addressed the first step toward entering UC—becoming eligible for admission. It did not address the second step, qualifying for the campus you wanted to attend. That decision was in the hands of each campus admissions office. In the wake of SP-1, getting admitted to the more selective campuses—Berkeley, UCLA, UC San Diego—was a very high hurdle for any minority or disadvantaged student who was not at the very top of the applicant pool. Many of these students were receiving offers of admission from the campus of their second or third choice; a rising number of eligible minority and disadvantaged students who once would have qualified for admission to Berkeley or UCLA now qualified only for admission to a less selective campus. As the 4 percent plan was being pondered in spring 1997, Dennis Galligani, assistant vice president for student academic services, wrote Provost King about this issue: "Redefining eligibility may change the ethnic composition of those who attain UC eligibility. . . . However, it will not by itself resolve the fundamental issue at the core of the admissions controversy, that is, not all UC eligible students can be admitted at the campus of [their first] choice."[8] This statement defined the problem UC faced in its most demanding form—not just acceptance at UC, but acceptance at the student's favored campus—but it was an important matter to students, families, and the legislature. Comprehensive review was intended to deal with this issue.

Considering students' achievements in terms of their life circumstances had also been one of the themes of the Task Force on Undergraduate Eligibility Criteria. Several versions of comprehensive review were already in use at the more selective campuses. The range of possibilities was defined by Berkeley on one end and San Diego on the other. Berkeley admitted half of its incoming class by "holistic" measures, assigning no fixed weights to various criteria but using them to come up with a single figure that determined who was accepted and who was rejected. San Diego considered all the factors Berkeley did but then assigned a number to each and used a formula to create a cumulative score. The practice at both campuses—and throughout UC—reflected different versions of a thirty-year policy of evaluating students in two tiers—admitting 40 to 60 percent of undergraduates on grades and test scores alone and selecting the balance on a combination of grades and test scores as well as personal qualities such as leadership skills or special talents. SP-1 shifted the proportion of students admitted solely on grades and test scores upward, from 40–60 to 50–75 percent, greatly increasing the weight of quantitative factors in the admissions process.

The comprehensive review ultimately approved by the Regents in November 2001 abolished this two-tier system. It instituted in its place an admissions process that would ensure, in the words of the proposal submitted to the board, that "students applying to UC campuses are evaluated for admission using multiple measures of achievement and promise while considering the context in which each student has demonstrated academic accomplishment."

ACADEMIC STANDARDS AND INSTITUTIONAL INTENT

Neither ELC nor comprehensive review won immediate acceptance from the Regents. When the ELC proposal was first explained to the board in May 1998, it was coupled with a tentative faculty proposal to minimize the weight high school honors and Advanced Placement courses carried in the admissions process. This was being considered because studies suggested the extra credit given for these courses inflated students' GPA without improving UC's ability to predict student performance. There was also the fact that many California high schools did not offer them. Some Regents were suspicious of the motivation for these potential changes, however. During a regental discussion in February 1999, Connerly wondered aloud if ELC were really a Trojan horse designed to circumvent SP-1 and Proposition 209; Governor Gray Davis and Regent John Davies, among others, worried about eroding academic standards. In the end, the Regents rejected the proposal to lower the bonus points for honors and advanced placement courses. But in March 1999, at a meeting attended by both Senator Hughes and Governor Davis, they approved Eligibility in the Local Context, to be effective in fall 2001.

Comprehensive review was a tougher case to make. It brought UC's admissions process closer to that of selective private universities, which meant that it was more flexible, less reliant on quantitative measures, and—a major source of regental and sometimes public suspicion—less transparent than UC's traditional measures. But even before SP-1, BOARS had been questioning some of the quantitative indicators used to assess student talent and promise: did they really yield enough information about students to justify the weight they carried in the admissions process? The answer, in the words of the Academic Senate, was to recommend "a more inclusive definition of merit that is . . . still geared strongly toward measures of academic achievement." BOARS's evaluations of the comprehensive review process in 2002 and 2003 concluded that, by virtually every quantitative measure, the academic preparation of students admitted under the program was exceptionally strong. At the same time, the proportion of disadvantaged students admitted to selective UC campuses was on the rise.

Quite apart from the policy question of affirmative action, the problem with SP-1 was that it favored certain goals of the UC admissions process over others. These goals have long stressed the importance of rewarding exceptional academic achievement or personal talent. But they also include enrolling a student body that reflects California's diversity and educating leaders for a pluralistic society,[9] as well as offering students a stimulating intellectual experience marked by a variety of values and perspectives.[10] SP-1 assumed that any student characteristic, like race and gender, that did not relate directly and demonstrably to objective measures of achievement—good grades and high test scores—violated the principle of fairness. In reality, no Ivy League university—in fact no selective US university at all—admits students solely on the basis of academic achievement. UC's admissions criteria were intended to recognize that many students with less than perfect grades or test scores bring intellectual or personal qualities that contribute to a vibrant learning environment; some show motivation and desire to learn that suggest they have academic promise and can do well at a place like UC. This was the point of UC's commitment to choose from "among" the top one-eighth of public high school graduates. It meant that a 4.0 GPA, even a greater than 4.0 GPA, did not trump every other qualification. SP-1's elevation of quantitative over other kinds of measures, as the Task Force on Undergraduate Admissions Criteria explained, outran the available evidence about the best ways to evaluate student achievement, talent, and promise. ELC, comprehensive review, and the later decision on the part of the Academic Senate to scrutinize standardized test requirements (discussed below) have helped repair the damage SP-1 inflicted on diversity at UC and realigned its admissions policies with the commitment to excellence and access that dates all the way back to the Organic Act.

Atkinson was careful to keep an open channel to the faculty throughout the debates over post–SP-1 admissions. On several occasions he visited with BOARS in person to explain his admissions proposals and seek its advice, an unusual occurrence in administration–faculty relations. In the wake of his February 2001 proposal to eliminate the SAT I admissions requirement, the Academic Senate embarked on a review of standardized testing in the University; his endorsement of broader measures of student potential in that same speech stimulated BOARS's interest in what became the proposal for comprehensive review. He had the good fortune of an exceptionally able and experienced faculty committee in BOARS that was willing to consider an idea even when it came from an administrator. In the aftermath of SP-1, the Academic Senate's collaborative relationship with the administration on admissions issues was an example of shared governance at work during a time when it was under serious threat.

Yet the reality is that SP-1 and, later, Proposition 209 have rendered the pursuit of diversity far more difficult. By the end of Atkinson's administration, the systemwide percentage of underrepresented minority students at UC had almost returned to its pre–SP-1 level. But this gain masked two serious problems. The proportion of minority students at several campuses, including Berkeley and UCLA, had not recovered from the drop in minority enrollment that followed SP-1. The gap between the percentage of underrepresented minority students graduating from California's high schools and the percentage of such students at UC is still widening, because the state's minority population continues to expand at a rapid pace. As Atkinson wrote in 2003, "Our experience to date shows that if race cannot be factored into admissions decisions at all, the ethnic diversity of an elite public institution such as the University of California may fall well behind that of the state it serves. And that is something that should trouble us all."[11]

Why did SP-1 happen at the University of California? Among the reasons cited by Brian Pusser in *Burning Down the House,* a detailed account of the events surrounding the Regents' action, two are related to governance. One is Connerly's successful challenge to President Peltason's claim, voiced in Peltason's November 1994 letter to the Regents, to be "the Board of Regents' *chosen and publicly designated agent* to . . . manage the University." Another is what Pusser sees as the inability or unwillingness of the Office of the President to join with students, labor unions, and other groups to oppose SP-1 and SP-2. Such a move, however, would have been antithetical to long-standing assumptions and practices within UC regarding the role of the central administration. This role was to make the case for its recommendations to the board but not to serve as a rallying point for its own positions, however strongly held.[12] One of Pusser's most intriguing conclusions is that over the long term UC's constitutional autonomy, intended to protect the

University from legislative interference, has had the ironic effect of making it more vulnerable to the political agendas of governors and interest groups.[13] But the end of constitutional autonomy, should that occur, would leave the University with an even longer list of potential intruders—there are many legislators with their own political agendas to push—without offering any real benefit in exchange.

In reflecting on his own experience in the 1995 drama of SP-1 and SP-2, President Emeritus Peltason was philosophical about the perils of academic governance. At UC, he said, an "Armageddon-like issue" surfaces every twenty years or so, like a subterranean virus in the body politic, that divides the Regents and plunges the University community into political turmoil. It had happened with the loyalty oath controversy in the late 1940s, the firing of President Clark Kerr in the 1960s, and, to some extent, the debates over UC's management of the Los Alamos and Livermore nuclear weapons laboratories and divestment from companies doing business in South Africa during the 1980s. Of these examples, SP-1 most resembles the loyalty oath controversy in raising fundamental issues about the nature of a public university and the responsibilities of a governing board. The Regents could rescind their resolution but not its consequences. These were, and continue to be, far-reaching.

Reinventing the Economy

One day Professor Terman remarked that many of the firms we visited, and many other firms throughout the country in this field [engineering], had been founded by men with little or no formal education. He suggested that someone with a formal engineering education, and perhaps a little business training, might be even more successful.

—DAVID PACKARD, 1965

The role of the university has shifted from the old tradition of the ivory tower that does not engage in commercial activity or in the economic activity of the region in which it operates to the entrepreneurial university, which takes a far more proactive, encouraging, and supportive role in the commercialization of technology. As a result, the research university . . . has become the major force for the development of technology, the generation of talent, and the creation of jobs and wealth.

—RAYMOND SMILOR ET AL., "THE RESEARCH UNIVERSITY AND THE DEVELOPMENT OF HIGH-TECHNOLOGY CENTERS IN THE UNITED STATES," 2007

In 1980 the San Diego economy, built largely on military contracts, banking, and the region's attractiveness to tourists and retirees, was locked in a deep recession. Yet it had several latent advantages that pointed to a brighter economic future. One was a nascent high-technology sector with start-ups in biotechnology and pharmaceuticals, telecommunications, computers, and electronics, many of them sparked by research conducted at UCSD, the Salk Institute for Biological Studies, and the Scripps Research Institute. Another was the robust individualism deeply etched in the culture of San Diego. According to Mary Walshok, dean of UCSD Extension during Atkinson's time and beyond, this self-reliance was already evident in 1917, when Secretary of the Navy Teddy Roosevelt visited San Diego and told civic boosters their city could never be a naval port because its bay was too shallow to accommodate oceangoing vessels. The city provided the funds to dredge the harbor itself. In 1902, before the advent of a public university in the area, E. W. Scripps established a marine biological institute in La Jolla, and the local chamber of commerce organized a fund-raising committee to support its work. This marine research center was the forerunner of the Scripps Institution of Oceanography, which in turn became the nucleus of the San Diego campus in the 1960s. The essential ingredients for a regional high-tech center—an entrepreneurial culture, a world-class research faculty, and a community interested in technology as an engine of economic growth—were in place in the 1980s.[1] UCSD's role in the emergence of San Diego as a thriving high-technology center was to become one of the defining goals of Atkinson's chancellorship.

What he contributed over a fifteen-year tenure was his active and highly visible support for closer relations with industry, his penchant for handing a problem to whoever he thought could solve it, and a set of ideas that had been evolving since his time at Stanford and NSF. The University of Chicago would always remain his ideal of the university as the conservator of humanistic learning. Stanford opened up another dimension, more dynamic, entrepreneurial, and outward-looking. It would be difficult, in fact, to overestimate the influence of Atkinson's Stanford years in shaping what he wanted to accomplish as chancellor. Fred Terman's strategy at Stanford of cultivating steeples of excellence, setting priorities, and seizing opportunities permeated the academic culture in which Atkinson began his career as a young academic. Long after leaving Stanford, he acknowledged a permanent debt to Terman:

> If there is a model for me in academic life, it is Fred Terman. I was a member of the Stanford faculty for almost twenty-five years. During much of that time, Fred was provost of the campus, working closely with President [Wallace] Sterling.... I was able to apply the knowledge I gained from Fred's work at Stanford years later when I became chancellor of the University of California, San Diego. I sought to use the "Terman Model" as a roadmap for UCSD's partnerships with the telecommunications and biotechnology industries that were beginning to spring up in the region, and as I encouraged the development of UCSD's own peaks of excellence.[2]

Terman's long reign was drawing to a close during Atkinson's time at Stanford. They were acquaintances, not close friends; Terman and his wife were interested in computer-assisted instruction and curious about Atkinson's work in that area. At MIT Terman had been the first Ph.D. student of Vannevar Bush, whose efforts to further industry–university partnerships in the Boston area helped create its famous Route 128. Bush's approach later inspired Terman to do the same thing at Stanford.[3] In 1946, after his four years in Cambridge as head of the wartime Harvard/MIT Radio Research Laboratory, Terman returned to Stanford deeply concerned about the dominance of East Coast industries in attracting wartime government contracts. If West Coast technology firms were going to compete successfully with their eastern rivals in the postwar world, they would need to be part of a community: "Such a community is composed of industries using highly sophisticated technology, together with a strong university that is sensitive to the creative activities of the surrounding industry. This pattern appears to be the wave of the future."[4]

The assumption that industry and universities are natural partners was as much a part of Atkinson's Stanford experience in the 1960s and early 1970s as the fundamental importance of teaching and research. The company he and Pat Suppes founded as a result of their work in computer-based learning, Computer Curriculum Corporation, gave him firsthand experience of academic entrepreneurship that was unusual among 1970s academics. Later, as UC president, he had no doubts about the legitimacy or desirability of research partnerships with industry and no fears that, if properly managed, they would distort the University's academic commitments or its research agenda. Silicon Valley had demonstrated how productive, not just economically but also intellectually, such collaborations could be.

It was at the National Science Foundation that Atkinson came to admire Vannevar Bush's formative role in the postwar relationship between American universities and American science. As President Franklin Roosevelt's science adviser during World War II, Bush was the prime mover in organizing scientists and engineers to advance the US war effort. He and Roosevelt feared that the enormous scientific successes of that effort could not be sustained without a clearly articulated strategy for supporting science in the postwar world. The aim of Bush's historic 1945 report on national science policy, *Science, the Endless Frontier,* was to establish what Bush described as a "pool of scientific knowledge" to ensure economic growth and the nation's defense. Much of its persuasive power derives from the bold simplicity of its rationale for supporting and applying research.

The federal government would fund basic science generally, not its applications.[5] Industry would be responsible for applied research. Bush reasoned that industry had little incentive to invest heavily in basic research because its results were not proprietary and might be profitably applied by rival firms. American research universities would produce the pool of fundamental knowledge on which industry and the military could draw. Federal support for university research would be channeled through a system of grants to individuals or teams of researchers, with each grant awarded to projects whose scientific merit had been endorsed through a process of peer review.[6] Graduate student training would become an integral aspect of government-supported research.

Science, the Endless Frontier gave research universities a dominant role in the American scientific enterprise, a reality that was never directly stated in that document. By the early 1960s, as Clark Kerr observed in his Godkin Lectures, the great postwar expansion of federal funding that poured into the nation's universities was transforming "the shape and nature of university research."[7]

Yet by the 1970s, the innovative engine Bush had set in motion seemed in need of repair. The 1973 oil crisis, rampant inflation, rising unemployment, and international competition throughout that decade left the US economy floundering and economic analysts speculating on what to do about it. The United States began a decline in output per worker per hour that reversed a nearly century-long global lead in productivity growth.[8] One reason US firms had enjoyed a competitive advantage over the rest of the world during the high-flying 1960s was that they reaped the rewards of the enormous postwar federal investment in research in American universities.[9] Other nations were catching up. Japan led the pack, not only in adapting and improving on existing American technology in products from cameras to automobiles but also in establishing its own scientific research base. Between 1967 and 1984 Japan was the only industrial nation in which the number of patents per scientist and engineer increased rather than decreased.[10] Numbers like these cast an entirely new light on European and Japanese practices of government assistance for emerging industries. Stiffening foreign competition—and especially Japan's extraordinary economic achievements, a few short decades after its devastation during World War II—were beginning to shake the ingrained American conviction that the market could take care of itself.

The economic alarms of the late 1970s were the backdrop for many of the NSF initiatives begun under Atkinson's directorship—the analytical studies that helped lay the groundwork for Bayh-Dole, the early industry-university research programs, the studies of tax credits and other incentives for technology transfer, the analyses of the role of R&D in economic growth. They were early signs of a trend toward a closer integration of American universities and American industry, something he had seen up close at Stanford and in Silicon Valley. Terman showed what could be accomplished by a judicious leveraging of institutional strengths and an entrepreneurial perspective. Bush defined the place of the research university in the larger landscape of American science, and Atkinson considered *Science, the Endless Frontier* "one of the great documents of American history."[11] But when it came to the daily task of institution building, it was Terman who mattered more and left a deeper mark. San Diego gave him the chance to test the Terman model in the real world.

THE ENTREPRENEURIAL CHANCELLOR

When Atkinson met California Governor Jerry Brown soon after becoming chancellor of UCSD, he made a case for a state initiative to encourage high-technology industries and industry–university partnerships. A strategy of promoting innovation and closer ties between universities and industry, he told the governor, would demonstrate his political commitment to restarting the stalled California economy. Brown sent his chief of staff, Gray Davis, to talk to Atkinson, who gave him a tour of San Diego's high-technology community and argued for a governor-appointed commission to develop a competitiveness strategy for California, with emphasis on the potential of the emerging sectors in electronics and biotechnology.

The California Commission on Industrial Innovation (CCII) was established by executive order in November 1981. Its charter was to propose "a blueprint for industrial innovation policy in California, in order to assure our continued leadership in the emerging technologies for old and new industries in the 1980's."[12] Brown chaired the commission and, in addition to Atkinson, appointed leaders from industry and academia, among them Steve Jobs of Apple Computer and David Packard of Hewlett Packard, Ruth Jernigan of the United Auto Workers, Chancellor Ira Michael Heyman of UC Berkeley, Charles Sporck of National Semiconductor Corporation, and Rene McPherson, dean of the Stanford Business School.[13]

The commission's report, "Winning Technologies: A New Industrial Strategy for California and the Nation," came down strongly on the side of free trade, legislation to promote research and development, and expanding the flow of capital into new companies. Its fifty recommendations ranged from trade policy to educating more technologically literate citizens. "Winning Technologies" focused on the international threats to American industry, but it had a local message as well.[14]

The nation was in the grip of the steepest recession of the postwar era, and San Diego's unemployment rate was spiraling into the double digits. The city's efforts to capitalize on its high-tech potential were not gaining much traction. In 1982 San Diego lost a national competition to be the site of the Microelectronics and Computer Consortium, a group of computer and semiconductor companies dedicated to supporting research that would blunt Japan's push to become the world leader in computing through its Fifth Generation Project. A few years later, the city lost again, this time in a competition for SEMATECH, a partnership between the US government and fourteen semiconductor companies, also aimed at countering the Japanese competitive challenge. Local venture capitalists were more likely to go to Silicon Valley, five hundred miles to the north, for investment opportunities. The San Diego Regional Economic Development Corporation, an alliance of business, government, and community leaders, came to Atkinson to enlist UCSD's help in attracting more high-tech industries and research to San Diego.

The campus's small industrial affiliates program, established in 1981, was not set up to encourage collaborative research. There were UCSD scientists and engineers founding their own start-ups or acting as consultants to the area's high-tech companies, but the campus lacked a business school, which would have served as a natural locus for a larger and more comprehensive partnership with local industries and entrepreneurs. Atkinson turned to Mary Walshok and UCSD Extension to help fill the gap. Extension was well known in the city of San Diego.

The University of California had sponsored Extension public service courses and programs in San Diego since 1920, and during World War II Extension helped with professional training for engineers, chemists, and other scientific personnel essential to the war effort. At Atkinson's request, UCSD Extension had already begun offering an executive education program for scientists and engineers who were CEOs of small- and medium-sized companies. Next was a more ambitious effort also mounted by Extension, UCSD CONNECT, a program open to anyone with a good idea who needed help in all aspects of organizing a start-up: writing a business plan, finding capital, learning how to run a company. As its name implies, the program brought together university researchers with entrepreneurs, angel investors, and venture capitalists from around the country. CONNECT was a prime example of the kind of strategy advocated in the "Winning Strategies" report—realizing the potential of young high-tech industries and making commercialization of university research easier and more vigorous.[15] Over time, CONNECT's record in generating successful high-tech start-up companies attracted increasing amounts of venture capital to San Diego.[16]

Atkinson regarded engineering as a foundational discipline for technical enterprises generally and a strong school of engineering as key to seeding a competitive high-tech community in San Diego. In 1980 no new engineering programs had been established in the University of California system for twenty years.[17] At San Diego engineering had no distinct identity; a few faculty members with engineering backgrounds were scattered among several programs and departments. Atkinson's goal was to organize these activities into a school. The faculty senate was reluctant at first, fearing that an engineering school might drain resources from other departments and that a school might isolate students from other disciplines. Atkinson promised that the school would be supported with new funds and that engineering students would be held to the same general-education requirements as other students. The faculty senate approved the reorganization into the Division of Engineering in 1982. It was renamed the School of Engineering in the early 1990s.[18]

Atkinson involved San Diego's business leaders in his search for faculty stars; they responded by endowing chairs and funding research. In 1985 the campus was chosen by NSF as one of four supercomputing sites in the nation. It added new interdisciplinary research capabilities through the industry-supported Center for Magnetic Recording Research (1983), the Center for Molecular Genetics (1983), and the Center for Wireless Communications (1995), whose organization and operations illustrate the kind of close research partnerships that were developing between the campus and the high-tech community:

The Center for Wireless Communications . . . was an answer for the "viscous" nature of tech transfer at UCSD. The center was launched and supported with funds from industry. Thus, all of the research was private. Members of the center had a right to "opt in" on any discovery made by researchers working on center funds. The members contributed equally to the patenting process. At the end of the patenting process, the "in" members shared the revenues equally with the university. Industrial members also contributed employees. These employees operated at the Center for Wireless Communication to assist in research and conduct private research using the center's equipment. Small companies could thus share the cost of expensive equipment that they could not otherwise afford.[19]

When many defense-related jobs fell victim to another recession in the late 1980s and early 1990s, an array of small high-tech companies around the campus and its environs took up the slack. Firms like QUALCOMM and Hybritech, Inc., were founded by former or current UCSD faculty; QUALCOMM soon rose to become a leader in wireless communications, and Hybritech was one of the founders of the biotechnology industry in the San Diego area. It is estimated that some forty communications and telecommunications companies were "either founded by students or faculty, or spun off from firms with ties to UCSD," during the 1980s and 1990s.[20] Budding companies could recruit from a growing pool of UC San Diego graduates skilled in high-tech fields. By the mid-1990s San Diego was no longer a one- or two-industry town but home to a growing mix of high-tech companies, from telecommunications to biotechnology.

A 2007 study of the birth and evolution of high-technology centers cited San Diego as an example and concluded that of the many factors required for success the most important is "a research university that can serve as instigator; promoter; collaborator; and magnet for talent, technological innovation, and entrepreneurial activity."[21] It was a good capsule description of the Terman model. It was an equally apt description of the roles UCSD filled in the region's transition from a near-exclusive dependence on military contracts, banking, and tourism to an economy built around high-technology, small companies, and entrepreneurial activities.

PRESIDENTIAL INITIATIVES

In one of his early statements as UC president, Atkinson sounded a note he would return to many times—the dynamic role of knowledge in contemporary life:

The role of knowledge in transforming virtually every aspect of our world has moved research universities like the University of California to center stage of American life. More than any other institution in our society, research universities are on the cutting edge in producing the well-educated people who drive our economy and the new research ideas that keep it growing. The tradition of research universities has been to value knowledge for its own sake. However, society's increasing need for applications of knowledge has placed new demands on these institutions, including the University of California.[22]

The idea of a knowledge-based society, mediated by the production and dissemination of increasingly sophisticated technologies, was not original with Atkinson. In the 1980s Peter Drucker had talked about a "knowledge economy," and in the mid-1990s Federal Reserve Chairman Alan Greenspan gave currency to the term "the New Economy."[23] The New Economy, grounded in the burst of technological innovation symbolized by the Internet, was identified with a structural trend in the United States away from traditional manufacturing to high-tech industries like biotechnology, advanced engineering, and computing. California was the epicenter of this phenomenon. The pessimism of the late 1970s and early 1980s vanished as the US economy began to expand at an average rate of 3.5 percent in 1997, 1998, and 1999, buoyed by low inflation and low unemployment.[24] A 1995 report by President Clinton's Council of Economic Advisers noted that 50 percent of US economic growth since World War II was due to advances in knowledge.[25] In a state that had served as the breeding ground of Silicon Valley, this statement was akin to a self-evident truth.

Evidence for the central role of knowledge in economic life was beginning to appear in a burgeoning subfield of economics called New Growth Theory. The Stanford economist Paul Romer's pathbreaking 1990 paper, "Endogenous Technological Change," explored the contribution of technology by starting with a question: why has American productivity—output per worker per hour—increased tenfold over the past century, whereas conventional economic theory would lead us to expect that growth would peak at some point and then level off or decline? Romer's answer: technological change. A century ago, he wrote, the only way to elicit visual pleasure from iron oxide was to use it as a pigment. Today it is applied to plastic tape to make videocassette recordings. Incremental improvements like these lie "at the heart of economic growth." Technical progress occurs at an increasingly rapid rate because successive generations of scientists and engineers learn from the accumulated knowledge of their predecessors.[26]

Further, technological change is driven in large part by market incentives. Even if you are a professor on a federal grant with no interest in applying your discoveries, should commercialization occur it will be because an individual or a private firm wants to make a profit. This is why Romer described technological change not as some external quantity injected into economic activity but as something endogenous—internal—to the economic system itself. Unlike land, labor, and capital, technological change created by human ingenuity holds out the potential of ever-increasing expansion in the wealth of nations. "The most interesting positive implication of the model," he concluded, "is that an economy with a larger total stock of human capital will experience faster growth."[27]

Some of the 1970s NSF-sponsored studies on the relationship of R&D to economic growth had laid the foundations. One of these was a 1977 analysis by Edwin Mansfield and colleagues on the social and private rates of return on industrial innovations—that is, the benefits that private firms gain from investing in new products and processes compared to the benefits that accrue to society. They found that the social rate of return was much higher than the rate of return to the firms themselves.[28] Toward the end of his career, Mansfield turned his attention to how basic research in universities stimulates technological change. He wrote an influential 1995 paper assessing how academic research contributed to industrial innovation in sixty-six firms in seven major manufacturing areas, from information processing to pharmaceuticals to petroleum. Mansfield found that academic research was responsible for a significant percentage of the new products and processes in the companies he studied.[29] A 1996 study of the origins of the first US biotechnology companies found that active, hands-on involvement of "star" scientists—scientists who had made original discoveries in the field and understood the techniques of working with recombinant DNA—was indispensable to the early expansion of the biotechnology industry.[30] These and similar studies helped shape government policy on technology and economic growth.

Governors and legislators who had never heard of Mansfield or Romer nevertheless were taking note of the practical benefits yielded by public investments in the new ideas and techniques coming out of scientific research. Governor Gray Davis of California was one of them.

Atkinson made it clear at the outset of his presidency that industry–university partnerships would be high on his agenda. Strong engineering programs were a priority, just as they had been in San Diego, and in 1997 he committed the University to expanding engineering and computer science enrollments by 50 percent within five years—from 16,000 to 24,000.[31] But what was the ultimate goal? An opinion piece Atkinson wrote with Ed Penhoet, cofounder of Chiron, one of the early companies that came out of the biotechnology revolution, put it this way:

> California is blessed with a combination of advantages that exists here and nowhere else. This state has more high-technology entrepreneurs, more venture capitalists, and more scientists and engineers than anyplace else in the world. We have the world's strongest basic research and graduate education, thanks to such premier institutions as Stanford, Caltech, the University of California, and the University of Southern California. What we haven't had, and urgently need, is a coherent program that will transform these advantages into a strategy to secure California's economic leadership.[32]

The search for "a coherent program" and a definition of UC's role in the state's economic competitiveness led in two distinct but related directions during Atkinson's administration. The first was a systemwide effort to spur research partnerships with industry, the Industry-University Cooperative Research Program (IUCRP). The second was a larger and more ambitious initiative, the California Institutes for Science and Innovation. In different ways, both led back to San Diego.

IUCRP

Atkinson announced the Industry-University Cooperative Research Program in January 1996, a little over three months after becoming president. In some ways IUCRP resembled its namesake NSF program from the 1970s, but it was also a lineal descendant of several earlier UC programs, one of which it incorporated— MICRO, a systemwide public-private effort founded in 1981 to improve the competitiveness of the state's electronics industry. California electronics firms, long world leaders, were among the US industries under challenge from the Japanese at the end of the 1970s. MICRO and other UC research partnerships were a factor in the industry's recovery and revitalization in the 1990s. In turn, MICRO benefited the University by giving UC researchers exposure to industrial designs and processes and a better sense of the kinds of technical problems private companies faced.[33] IUCRP's aim was to extend this approach systematically to other high-tech areas important to the California economy.

With initial funding of $3 million from the University and $5 million from the state of California, the IUCRP brought UC researchers and high-tech companies together to collaborate on commercializing scientific discoveries. UC investigators presented research proposals, and interested industrial partners had to commit to supporting at least half the costs of the project. It was a three-way collaboration among the University, industry, and government: UC contributed the research expertise of its faculty, the state seed funding and tax credits, industry a three-to-one match for every state dollar invested in IUCRP. The program focused on early-stage research in areas chosen for their potential for commercialization— biotechnology, communications, digital media, electronics materials and manufacturing, and information technology for the life sciences—and one of its key functions was to spur the creation of new entrepreneurial companies. IUCRP was unusual in at least two respects: the use of peer review in selecting projects and a strong emphasis on the academic character of the research it supported, with no exceptions to attract business interest or funding. Industry gained access to UC researchers as well as UC graduate students and postdoctoral fellows (roughly two-thirds of the grant money spent on personnel went to research assistantships for graduate students and postdocs). At the end of Atkinson's tenure in 2003, the

Industry-University Cooperative Research Program was operating on an annual budget of $280 million and supporting nearly six hundred projects. There were differences in motivation among the participants; most biotechnology companies, for example, were interested in advancing a new avenue of research, while research sponsors from the semiconductor industry were more likely to be looking for promising students to recruit. A majority of companies ranked the quality of the research as the most important reward for their investment, followed by the useful expertise contributed by UC scientists and engineers and an early window on new knowledge and scientific breakthroughs.[34]

THE CALIFORNIA INSTITUTES FOR SCIENCE AND INNOVATION

In 1999 two San Diegans, Regent John Moores, a successful businessman (and owner of the San Diego Padres baseball team), and Richard Lerner, president of the Scripps Research Institute, proposed an idea first to Atkinson and then to Governor Davis. What if a series of laboratories were created within the University of California system, staffed by a critical mass of researchers from many disciplines, institutions, and industries, all dedicated to creating the scientific discoveries required for the economic and social prosperity of California? The model they had in mind was the renowned corporate research giant Bell Laboratories, responsible in its heyday for such key scientific advances as the transistor and fiber optics. The era of the big industrial laboratories—Xerox and RCA, as well as Bell Labs—was over. But a key lesson of Bell Labs's phenomenal success was the utility of scale in making rapid progress toward the solution of scientific or technical questions. Embedded in the University of California and set in the midst of a university campus, these new laboratories could serve the needs of the high-tech California economy of the future by replicating the intense and focused research that had proved so essential to the success of Bell Labs.

The governor was enthusiastic. He and Atkinson shared a belief in the economic importance of California's research universities and a personal relationship that began with their collaboration on the California Commission on Industrial Innovation in 1981. Atkinson's principal concern—that the new laboratory facilities would have to be carved out of UC's existing capital budget—was put to rest when Davis agreed to provide the money to build them. The state contributed $100 million in capital support for each institute, with the requirement that the institutes raise matching funds on a two-to-one basis to the capital funds.

Davis announced the establishment of the California Institutes for Science and Innovation in December 2000.[35] The four new interdisciplinary research institutes were chosen by a competitive process and funded through a three-way partnership: government, industry, and the University. All four collaborate with a wide variety of researchers, students, and private companies in conducting fundamental and applied research across many disciplines. Each institute involves two or more UC campuses, with one campus taking the lead:

- The California Institute for Telecommunications and Information Technology (Calit2), with UC San Diego as the lead campus in partnership with UC Irvine;
- The California Institute for Quantitative Biomedical Sciences (QB3), with UC San Francisco as the lead campus in partnership with UC Berkeley and UC Santa Cruz;
- The California NanoSystems Institute (CNSI), with UCLA as the lead campus in partnership with UC Santa Barbara; and
- The California Institute for Information Technology Research in the Interest of Society (CITRIS), with UC Berkeley as the lead campus in partnership with UC Davis, UC Merced, and UC Santa Cruz.

Like CONNECT and IUCRP, the California Institutes are an attempt to reflect the competitive realities of the national and global marketplace and the demands it imposes on research universities. Among these expectations is the need for more interdisciplinary research, conducted with industrial partners to help translate basic science into new products, processes, and start-up companies—to repair the weak link in the 1945 Bush model, which was technology transfer. Another is the expectation that research universities will make explicit efforts to take a longer view of the scientific and technological discoveries that will prove essential to the economy ten or twenty years into the future. A third is that they will educate students who are proficient not only in science and technology but also in entrepreneurship.

The California Institutes are an experiment in a new research paradigm that recognizes these multiple demands. Their cross-disciplinary mandate has required them to challenge the faculty specialization and physical isolation within a department typical of research universities. The California Institute for Information Technology and Communications, for example, is a leader in taking Internet technologies to the next level; twenty-four academic departments work across disciplines to tackle complex problems, many of which lead to the movement of intellectual discoveries into the marketplace. The colocation of researchers from university, industry, and public agencies—the institutes work on societal challenges as well as economic ones—generates a dynamic environment for thinking about old problems in new ways. It has also created new kinds of learning and career opportunities for students. The institutes are a magnet for both undergraduate and graduate students interested in combining traditional in-depth knowledge of a single field with broad experience of one or two other fields. Business students seeking an education in entrepreneurship and innovation find the institutes a rich source of ideas, advisers, and mentors.

The California Institutes have received high marks for the innovative importance of their research accomplishments. Their progress toward the goal of contributing to the technological infrastructure for the next economy is harder to assess and perhaps premature. As of 2010, a decade after their founding, the institutes' most pressing problem was operating funds. Although they have more than succeeded in attaining a two-to-one match for state funds, California's multibillion-dollar deficits have left virtually all public entities, including the University of California, on the edge of a fiscal precipice.

THE POLICY FRAMEWORK

There was a third major initiative during the Atkinson administration: an effort to create the right policy framework for guiding the University's involvement with industry. Many of UC's policies in this area dated to the 1980s. In 1982 President Donald Kennedy of Stanford University invited the presidents of four other research universities—Harvard, MIT, Caltech, and the University of California—to meet for a discussion of the future of industry-university research, a meeting known as the Pajaro Dunes conference. Kennedy was interested in starting a conversation about what the policy response should be to a cascade of change in academic science: the passage of Bayh-Dole, the extraordinary commercial potential of advances in biomedical sciences, and the proliferation of ties between businesses and universities in many technical disciplines. The old rules governing institutional responsibilities and professional faculty conduct did not always fit this emerging new world of campus patent offices, entrepreneurial faculty businesses, and profitable research agreements with industry. A central question, as Kennedy summed it up, was "the effect of proprietary influences on the conduct of science."[36] Participants in the Pajaro Dunes conference (including UC President David Saxon and Berkeley and Santa Cruz Chancellors Ira Michael Heyman and Robert Sinsheimer) offered few prescriptions and no specific policies, leaving that to individual universities. But they defined the goals any future policies would need to serve:

> The overriding concern of the participants was to explore effective ways to satisfy the university community and the public that research agreements and other arrangements with industry be so constructed as not to promote a secrecy that will harm the progress of science; impair the educational experience of students and postdoctoral fellows; diminish the role of the university as a credible and impartial resource; interfere with the choice by faculty members of the scientific questions they pursue; or divert the energies of faculty members and the resources of the university from primary educational research missions.[37]

Saxon had already appointed two policy groups before the Pajaro Dunes conference began, one on UC's relationships with industry and the other on intellectual property rights.[38] Most but not all of their recommendations were ultimately embodied in a 1989 policy, Guidelines on University Industry Relations.

One of the recommendations was to give chancellors more control over patenting activities, at that time centralized in the Office of the President. Little came of that recommendation until 1994, when campus unhappiness over some of the operations of the systemwide patent office came to a boil. A committee appointed by President Peltason, recognizing that each campus had different needs and different levels of expertise for dealing with technology-transfer issues, recommended a dual solution. The Office of the President would provide support for campuses that wanted it; campuses that did not could establish their own technology transfer offices but were required to meet certain criteria set by the Office of the President. Some issues, such as a decision to take equity in a company, continued to require UCOP approval.[39]

But the larger issue was that the research environment was changing: industry-sponsored research was growing rapidly, and so was patent activity. Electronic technologies like the Internet, now ubiquitous, raised new questions about copyright. At the same time, some private companies were reporting that they found the path toward research collaborations involving UC strewn with bureaucratic obstacles. It was clear that the University would be doing more technology transfer and industry partnering in the future and needed to scrutinize its policies and practices in light of these realities. All of which meant that the 1989 guidelines were no longer adequate.[40]

These were the reasons Atkinson convened a University-wide retreat in January 1997 on UC's relationships with industry. The purpose of these relationships, as Senior Vice President Wayne Kennedy reminded the participants, is "not simply to generate royalty revenue, but rather to create a stimulus for the expansion of the economy in California, to create relationships with industry that will help the faculty in pursuing their research activities, and to develop a channel for getting our technology out into the marketplace."[41] The overriding message of the retreat was that the University should become less risk-averse in seeking partnerships with industry, consistent with an open academic environment in which graduate student participation would be routine. A more aggressive approach to attracting industry partners and greater entrepreneurship within the University had to be balanced by policies ensuring accountability on the part of faculty and anyone else involved. Ultimately the UCLA meeting resulted not only in a revised patent policy but in a new policy framework for industry partnerships generally. This included policies on faculty conflict of interest and conflict of commitment, intended to ensure that faculty involvement in outside activities does not occur at the expense of other University responsibilities.

The redefinition of UC policies in the 1990s clarified faculty and institutional responsibilities in the area of industry-university relations, technology transfer, and patenting. What policies cannot guarantee, however, is that faculty and researchers are systematically following them. Compliance is an ongoing and formidable responsibility for UC and research universities everywhere.[42]

A survey done by IUCRP in 2002 reflected how central the University of California had become to the state's research-intensive industries. One in six communications firms was started by a UC scientist. One in four biotechnology firms had a UC scientist-founder, and 85 percent of California biotech firms employed UC alumni with graduate degrees.[43] UC has long been the most prolific producer of patents of any American university. In 2008 the University of California system earned $146,314,433 in licensing revenue, with 1,913 active licenses, 224 issued in 2008, and 899 new patent applications. UC research produced fifty-five start-up companies that same year.

Atkinson's career as chancellor and president coincided with an era in which American research universities were becoming increasingly visible as potential contributors to economic life. In terms of the issues that dominated his administration, it would be hard to imagine a more striking contrast to the affirmative action question. The fight over who would be admitted to the University cast a harsh light on the cultural dissonance at the heart of California's multicultural society. The New Economy, built on ever more powerful technologies and on the translation of fundamental scientific knowledge into new products, played to the University's strengths in research. It encouraged cooperation among the University, the state, and the business community. For these reasons alone, the University's role in the California economy would probably have been important to anyone who was UC president in the mid-1990s.

For Atkinson, however, the argument that research universities have a special role to play in advancing innovation and economic prosperity was far more than a strategy for garnering public and legislative support. It was, like Robert Gordon Sproul's commitment to the one-university idea, an orienting conviction, and it guided some of his most important decisions as president of the University. He saw the entrepreneurial university as a phenomenon with a historical logic of its own.

8

An Idea and Its Consequences

The untold story of the SAT is really about how the concept of aptitude was at first embraced, then simply assumed, then became an embarrassment, and, most recently, abandoned. . . . The root of the problem is that Carl Brigham adopted the word aptitude *in his test without a good theory of what aptitude might be.*

—DAVID E. LOHMAN, "APTITUDE FOR COLLEGE: THE IMPORTANCE OF REASONING TESTS FOR MINORITY ADMISSIONS," 2004

Anyone involved in education should be concerned about how overemphasis on the SAT is distorting educational priorities and practices, how the test is perceived by many as unfair, and how it can have a devastating impact on the self-esteem and aspirations of young students. . . . In many ways, we are caught up in the educational equivalent of a nuclear arms race. We know that this overemphasis on test scores hurts all involved, especially students. But we also know that anyone or any institution opting out of the competition does so at considerable risk.

—RICHARD C. ATKINSON, "STANDARDIZED TESTS AND ACCESS TO AMERICAN UNIVERSITIES," FEBRUARY 2001

Test scores have served as an irresistible shorthand for the elusive "merit" that makes a student desirable to colleges.

—NATIONAL RESEARCH COUNCIL, "MYTHS AND TRADEOFFS: THE ROLE OF TESTS IN UNDERGRADUATE ADMISSIONS," 1999

"The admissions policy at the University of California is going through more proposed rewrites than a Hollywood script," the *Chronicle of Higher Education* noted in March 2001.[1] It was true that, as academic timelines go, UC admissions issues were moving along with unusual dispatch. Between the passage of SP-1 in summer 1995 and fall 2000, the University had embarked on an unprecedented effort to qualify thousands more K–12 students for UC, created a new path to admission through Eligibility in the Local Context, and begun Academic Senate review of a second, the Dual Admissions Plan. The *Chronicle* was not referring to any of these, however. The policy in question was President Atkinson's call to eliminate the SAT I as a requirement for admission to the University of California.

Announced in a February 2001 speech at the annual meeting of the American Council on Education (ACE) in Washington, DC, the SAT proposal generated a media firestorm of unexpected intensity that, in retrospect, probably should not have surprised anyone. What Atkinson had to say—that the nation's largest user of the SAT I was considering dropping it—was an education bombshell.

The impact of his announcement was amplified by the leak of the penultimate draft of his speech to the Associated Press by a departing Office of the President employee. As a result, the news was reported on the front pages of the *New York Times,* the *Washington Post,* the *Los Angeles Times,* and other major newspapers on Saturday, February 17, the day before Atkinson was to deliver it. That same day he was interviewed by ABC, CBS, and CNN in the lobby of the Marriott Hotel. When he arrived at the ACE meeting the following afternoon, he found an audience of more than a thousand people—the largest number to attend a keynote address in the history of the American Council on Education, which had featured such speakers as Bill Clinton, Kofi Annan, Alan Greenspan, and Jesse Jackson.

Atkinson made four major points in his widely quoted address, "Standardized Tests and Access to American Universities." Although standardized tests have an important role to play in admitting students to college, the SAT I was based on the dubious premise that it is possible to express academic potential in a single score; its claims to accurately assess student talent had no reliable scientific basis. In a democratic and meritocratic society, students should be judged on what they had actually achieved in school, not on "ill-defined notions of aptitude." The national obsession with the SAT I and the ensuing teach-to-the-test mentality were destructive to genuine learning and thus to schools and students alike. Atkinson was therefore asking the Academic Senate of the University of California to drop the test as a requirement for admission to UC. UC campuses would move away from "processes that use narrowly defined quantitative formulas and instead adopt procedures that look at students in a comprehensive way," including standardized admissions tests that emphasize achievement rather than aptitude.

Atkinson did not give the sponsor of the SAT, the College Board, advance notice of his speech, although his remarks included some words of praise for the technical expertise of the Educational Testing Service (ETS), the company that prepared the test for the College Board. His choice of ACE as the forum for issuing a public challenge to the SAT added a minor footnote to the history of the test. During the postwar years, ACE and the College Board had been locked in combat over which organization would control what became the Educational Testing Service—a battle ACE ultimately lost.[2]

Gaston Caperton, president of the College Board, compared jettisoning the SAT I to throwing grades out of the admissions process and promised a vigorous defense of the test. With no foreknowledge of Atkinson's topic, ETS had decided to host a reception for conference delegates immediately after the ACE keynote address. The overflowing throng talked of little else besides the speech they had just heard about ending the supremacy of ETS's most famous test.

When the hoopla subsided and Atkinson returned to California, he found an avalanche of letters from people he had never met describing their unhappy experiences with the stigma of a low SAT score. He heard from researchers who sent data that supported or refuted his position, K–12 educators who applauded his initiative in taking on the College Board, cognitive scientists who congratulated him on his leadership in sparking a national debate on the issue of aptitude versus achievement in college testing. Forty-one members of the California Assembly wrote thanking him for his "courageous stance" on eliminating the SAT I and calling for replacing the test with a comprehensive look at students' records. *Time* and *Newsweek* did major stories on his announcement; *Time* wanted to put him on the cover, but he refused. Instead, the magazine featured an article with side-by-side photographs of Atkinson and President George W. Bush, with the caption "What do these two men have in common?" Answer: they shared an interest in testing. *Time* also published the SAT scores of President Bush (1206 out of 1600), former Vice President Al Gore (1335), Sun Microsystems CEO Scott McNealy (1420), and a host of other prominent citizens. Atkinson, a graduate of the University of Chicago, never took the SAT.

He also heard from those who believed he was simply wrong or misguided about the test, or who were convinced his attack on it was motivated by a desire to dilute academic quality in the interests of boosting minority enrollment. Some took their complaints directly to the Regents. "Atkinson is a leftist who wants to lower standards in order to accommodate the Third World," one angry alumnus wrote Board of Regents Chair Sue Johnson, adding, "Atkinson should resign or be fired." What most surprised Atkinson was the explosive reaction among ordinary citizens who had no particular connection to higher education or the arcane details of college admissions. Months later, he summed up the polarized public reaction to his speech: "Clearly, the SAT strikes a deep chord in the national psyche."[3]

APTITUDE

Behind that statement lay the long and tangled history of psychological testing and its growing prominence in American higher education. General intelligence, or "aptitude," testing began on a large scale in the United States during World War I, when the army used examinations originally developed by Stanford University professor Lewis M. Terman to sort 116,000 recruits into different ranks and occupations. Terman's research sought to build on the work of a French psychologist at the Sorbonne, Alfred Binet, who had used simple reasoning tests to diagnose educational deficiencies among French schoolchildren. The purpose of the tests was to help schools identify students with learning problems that needed special attention. Binet never intended his tests to be used as an instrument to measure innate intelligence, or IQ, as it came to be known, because he did not believe such quantification was possible. "Intellectual qualities . . . cannot be measured as linear surfaces are measured," he wrote in 1905.[4] In fact, Binet had some remarkably prescient worries about the tests he created. One was that teachers might be tempted to use low performance on the tests to marginalize rather than assist difficult or unmotivated students. Another was that a low IQ score would become a psychologically damaging label that would scar a student for life.[5]

In its early days, intelligence testing was riddled with all kinds of anti-immigrant and xenophobic assumptions and was often used to validate the most obnoxious racial and ethnic stereotypes. The Harvard evolutionary biologist Stephen Jay Gould chronicled this dark aspect of its history in his 1981 book, *The Mismeasure of Man,* which described in telling detail the shortcomings of the tests and the sometimes bizarre interpretations imposed on the results. The idea these tests embodied—that intelligence is a permanent, measurable entity, largely unqualified by environment—is, he wrote, a particularly pernicious form of biological determinism. "Biological determinism is, in its essence, a *theory of limits.* It takes the current status of groups as a measure of where they should and must be (even while it allows some rare individuals to rise as a consequence of their fortunate biology)."[6]

In the hands of Terman and like-minded psychologists, however, IQ testing was envisioned as the royal road to a society organized around intellectual merit. Although a number of US colleges performed intelligence testing in the 1920s for institutional purposes, such tests were not used to decide on the admission of individual students.[7] But in 1923 Princeton University professor Carl C. Brigham, who had helped administer the army's World War I testing program, published *A Study of American Intelligence,* which celebrated the army tests as scientifically valid assessments of intelligence whose use should be extended to other domains of American life. His book attracted the attention of the College Entrance Examination Board—now known as the College Board—a nonprofit organization that had been organized in 1900 by the heads of twelve leading northeastern universities. The College Board's purpose was to rationalize the profusion of admissions requirements at American colleges and universities by offering essay examinations in academic subjects for high school students.[8] In 1925 the College Board asked Brigham to head a commission to look into an intelligence test that could be used to screen college applicants. Brigham recommended an examination modeled on one used by the army, called the Alpha test. He called the new college entrance examination the Scholastic Aptitude Test, or SAT. Eight thousand young men took it in 1926.

The first of several ironies in the SAT's history is that a year later, in 1927, Brigham reversed course and repudiated his original claim that the test could measure biologically inherited intelligence. He also deplored the establishment of the Educational Testing Service, the test-development arm of the College Board, despite the fact that he had been instrumental in its birth. None of this stopped the SAT from establishing itself as *the* college entrance examination in the United States. Its rise to preeminence was given a significant boost in the 1930s by James B. Conant, president of Harvard. Moved by the complaints of Harvard alumni from western states about their alma mater's "exclusively Eastern orientation," Conant decided to establish a generous national scholarship to attract promising boys from other parts of the country. Conant was looking for a way to admit bright students who had not enjoyed the advantages of wealth or private schooling. It has been argued he was also looking for a way to put a lid on Harvard's growing Jewish enrollment by focusing the geographic reach of the National Scholarship Program on places of traditionally low Jewish population.[9] Whatever his motivation, Conant's strategy was to expand the traditional requirements of grades and recommendations to include a test that did not rely on specific knowledge of a particular subject or academic course. Such a test would be designed to level the educational playing field by reflecting general intelligence or aptitude, and thus hidden academic potential.

Conant was immediately challenged by a member of the Harvard governing board, who asked how he could be sure that the students selected were in fact the most academically gifted students. Most of Harvard's largely East Coast students came from private boarding schools, so their academic preparation for college was a known quantity. The National Scholarship Program students would be drawn predominantly from public schools, with much less predictable results.

Conant proposed a wager: once a selection mechanism had been devised, the scholarships would be offered for four years, and if the individuals chosen were not among the top performers in the senior class, the whole idea would be abandoned. For the first round of scholarships, the students selected would be limited to the Midwest, which Conant quaintly referred to as the states that made up "the old Northwest Territory—the states of Minnesota, Wisconsin, Michigan, Illinois, Indiana, and Ohio."[10] He turned to two Harvard assistant deans, Wilbur J. Bender and Henry Chauncey, to examine how other colleges and universities selected students:

> I could not have put the fate of the idea into better hands. These two young men were able to look at examination procedures with a fresh eye. . . . They were particularly

impressed with what Carl Brigham had been doing at Princeton. . . . The Scholastic Aptitude Test, which he had been instrumental in developing and which was already offered by the College Entrance Examination Board, seemed a promising device.[11]

It soon became apparent that a four-year trial was unnecessary; the "promising device" was an immediate success. Within two years Harvard, in cooperation with Princeton and Yale, was offering a one-day battery of college entrance tests that began with the SAT in the morning and continued with achievement tests in various subjects in the afternoon. "The examination was so well received by many colleges that it began to be used for admission of those who were not applying for scholarships," Conant wrote, and by 1938 twenty-eight institutions were using the tests and some four thousand students had taken it, double the number of the previous year. "The record seems to show," Conant concluded, "that Harvard's interest in the use of objective tests for selecting national scholars was an important factor in promoting the use of these tests for general admission purposes."[12] By "objective," Conant meant "aptitude," and he was right: the Harvard stamp of approval hastened the adoption of the SAT I in colleges and universities around the country. But another institution of higher education also played a crucial if unintended role in the rise of the SAT—the University of California.

THE SAT IN CALIFORNIA

The College Board, which opened an office in Berkeley as early as 1947, saw California as a dazzling market opportunity for the SAT. Henry Chauncey once compared standardized testing to the standard gauge used by railroads, adding that California was the "golden spike" that would nail down the SAT's national dominance of college entrance examinations. The SAT was first taken by UC applicants in 1960 as an experiment, to assess whether standardized test scores—which up to that point had not been part of the University's admissions requirements—could help manage some of the problems of selecting students. For UC, the most pressing of these problems were burgeoning enrollment and the nationwide phenomenon of grade inflation in the high schools, which complicated the task of assessing students' real academic achievement. The UC experiment was aimed at determining whether the SAT would yield improvement in predicting first-year college grades, as an indicator of whether a student was likely to succeed in college. By that time, the SAT had long since become two different examinations, the SAT I—a three-hour, multiple-choice test of verbal and mathematical reasoning—and the SAT II—a battery of achievement tests in specific subjects also produced by the College Board's Educational Testing Service. The faculty concluded that both were of only marginal utility in the task of selecting students.

Although UC began requiring the SAT I and several SAT II tests in 1968, they were used principally to give a leg up to promising students who did not meet one or another of the University's admissions requirements. Only in 1979 did the SAT I and SAT II become part of the University's regular admissions process. And even then the main reason for this step was to corral its undergraduate admissions numbers within the 12.5 percent of California high school graduates required by the Master Plan. UC, one of the nation's largest public universities, became the College Board's biggest client, not only for the SAT I, but also for the SAT II. In 2000 California high school seniors made up 12 percent—156,000—of the 1.3 million students who took the SAT I nationwide.[13]

As a faculty member at Stanford University in the 1960s and 1970s, Atkinson followed the ebbs and flows of the SAT debate; the subject of standardized testing interested him, and he was teaching and doing research in the same department in which Lewis Terman had created the Stanford-Binet Intelligence Scales. He had taught a course in psychometrics—the theory and technique of measuring mental abilities—titled "Mathematical Foundations of Test Theory," and for some time his own views about aptitude tests were uncertain. One of his undergraduate memories from his Chicago years was the vocal opposition of leading members of its faculty to the SAT. They favored examinations that measure mastery of a particular subject rather than aptitude, whatever that ambiguous word might mean. There may have been a touch of academic competitiveness in this opposition to a test endorsed by Harvard, but in any case Atkinson never forgot the vigorous stand some members of the faculty took on the superiority of achievement tests.[14] He ultimately came down on the side of Binet and others who argued that such tests are strictly tools to be employed in a clinical setting for diagnosing learning difficulties. As a reliable measure of mental ability or as a means of ranking or making fine distinctions among students, they have significant limitations.

By the time Atkinson became UC president in 1995, discontent with the SAT was brewing in several quarters of the University. Minority groups had long considered the SAT I an unfair barrier to Hispanic, African American, and Native American students. African American and Latino students in the highest income categories routinely posted lower scores than low-income whites and Asians. The College Board argued that this was the inevitable outcome of the inferior schools and diminished educational opportunities minorities faced in twentieth-century America.

Eugene Garcia, dean of UC Berkeley's graduate school of education, had taken the SAT when he was a student at Grand Junction High School in Colorado at the suggestion of his baseball coach, who thought he might qualify for a college athletic scholarship. When his SAT scores arrived, Garcia did not understand their import, but his coach explained—in a "very supportive way," Garcia says—that they were low, and that was okay, but he would never be, say, a college professor.[15] To many members of minority groups, Garcia's experience and his later success in higher education were emblematic of both the SAT's stigmatizing effect and its failure as a predictor of academic accomplishment.

In 1992 Garcia chaired a task force appointed by the Regents to look into the persistently low rates at which Latinos qualified for the University. When Garcia presented the Latino Eligibility Task Force's final report to the Regents in September 1997, this figure— 3.8 percent—was still essentially the same as it had been when the group began its work five years earlier.[16] The report's first recommendation was to eliminate the SAT I as a requirement for admission. The task force claimed, based on a study of retention and graduation at UC, that the SAT I did not accurately predict graduation rates for minority students, especially Latino students. There was no correlation between SAT and cumulative grade-point average (GPA) scores and the rate at which students graduated from college. Yet low SAT I scores kept Latinos out of selective UC campuses and concentrated in less elite UC campuses like Santa Cruz or Riverside. Eliminating the SAT I, Garcia said, would increase the Latino eligibility rate by 60 percent, from 3.9 percent to 6.3 percent.[17] The report argued that UC should replace the SAT with other measures of student potential, such as the Golden State examination, that reflected the high school curriculum and thus reinforced school reform efforts, then a public priority in California.

The proposal clearly caught the president's attention. During the ensuing discussion, Atkinson said eliminating the SAT I was a "powerful suggestion" that the University-wide Academic Senate should look into. He added that aptitude tests had originally been devised to identify talented students who were not performing up to their potential and that "too much emphasis was being put on minor differences in SAT scores" in determining admission to college.[18] The task force report ultimately had little influence on the debate within UC, in part because technical assessments did not support its argument that abandoning the SAT I would increase minority student enrollment. But the discussion it generated included Atkinson's first public statement to the Regents about his views on the SAT I. Those views had been crystallized by two events.

In the early 1990s Atkinson had served as the founding chair of the National Academy of Sciences's Board on Testing and Assessment (BOTA). BOTA's charge is to advise the federal government and public agencies on testing issues, including the civil rights implications of specific tests and new methods of assessment. It was an experience that gave him an entirely new awareness of standardized testing and its role in college admissions. At one meeting in Washington, representatives of the College Board and of the Educational Testing Service talked about the SAT and its ability to predict first-year college grades. It was a presentation in which,

Atkinson says, "the notion that the SAT I was a 'true measure of intelligence' dominated their perspective." And they seemed oddly unaware of several recent studies that had challenged the superiority of aptitude tests in predicting first-year college grades.[19] In 1988, for example, James Crouse and Dale Trusheim, both of the University of Delaware, had expressed a highly skeptical attitude toward the test in *The Case against the SAT*. A key point of their argument, based on six years of research and buttressed with forty tables of regression analyses and other statistics, was that the College Board and ETS were aggressively pushing a test that added little to the usefulness of high school records in predicting a student's future college performance.[20]

After the meeting, Atkinson flew to Florida to visit his daughter and her family. He found his twelve-year-old granddaughter studying verbal analogies to prepare for the SAT I. The amount of time she was devoting to memorizing vocabulary words and constructing analogies surprised and dismayed him. The College Board asserted that the analogies were a good measure of verbal reasoning. Atkinson thought that a dubious claim. If you did not know the definition of the word you were being asked to compare with another, you could not reason about it; if you did know the definition, the reasoning involved was trivial. The history of testing intelligence had been largely a history of testing vocabulary, which heavily favored the middle and upper strata of American society. Although the College Board no longer claimed the SAT I measured native intelligence, the emphasis on vocabulary was a vestige of this history, with no solid basis in contemporary cognitive science. The analogy section was not only flawed as an indication of a student's verbal abilities; it was a distraction from the real task of schooling, which is to instill the basic skills of writing and mathematics.

He spent the flight home to California outlining an op-ed piece about college admissions tests. It began with the assertion that "aptitude" tests do not reveal what they purport to measure—generalized intelligence. It went on to urge that the whole muddied history of intelligence testing be left behind in favor of achievement tests that reflect what students have actually learned in high school. Students should be tested on the two key skills for success in college, writing and mathematics, by including an essay and a more advanced level of mathematics than the SAT I's eighth-grade introduction to algebra. A fundamental aim of college entrance testing was to convince students, parents, and teachers that the ability to write and to do at least tenth-grade mathematics was indispensable to success in college. The draft concluded with a proposal to refer the issue to the National Academy of Sciences for further study. Atkinson eventually decided "the time was not right" to challenge aptitude testing, however, and put the draft aside.[21] But he collected several versions of the SAT I tests and began taking them at home in his spare time.

BOARS AND TESTING

Reservations about the SAT I surfaced from time to time in the discussions of the Academic Senate's committee on undergraduate admissions, the Board of Admissions and Relations with Schools. In the mid- to late 1990s, on the advice of BOARS, the University's faculty took several steps to limit the influence of the SAT I in admissions decisions, one of which was to increase the weight of the SAT II examinations relative to the SAT I in response to studies indicating that the SAT II was a better predictor of student performance. In addition to these technical concerns about the SAT I's predictive validity, some of BOARS's dissatisfaction focused on the analogies and whether they yielded good evidence, as the College Board claimed, about students' critical thinking skills and therefore their readiness for college-level reading and writing. On several occasions, BOARS had raised questions about the analogies with representatives of the College Board; the reaction was disappointingly defensive. BOARS began talks with the College Board about the possibility of an SAT I developed especially for California that would exclude the analogies.

The larger issue percolating up through BOARS's discussions was a growing unease with the University's standardized-test requirements in the increasingly competitive world of UC admissions. The chair of BOARS from 1999 to 2002, Professor Dorothy Perry, was the administrative head of the only undergraduate program—dental hygiene—at UC San Francisco, a campus devoted to professional and graduate education in the health sciences. In this respect she was an unusual choice to head BOARs, and she sensed a distinct hesitation among her faculty colleagues about appointing her chair of a Senate committee focused on undergraduate admissions issues. But her own educational trajectory had followed the kind of ideal path envisioned by the Master Plan—she was a transfer student from Ventura Community College who had gone on to earn a Ph.D. in testing and measurement—and she had an ingrained commitment to fostering opportunity at all levels of schooling.

Perry's concerns about standardized tests and the SAT I had more to do with educational policy than with cognitive theory. In 2000 UC was inundated with 71,000 freshman applications for fall 2001, the largest number ever; in that same year the Berkeley campus alone had applications from four times as many students as it had places. As student demand rose and the campuses became more and more selective, admissions officers were faced with choosing among large numbers of applicants whose high school grades were good to outstanding. In many cases, the only way to select from among these well-qualified applicants was to give more weight to indicators of student performance other than grades—Advanced Placement courses and standardized test scores, for example. This meant that SAT I scores were taking on more weight in admissions decisions, and some members of BOARS worried about that development, especially since there was little good data about the predictive validity of the SAT I compared to the SAT II achievement tests.

Perry was troubled by another question. She had been a member of BOARS in July 1995, when SP-1 was approved, and had helped revise the University's guidelines for admission in those harried months between July and December. The backers of SP-1 and Proposition 209 had made fairness their prime argument. It was unfair, they said, to give a leg up to certain minority students when poor white and other deserving students, including minorities who were not considered "underrepresented," got none. But standardized testing raised a fairness issue too. Was it fair to students and schools to demand achievement in certain subjects and then test on reasoning ability or an aptitude for mathematics? The University required students to take certain courses to qualify for UC but then tested them with an examination unconnected to the curriculum. Nationally, the SAT had an influence far out of proportion to its significance as an indicator of students' ability to succeed in college-level academic work. The test was sensitive to how much students' parents earned and whether they had a college degree. Scores could be improved through coaching, although by how much was a matter of dispute. Keith Widaman, an expert in developmental psychology and Perry's predecessor as chair of BOARS, told the Regents in February 1998 that his research suggested that coaching could boost SAT I scores by about 10 points.[22] His estimate was conservative; others ranged from the College Board's 26 points to the test-preparation company Princeton Review's 140 to 150 points.[23] Either way, coaching gave students in more affluent schools an edge over students from poorer ones. And the SAT's long dominance of the college-testing scene had bred an unquestioning faith among the public and throughout much of higher education in its utility as a barometer of student promise.

The relationship between fairness and standardized testing was not just a UC issue; it was at the heart of the growing national debate about affirmative action. In 1996 the Fifth District Court struck down affirmative action in Texas, Louisiana, and Mississippi in *Hopwood v. Texas;* Governor Jeb Bush ended affirmative action in Florida by executive order; and two landmark cases involving admission at the University of Michigan, *Gratz v. Bollinger* and *Grutter v. Bollinger,* were making their way toward the Supreme Court. In this heated atmosphere, the National Research Council was moved to sound a cautionary note about standardized testing. The NRC consisted of members drawn from the National Academies of Science and Engineering and the Institute of Medicine, and its 1999 publication, "Myths and Tradeoffs: The Role of Tests in Undergraduate Admissions," drew on BOTA's investigations of standardized testing. Among other things, the NRC was concerned about widespread misunderstanding of the statistical implications of standardized test scores. Noting that more than eight million students were enrolled in four-year colleges and universities in 1996, the NRC described the role of standardized tests as "one of the principal flashpoints in discussions of its fairness."[24] The report rejected the claim that the disparities in test scores among different ethnic and racial groups were the result of bias in standardized tests. But it also concluded that such tests, while a valuable way to compare students' performance within an enormously varied school system, were subject to being interpreted as more significant than they really were. The most widely used standardized tests could not measure such important qualifications as "persistence, intellectual curiosity, and writing ability." Nor were they useful as a tool for discriminating between students with roughly similar scores. Their principal value was in organizing applicants into three large groups—those highly likely to succeed, those highly unlikely to succeed, and those in the middle.[25] Yet the SAT I, more than any other college admissions examination, was regarded throughout the country as the gold standard for predicting which students had the talent to benefit most from a college education.

In fall 2000, however, the SAT I was nowhere near the top of BOARS's crowded agenda. SP-1 had moved admissions issues to center stage at UC, and there were many issues besides the SAT clamoring for the faculty's attention. And while some on BOARS criticized one or another aspect of the SAT I, opposition to the test was unlikely to coalesce around a policy position the entire board would support. Whatever the sentiments of individual members, nothing official was likely to come out of BOARS regarding the SAT.

THE ATWELL LECTURE

The draft opinion piece sat in Atkinson's desk drawer until fall 2000, when he began thinking about the Atwell Distinguished Lecture he had been invited to present the following February at the American Council on Education. One morning he and his associate president, Pat Hayashi, discussed the pros and cons of making the SAT I the subject of his address. They went over the reasons for making Atkinson's critique of the SAT I public. His ideas about the test had matured. It was a cause he cared deeply about. His position as president of UC, the major user of the SAT, and his credentials as a cognitive scientist made him one of few individuals in the country who could challenge the powerful College Board on this issue.

The draft version had urged putting the testing issue in the hands of the National Academy of Sciences for further study. But Atkinson decided to propose the much bolder step of eliminating the SAT I at the University of California. He knew the hazards of such a move at UC, with its powerful faculty and potentially unsympathetic Board of Regents. He needed the approval, or at least the neutrality, of both; the president could propose ending use of the SAT I, but he could not mandate it. He was thinking about retiring as president the following year, so if he were going to act, it had to be soon. Faculty review could take months or even years;

regental approval, especially in the mercurial atmosphere of post–Proposition 209 California, was uncertain. Timing and strategy were crucial, and for help with both he turned to Pat Hayashi.

Hayashi had spent many years at the Berkeley campus in the area of admissions and knew UC's admissions policies and practices well. He was also a veteran of the early years of affirmative action at Berkeley, and in the 1980s he had been a key contributor to resolving a politically charged dispute between the Berkeley administration and several Asian American organizations over whether the campus's admissions policies and practices had discriminated against Asians. In 1995 he had served on the task force on undergraduate admissions criteria that revised UC's admissions policies to conform to SP-1. His experience in admissions and affirmative action was amplified by a keen political sense and a talent for organizing people to tackle complicated projects. In the early 1990s he had been a member of the College Board's Commission on New Possibilities for the Admissions Testing Program, cochaired by then–UC President David Gardner and Harvard President Derek Bok. The commission's main charge was to consider adding an essay to the SAT, either as part of the SAT I or as one of the SAT II achievement tests. *Beyond Prediction,* the commission's final report, did not include an essay among its recommendations for revising the SAT, in large part because Hayashi persuaded his fellow commissioners that such a test would disadvantage non-native speakers, principally Asians. Hayashi's work with the commission, and later as a trustee of the College Board, gave him valuable experience with both the politics of testing and the politics of the College Board. In the months to come, he would be indefatigable in guiding Atkinson's proposal through the web of UC's Academic Senate and Board of Regents and negotiations with the College Board.

One of their first steps was to enlist the help of Saul Geiser, a sociologist by training who was director of research and evaluation in the academic affairs division of the Office of the President. Atkinson wanted to know about the SAT I's predictive validity—that is, its reliability as a forecaster of freshman grades—compared to that of the SAT II. Predictive validity was a far from perfect measure of whether a student would do well in college, but it added information admissions officers found useful in evaluating students. Although there had been many studies of the SAT I's predictive validity, there had been few efforts to do a cross-comparison with the SAT II—an experiment that would yield useful technical evidence about the relative value of aptitude and achievement tests. Atkinson wanted to know what insights could be gained from a look at UC's experience with the two kinds of examinations.

When Geiser arrived in his office, Atkinson handed him a piece of paper with an equation written on it. The point of the equation was to compare the predictive validity of the SAT I and the SAT II for UC students as a whole and then for minority students, using the records of 77,893 freshmen who entered the University between fall 1996 and fall 1999. Because UC had been administering the test for so long, it had large amounts of data on students' test scores on the SAT I, the SAT II achievement tests, and their subsequent freshman grades. By the time Atkinson gave the speech in February, Geiser had only preliminary answers to the question; the full analysis was not completed until October 2001. But the early analysis pointed in a single direction—that the SAT II achievement tests were a better predictor of freshman grades than the SAT I aptitude test.

THE ARGUMENT

There were four principal ways to make the case against the SAT I. You could argue that it was based on flawed and outdated cognitive theory; that achievement tests offered greater predictive validity and encouraged schools to focus on academic subjects; that minority perceptions of the unfairness of the SAT argued against its use in a racially diverse society; or that aptitude tests like the SAT I went against the grain of American democratic values. Atkinson employed all of these arguments in his Atwell Lecture. He made a deliberate decision, however, to use values as the keystone of his case: aptitude tests are incompatible with a democratic philosophy because opportunity should be awarded on the basis of academic accomplishment, not the promise of academic accomplishment.

Atkinson's SAT speech had its origins in his experience and convictions as a cognitive scientist. But it brought together in one economical statement a number of issues he and the University had been struggling with throughout the five years of his presidency. The end of racial and ethnic preferences had forced the University to reconsider virtually every aspect of how it judged and selected students. This institutional discussion raised fundamental questions, and none was more fundamental than the philosophy that underlay UC's admissions requirements.

This philosophy, he stated in the Atwell Lecture, sought to combine meritocratic and egalitarian values. The University's admissions criteria were meritocratic because they gave the greatest weight to grades earned in demanding high school classes. They were egalitarian in that they were designed so that hardworking students in any comprehensive California high school could meet them. The role of standardized tests in the admissions process was to help correct for differences in grading practices among California's one thousand high schools.

The problem was that the American obsession with test scores, especially SAT I scores, had begun to subvert these twin values. In the words of the National Research Council report, standardized test scores had become "an irresistible shorthand" for academic merit. The lesson of the University's endless internal debates about race-blind admissions was that there is no such thing as a shorthand for academic merit. On the contrary, a highly selective public university must look at each individual in the broadest possible way. This meant judging them not only on grades and test scores but also on what they had made of their opportunities to learn, whether many or few.

Then there was the University's relationship with the K–12 public schools. In the early 1900s UC had accredited high schools to ensure their curricula were appropriate for college-bound students; at the national level, the College Board set standards for each academic subject, including a syllabus that students could use to prepare for college entrance examinations. An unintended irony of the SAT is that it had become one of the reasons this kind of close working relationship between universities and the schools eroded in the postwar era of widespread standardized testing. By 2000 the ties between universities and the schools were more tenuous in the United States than in many other countries.[26]

The University's Outreach Task Force had argued that in a post-209 world, bringing more poor and minority students into higher education ultimately depended on improving their preparation—which meant strengthening the state's beleaguered K–12 public schools. School reform, the policy centerpiece of Governor Davis's administration, was beginning to pick up strong political momentum in California. The SAT I was looking less and less like the right test for achieving that goal.

The superiority of achievement tests, Atkinson argued in his speech, is that they are fairer to students and easier for schools to integrate with the daily activities of teaching and learning academic subjects. A poor achievement test score can be the spur to work harder and do better the next time. A lackluster showing on an aptitude test, however, can have "a devastating impact on the self-esteem and aspirations of young students," without providing any clues about how to improve. And students are not the only victims. National rankings routinely penalize colleges and universities for admitting students with low SAT scores, a judgment with powerful implications for the bottom line. In one of his most frequently quoted metaphors, Atkinson compared the national frenzy over the SAT I to a nuclear arms race: "We know that this overemphasis on test scores hurts all involved, especially students. But we also know that anyone or any institution opting out of the competition does so at considerable risk."

One of the strong messages of the speech, which went largely unreported in the media but which caught the attention of UC's faculty, was that colleges and universities should be explicit about the principles that guide their test requirements. Equally important, they should take steps to see that test scores "are not overvalued, but rather used to illuminate other aspects of a student's record." Students were entitled to a comprehensive review of their academic record, one that takes into consideration the challenges they have met and the obstacles they have overcome.

If UC eliminated the SAT I as a requirement for admission, what would take its place? Atkinson's answer was to substitute the SAT II achievement tests until an appropriate replacement for the SAT I could be developed. He concluded with an acknowledgment that the changes he proposed would be "labor intensive and therefore expensive. . . . But the stakes are too high not to ensure that the job is done right."

THE SAT, THE FACULTY, AND THE COLLEGE BOARD

Despite the victory in Washington, prospects for success in California were clouded. Most of the ten chancellors were reluctant to support the proposal, worried that its political risks—especially the risk of appearing to lower standards—outweighed any possible benefits. Campus admissions officers, many of whom regarded this as an infringement on their territory, were almost universally opposed. Dorothy Perry was immediately enthusiastic, and under her leadership BOARS was likely to be favorable, but the Academic Senate as a whole was sure to be divided. Without the Senate's endorsement, there was no point in taking the case for change to the Regents—and even if the proposal made it to the board, it was impossible to predict how the vote would go. Ward Connerly registered his suspicion about the motives behind the SAT proposal early on, in an op-ed that said, in effect, tinkering with the SAT I was just one more effort to undermine the ban on affirmative action.

The immediate issue was how to move the SAT proposal through the University's complex academic machinery, which required a multilayered review of the proposal by BOARS, the Academic Council (the executive body of the systemwide Academic Senate), campus senates, and the Assembly of the Academic Senate (the legislative body of the Senate). The role of the Academic Senate was a particularly delicate matter. Admissions requirements lie within the purview of the faculty, who generally do not welcome suggestions from the president. If the SAT proposal survived the Senate, the next and final stop was the Board of Regents.

Atkinson put his proposal before the Academic Senate on February 15, a few days before he gave the Atwell Lecture, in a letter addressed to its chair, Michael Cowan. He asked the faculty to consider two changes in UC admissions policy. The first was to "require only standardized tests that assess mastery of specific subject matter rather than undefined notions of 'aptitude.'" The second was to endorse admissions procedures that look at students in a broad and comprehensive way rather than concentrate on "quantitative formulas." Doing so would ensure that "standardized tests are not given undue weight in admissions decisions."[27] The SAT proposal was on its way.

On March 16 Gaston Caperton came to Atkinson's Oakland office. The two had met soon after Caperton arrived at the College Board in 1999, when Atkinson had taken the opportunity to mention his reservations regarding aptitude tests and urge revising the SAT I to include a writing sample and higher-level mathematics. The response was noncommittal.

Caperton had been a successful businessman and governor of West Virginia, a post he used to bolster the state's public schools. His academic background was sparse, and he was not an expert on testing, but he had excellent political instincts and a persuasive charm. He was ready to use both on behalf of the test. He had tried unsuccessfully to reach Atkinson on February 17, the day before his Atwell Lecture, and this was the first opportunity since the speech for the two men to talk. Atkinson was polite and low-key during the March 16 visit, explaining there had been nothing personal in his attack on the SAT I and suggesting that UC was ready to work with the College Board on developing a new examination, perhaps an SAT II–type achievement test geared to California curricula. Caperton was cordial and pledged to keep channels of communication open. That same day, he stopped by the Berkeley campus for a meeting with Chancellor Robert Berdahl, who delivered the same message about the SAT I: the analogies section should go.

Privately, the College Board was busy lining up support for the SAT I. In an opinion piece titled "The Case for Not Scrapping the SAT," Bob Laird, a former admissions director at UC Berkeley and at the time a consultant to the College Board, asserted that Atkinson had unveiled his proposal at a national forum because he was more concerned about "making the Big Splash" than about creating support for his idea within the University. Laird repeated this charge in a book he subsequently wrote about affirmative action, charging (erroneously) that Atkinson had made his proposal without having a reasonable alternative to the SAT I to offer.[28] Several UC faculty who were prominent in the area of admissions and testing were approached by College Board representatives interested in persuading them to take a public stand opposing Atkinson's proposal.

Publicly, the College Board continued to hammer away at the argument it had made for years in response to various criticisms of the SAT I: the fault lay with the schools, not the test. "What we have is an unequal educational system," Caperton told the *Chronicle of Higher Education* in October 2001. "It's not the kids. It's not the test."[29] Nonetheless, as the months passed after the Atwell Lecture, there were signs that the College Board's resistance might be weakening. At a meeting in Sacramento in September 2001 Wayne Camara, a vice president of the College Board, let UC officials know that the College Board might consider adding a writing component to the SAT I. There was a certain amount of wariness among UC people because of the College Board's recent history of delays and stonewalling of their complaints about the verbal analogies and other aspects of the SAT I. Now College Board officials repeatedly promised cooperation in moving toward a new test that would meet the requirements Atkinson spelled out in the Atwell Lecture and that BOARS had endorsed. These assurances were typically followed by mailings from the College Board describing research that supported the claims of the current SAT I. As the months drifted by, it began to look as if the College Board was playing a waiting game, in the hope that the momentum for change would wind down, or that Atkinson would retire and the issue would simply go away. BOARS was wavering; most members were receptive to the Atkinson proposal and impatient with the maneuvering of the College Board, but they also worried about the specter of lowering standards and the uncertainties of developing an entirely new test. Many took a wait-and-see attitude.

November 2001 was a turning point. A two-day conference at UC Santa Barbara, convened by BOARS to air some of the major issues involved in standardized testing and the SAT I, brought together Atkinson and Caperton, as well as UC faculty and representatives of the College Board, rival testing company ACT, Inc., and other organizations, such as FairTest, with a stake in testing. Both Atkinson and Caperton departed from their prepared texts and spoke informally and in personal terms, Atkinson about his French-born mother who knew no English when she arrived in this country and Caperton about the transformations wrought by 9/11 and his views on their link to the SAT. In the afternoon session, College Board representatives presented data they used to argue that substituting the SAT II subject tests for the SAT I would mean that Latinos would be admitted to UC in much greater numbers because of the SAT II Spanish test and the advantage it gave students who were native speakers. Saul Geiser presented a paper, written with his colleague Roger Studley, that laid out the results of his long-awaited analysis comparing the predictive validity of the SAT I and the SAT II. This analysis was, Atkinson later said, "a ticking time bomb." Every claim about the superiority of the SAT I ultimately rested on its strength as a predictor of first-year college grades. The Geiser paper cut the ground out from under this argument and, in the process, went a long way toward shattering the notion that the SAT I was the gold standard of college entrance examinations. In Atkinson's words:

> In brief, the study shows that the SAT II is a far better predictor of college grades than the SAT I. The combination of high school grades and the three SAT IIs accounts for 22.2 percent of the variance in first-year college grades. When the SAT I is added to the combination of high school grades and the SAT IIs, the explained variance increases from 22.2 percent to 22.3 percent, a trivial increment.
>
> The data indicate that the predictive validity of the SAT II is much less affected by differences in socioeconomic background than is the SAT I. After controlling for family income and parents' education, the predictive power of the SAT II is undiminished, whereas the relationship between SAT I scores and U.C. grades virtually disappears. The SAT II is not only a better predictor, but also a fairer test insofar as it is demonstrably less sensitive than the SAT I to differences in family income and parents' education.

These findings for the full U.C. data set hold equally well for three major disciplinary subsets of the data, namely for (1) physical sciences, mathematics, and engineering, (2) biological sciences, and (3) social sciences and humanities. Across these disciplinary areas, the SAT II is consistently a better predictor of student performance than the SAT I.

Analyses with respect to the racial-ethnic impact of the SAT I versus the SAT II indicate that, in general, there are only minor differences between the tests. The SAT II is a better predictor of U.C. grades for most racial-ethnic groups than the SAT I, but both tests tend to overpredict freshman grades for underrepresented minorities to a small but measurable extent. Eliminating the SAT I in favor of the SAT II would have little effect on rates of U.C. eligibility and admissions for students from different racial-ethnic groups.

The U.C. data yield another interesting result. Of the various tests that make up the SAT I (verbal and quantitative) and the three SAT IIs, the best single predictor of student performance was the SAT II writing test. Given the importance of writing ability at the college level, it should not be surprising that a test of actual writing skills correlates strongly with college grades.[30]

The College Board representatives departed right after Geiser's talk and did not appear at dinner or for the presentations the next day. It might have been nothing more than a coincidence. But to the UC participants, it felt as if the College Board had left the field.

BOARS WEIGHS IN

A few months after the Santa Barbara conference, in January 2002, BOARS issued its first official report in response to the SAT proposal. Atkinson had made his case on the SAT and standardized testing to the faculty-at-large Academic Senate meetings and also met with the members of BOARS to discuss it. The BOARS discussion paper reviewed the history of admissions tests at UC and the statistical evidence justifying their use. Given the small differences in predictive power between aptitude and achievement tests, the paper concluded, a decision about which to use should be made not on the basis of predictive validity but on educational policy grounds. From that perspective, achievement tests are "philosophically preferable" to aptitude tests like the SAT I. They impress on students the importance of mastering the academic courses UC demands (called the A-G requirements) and offer the K–12 schools a strong incentive to build rigorous curricula and reward good teaching. The report also laid down a set of principles that should guide which tests were selected as admissions requirements, making UC one of the first universities in the country to spell out exactly what it would use admissions tests for and what characteristics they should have. The BOARS report recommended revising UC's test requirements to incorporate an achievement examination on mathematics and reading and writing that would include an essay, as well as two one-hour examinations in academic subjects. The next step was determining exactly what achievement test UC should adopt, and the report concluded with a recommendation that UC work with both the College Board and ACT on a new array of admissions tests.

BOARS's endorsement of achievement tests as a replacement for the SAT I meant that the action shifted to the campus academic senates. Early in 2002, Perry, Hayashi, and Geiser began a series of pilgrimages to each of the University's campuses to explain BOARS's rationale and field questions. Perry and her faculty colleagues made their case before the Regents at several meetings that included presentations by the College Board and ACT. More than a year had passed since Atkinson announced his proposal, and for both the Academic Senate and the president it was beginning to feel like an endless uphill climb.

Then events began to move quickly. The Academic Senate approved the BOARS proposal in May, clearing the way for the Regents to vote at their July meeting on whether to drop the SAT I. On a sunny day in June, while Perry was at Irvine to meet with the campus academic senate, the news came out: the College Board had voted to change the SAT I. The revised test would eliminate the analogies, include higher-level math, and give greater emphasis to reading comprehension. After field testing, the new SAT I would be used for students entering college in fall 2006. The revisions were clearly intended to address the criticisms Atkinson made in the Atwell Lecture and the criteria BOARS proposed in its report on the use of standardized tests in admissions.

In a public statement, Atkinson welcomed the decision and praised Caperton and the College Board for their courage in making it. He acknowledged that some would feel the changes did not take the SAT I far enough in the direction of an achievement test; in fact that included some members of BOARS. But he hailed the reforms as "the foundation for a new test that will better serve our students and schools."

In July 2003 the Regents brought the SAT proposal to its official conclusion by approving the faculty's recommendations for changes in the University's standardized test requirements. UC would accept the new SAT I—eventually known simply as the New SAT or the SAT-R, for "reasoning"—or the ACT with Writing as satisfying its core test requirement for an experimental two years, beginning with the freshman class of 2006.

THE SAT AND THE ROLE OF THE PRESIDENT

More than any other action in his presidency, the SAT initiative showed Atkinson at his most characteristic. It was not only his skepticism about received ideas and his single-mindedness in pursuing a goal he cared about (which came as some-thing of a surprise in a man of such legendary impatience). It was also his willing-ness to risk public failure on a national scale by embracing a controversial issue without arming himself beforehand with a detailed plan of action. Perhaps no such strategy was possible, given the unpredictability of the situation. Either way, Atkinson and his colleagues relied largely on instinct and course corrections to bring them through in the months following the Atwell Lecture.

The SAT initiative was untypical in one sense: he broke his own administrative axiom that the president should never get out in front of the faculty. In the case of the SAT, however, he acted on an even more fundamental reality of academic life. By announcing his proposal at a national forum, with minimal forewarning, he forced a hearing for his ideas within the University and among the public. Once that was done, even the long process of discussion and debate ultimately worked in his favor. Delay involved the risk that his proposal would be buried by institutional inertia and resistance to change. But it also gave him the opportunity to explain the logic of the SAT recommendation and how it was part of a reasonable and coherent philosophy of academic merit. It gave the faculty and the Regents the chance to get used to what at first sounded like a very radical idea. And it gave UC and the College Board the time to redefine their positions and come to a resolution on the issue.

THE PUBLIC AND THE SAT

Why did the challenge to the SAT I capture the public imagination? Most of Atkin-son's criticisms of the test had already been made, in one form or another, by oth-ers. David Owen's *None of the Above*, published in 1985, was a witty and withering critique of the flaws of the SAT I and its inflated claims to measure intelligence and predict academic performance (he points out that researchers at the University of Michigan in the 1960s found a blood test that did a better job than the SAT I of predicting the likelihood of graduation from college).[31] James Crouse and Dale Trusheim's *The Case against the SAT*, which appeared in 1988, was a more scholarly appraisal of the limitations of the test. And just a few years before Atkinson's At-well lecture, Nicholas Lemann's *The Big Test* and Peter Sacks's *Standardized Minds* both took aim at the SAT and the College Board with deadly effect.[32] As Lemann has said, however, Atkinson's was by far the most powerful challenge in the history of the SAT I.

The overwhelming public reaction to Atkinson's proposal, which spilled over in months of articles, interviews, opinion pieces, and letters to the editors of major newspapers, was due in part to his status as president of the nation's most dis-tinguished public university in the nation's most populous state. In part it was a function of UC's position as the largest user of the SAT I. This gave Atkinson an important strategic advantage. He could, and did, do more than criticize the test: he threatened the College Board's bottom line by proposing to eliminate it as a UC requirement. The financial peril the College Board faced required that it pay attention to the SAT I initiative. The ensuing publicity galvanized antitesting organizations that had protested the SAT but had little leverage to compel change, which in turn focused even more public attention on the controversy over the SAT.

The most important difference between Atkinson's proposal and earlier challenges to the SAT I was not the cogency of the critiques. It was the growing, and incredibly intense, competition for admission to elite universities, public and private, that has taken place over the past few decades. In this environment, standardized test scores are often seen as the tipping point in deciding success or failure in life. According to a recent study of admissions at several Ivy League institutions, "The underlying source of the enormous stress surrounding college admissions is that even the privileged classes are no longer confident that they can pass their position on to the next generation. . . . It is no exaggeration to say that the current regime in elite college admissions has been far more successful in democratizing anxiety than opportunity."[33] Lemann makes a similar case: "Americans' preoccupation with admission to selective colleges has gone past the bounds of rationality," he writes in *The Big Test*. "The culture of frenzy surrounding admissions is destructive and anti-democratic; it warps the sensibilities and distorts the education of the millions of people whose lives it touches."[34] Atkinson's message that the SAT I had become a destructive national obsession tapped into a vast reservoir of anxiety about the future. And his proposal to link admission to achievement rather than aptitude came across as a plea on behalf of returning a measure of rationality and perspective to the unrelenting competitiveness of elite college admissions. It was a message the public was more than ready to hear.

THE SAT EVOLVES

Atkinson was initially pleased with the New SAT unveiled by the College Board in March 2005. The verbal analogies were gone. The mathematics section incorporated more demanding algebra problems. Most important, writing was included for the first time. The SAT II writing exam, the strongest predictor of first-year grades among the tests UC required, was imported wholesale. But the New SAT also featured a critical-reading section that closely resembled the verbal reasoning portion of the old test, and the addition of the essay stretched the time required to complete it by almost an hour. Still, in the test's first few years, the changes in math and writing appeared to have encouraged a greater emphasis on those subjects in many K–12 schools around the country.

A 2008 assessment of the New SAT by the College Board, however, found that the test exhibited no gain in predictive power over the previous version—a surprising outcome, given the inclusion of the strongly predictive SAT II writing exam. A study done by researchers at the University of Georgia that same year suggested a possible explanation: inclusion of the writing test had made the critical-reading section virtually redundant. As a result, that portion of the New SAT added nothing to its predictive ability.

In the meantime, Saul Geiser and his colleagues were continuing to study the relative merits of aptitude- and achievement-based tests.[35] This work, and indeed a decade of research done at UC, consistently supported the conclusion that achievement tests are better than SAT-type tests along three dimensions: predicting student performance in college, fairness to low-income and minority students, and sending students the crucial message that effort is the most important ingredient in academic success. A 2009 national study of college completion, which looked at a large population of students at public colleges and universities, confirmed the UC findings about the superiority of achievement tests over aptitude-based examinations.[36]

Atkinson and Geiser wrote a paper together in 2009 that distilled the conclusions they had reached about the New SAT and the lessons to be gleaned from a century of experience with standardized testing in college admissions.[37] They were not favorable to the New SAT. Although a clear improvement over earlier versions, they wrote, it nonetheless does not go far enough in the direction of an achievement test, and its origins in IQ-based testing continue to thwart its evolution into an examination more closely aligned with the high school curriculum. They saw it as an ultimately unsatisfactory hybrid of old (the verbal reasoning test, reincarnated as critical reading) and new (the writing portion): "The College Board could and did tell admissions officers that the critical-reading and math sections of the New SAT were comparable to the verbal and mathematical reasoning sections of the old SAT I. If admissions officers disliked the New SAT, they could ignore the writing exam and then for all practical purposes the old and new SAT would be equivalent."[38] Atkinson and Geiser noted that the National Association for College Admissions Counseling has called for less reliance on testing agencies and more independence on the part of American colleges and universities in designing the college entrance examinations of the future.

THE SENATE'S CHOICE

When BOARS and the Academic Senate assessed the performance of the SAT-R in 2009, three years after its introduction, they endorsed its continued use in UC admissions. Although it did not totally conform to the principles for standardized testing adopted in 2002, the Senate concluded that it was as close as any national test could come. Further, the new writing and mathematics portions had made it a more useful test for UC.

The Senate's next recommendation was more surprising: UC should drop the achievement-based SAT subject tests as a requirement for admission. The Senate agreed that strong evidence points to high school GPA as the single best predictor of college performance and that, where tests are concerned, curriculum-based achievement tests should be preferred. But it reasoned from these premises that three tests—the SAT-R and two subject tests—were an unnecessary burden on students. A single test would be sufficient, and that should be the SAT-R. Moreover, many otherwise qualified applicants fail to take the two subject tests. This means, in the Senate's view, that requiring them "arbitrarily excluded many high-achieving students, particularly those from under-represented groups."[39] These testing recommendations are part of a larger set of revisions in the admissions process, effective in fall 2012.

9

History's Coils

The Nuclear Weapons Laboratories

If we get rid of bomb making, plutonium, and New Mexico, I would be very happy.
—UC PRESIDENT ROBERT GORDON SPROUL, 1946

Operation of the Laboratories has for decades been a divisive influence affecting important sectors of the University community. Disputes over the Laboratories have not been mere academic differences of opinion but divisions of a deep and enduring kind over fundamental questions of value. They have divided students from faculty and from administration, faculty from faculty and from administration, and caused divisions within the Board of Regents.
—REPORT OF THE ADVISORY COMMITTEE ON THE UNIVERSITY'S RELATIONS WITH THE DEPARTMENT OF ENERGY LABORATORIES, 1989

The University has never competed for this contract. We've always viewed it as a national service. We were asked by the Federal government to do this.... And the University, when it entered into this arrangement entered into it with a view that it would be a cooperative relationship, there'd be an effort on the part of the Federal Government to work closely with the University to identify and resolve problems, and that was the relationship that evolved and I think was a very successful relationship. In the last decade ... that relationship has changed.
—UC PRESIDENT RICHARD C. ATKINSON, TESTIMONY TO THE U.S. HOUSE OF REPRESENTATIVES, SUBCOMMITTEE ON OVERSIGHT AND INVESTIGATIONS, MAY 2003

In fall 1998 Director John Browne of the Los Alamos National Laboratory (LANL) testified before a congressional committee worried about the safety of the nation's nuclear secrets. LANL and a second nuclear weapons research laboratory—the Lawrence Livermore National Laboratory, or LLNL—were both managed by the

University of California for the US Department of Energy (DOE). Between them, these laboratories had invented every weapon in the nation's nuclear arsenal. Spies and nuclear weapons have a natural affinity for each other, and the backdrop of Browne's testimony was a fight simmering in Congress over the Clinton administration's decision in the early 1990s to ease some of the restrictions on visits from foreign scientists to American laboratories. Republicans were arguing that the Clinton directives amounted to an open invitation to espionage, especially by China. The end of nuclear testing in the early 1990s, as a result of the Comprehensive Test Ban Treaty, meant that the two UC weapons laboratories depended more heavily on high-performance computers and computer simulations to monitor the safety and reliability of the nation's nuclear stockpile. Computer security was therefore an especially sensitive issue; advances in computer technology were so rapid that keeping intruders out was an ever-mounting challenge. On a number of occasions the General Accounting Office had criticized the nuclear weapons laboratories for being insufficiently strict about overseeing Chinese and Russian visitors to ensure they were barred from access to classified information.

Browne sought to reassure his listeners by explaining the security procedures at LANL: no foreign nationals were allowed access to classified information, and the laboratory had recently created a new counterintelligence office to monitor foreign visits. He described the scientific contributions of foreign scientists who came to the laboratories as postdoctoral students or as visitors, the range of expertise they brought to the American research enterprise, and the important international partnerships they helped nurture. He pointed to recent visits from Russian scientists who were working with LANL colleagues to ensure that the nuclear stockpiles of the former Soviet Union remained secure and out of the hands of rogue nations. It was in the nation's interest not to shut out foreign scientists because no laboratory can hope to remain at the top without playing an active role in the international scientific community. The degree of openness at Los Alamos, he insisted, was compatible with both good security and good science.[1]

What Browne did not say in his public testimony—and could not say, under threat of penalty from the Federal Bureau of Investigation—was that he had known for a year that the DOE and the FBI suspected a spy was active in X Division, the unit responsible for Los Alamos's nuclear weapons designs. The FBI insisted that Browne neither remove the suspect—a nuclear scientist named Wen Ho Lee—from his sensitive position nor inform other UC officials, including the president of the University, about the FBI investigation. Atkinson learned about Wen Ho Lee a day or so before the *New York Times* ran a story in March 1999 about his dismissal from the laboratory for alleged security breaches.

Lee was not a foreign visitor but a long-term LANL employee, originally from Taiwan, who had become a naturalized American citizen. His work involved constructing computer codes that simulate what happens inside nuclear weapons—atomic bombs and hydrogen bombs—when they explode. He was, the *Times* reported, a "prime suspect" in an FBI investigation of alleged thefts of US nuclear secrets by China.[2] After his arrest in December 1999, Lee spent 278 days in prison, many of them in solitary confinement. The FBI's investigation, called Kindred Spirit, was a long and desultory affair that centered largely on circumstantial evidence, much of it shaky, and was flawed by a hasty and near-exclusive focus on Lee as the primary suspect. Presiding Judge James Parker concluded that Lee's arrest and incarceration amounted to a major miscarriage of American justice. On September 13, 2000, Judge Parker told Lee he was a free man, adding that the government's actions "have embarrassed our entire nation and each of us who is a citizen of it." In exchange for pleading guilty to one count of downloading classified information, Lee was sentenced to the 278 days in prison he had already served.

Whether or not Lee was a spy, he had in all likelihood committed the most serious security breach at the weapons laboratories in three decades. The circumstances of his case prompted a June 1999 report from the President's Foreign Intelligence Advisory Board, chaired by Senator Warren Rudman, which indicted the laboratories for a long-standing pattern of lapses in security, large and small, and the Department of Energy for arrogance, inertia, and bureaucratic stonewalling.[3] Rudman's report bore the descriptive title *Science at Its Best, Security at Its Worst,* and it was careful to point out that his criticisms were not aimed at the science performed at the weapons laboratories, which were described as "national jewels." It was the management issue that concerned Rudman and his colleagues, and their concerns ranged far beyond the specific details of the Lee incident and the Los Alamos laboratory. "The predominant attitude toward security and counterintelligence among many DOE and lab managers has ranged from half-hearted, grudging accommodation to smug disregard," the report charged, leading to "substantial" opportunities for the loss of sensitive information.[4] The most withering blasts were directed to DOE, but there was plenty of criticism for the weapons laboratories as well, reinforcing an image of sievelike laxity about the nation's nuclear secrets.

The Lee case opened the door to the idea that the University of California, despite the laboratories' brilliant accomplishments in nuclear physics and a host of other disciplines, was not the only—perhaps not even the best—possible manager of Los Alamos and Livermore. UC had run them, without competition, for almost sixty years. Even before the Lee incident, DOE had begun dropping hints to UC officials that it might consider opening the laboratory management contracts to other competitors. A non-UC manager for the third DOE laboratory run by the University, the Lawrence Berkeley National Laboratory (LBNL), was unlikely; LBNL, which conducts unclassified energy-related research, had been located on the UC Berkeley campus since its establishment in the 1930s, and many of its scientists were also Berkeley faculty. But the weapons laboratories were separate institutions, and Los Alamos, located high in New Mexico's Jemez Mountains, was not even in California.

The spy scandal and its aftermath set off an alignment of powerful forces that undermined the case for UC's management: hostile elements in DOE, political agendas in Congress and the Clinton and George W. Bush administrations, even the continuing fallout from the geopolitical realignment ushered in by the end of the cold war. What happened was also the culmination of a sea change in UC's relations with the Department of Energy and sixty years of conflict over the morality and the management of research on weapons of mass destruction.

SECURITY

The immediate result was a new and stricter regime of DOE-mandated security measures at the national laboratories. At the same time, DOE commissioned an investigation of the Lee case and security at Los Alamos by the Inspector General. While noting the recent improvements Secretary of Energy Bill Richardson had mandated, the Inspector General's report revealed a DOE riddled with systemic problems in dealing with counterintelligence issues and hobbled by widespread confusion about individual roles and responsibilities in various aspects of the Lee case. Communications within DOE, and among DOE, the FBI, and the laboratory, were muddled by conflicting versions of the same events, misunderstandings, poor judgments, and inadequate or nonexistent follow-up. This account reflected a reality the University and the laboratory had already learned the hard way: the division of authority for security between DOE and the UC laboratories, including the highly sensitive area of cybersecurity, was ambiguous at best. Under its contracts with DOE, UC was responsible for complying with DOE security regulations and directives. But how was the University to carry out its responsibilities when—as in the case of Wen Ho Lee—only one UC person (in this instance, the LANL director) was permitted to know about the potential security breach? Although blame was difficult to assign in this murky managerial environment, the Inspector General identified nineteen individuals at DOE and LANL with "a degree of responsibility" for the fiasco. Richardson, frustrated that "the factual record isn't clearer about who knew what when," wanted the University to discipline three of them.[5]

Richardson, whose handling of the Lee case may or may not have been influenced by his rumored aspiration to be Al Gore's running mate in the 2000 election, had a list of LANL employees that he wanted Browne to fire. One of them was a former LANL director, Siegfried Hecker. When Browne refused, Richardson proposed that they meet for breakfast at a restaurant in Santa Fe to discuss it. Browne arrived first. Before long Richardson appeared, trailing an entourage of television and print reporters, and proceeded to demand on camera that Browne fire the offending employees. Browne refused.[6]

The following month, DOE awarded LANL a satisfactory rating—the highest possible—on security, and noted that the Livermore laboratory was much improved and on the way to a satisfactory rating as well. "Our reforms are beginning to work," Secretary Richardson declared.

These reforms had included greater restrictions on foreign visitors and, to snare potential spies at the outset, the extension of polygraph testing to thousands of laboratory employees. Atkinson was alarmed by the chilling effect these steps could have on the morale and the quality of science performed at the laboratories, and he was not alone. The National Academy of Sciences warned against "potentially inappropriate restrictions" on foreign visitors and the damage such restrictions would inflict on America's scientific and security interests alike. Atkinson's principal advisory group for the laboratories, the UC President's Council on the National Laboratories, echoed the Academy's concerns in a November 1999 report that also cut through the ambiguity of the overlapping roles of DOE, the FBI, and UC in security matters. It asserted that UC must assume full responsibility for safeguarding nuclear secrets, devoting as much attention to security as it did to physical safety and environmental protection at the laboratories. The report endorsed many of the steps DOE had already taken but disputed allegations that the laboratories had neglected or downplayed security. Richardson had written Atkinson the previous summer demanding assurance that the University was fully committed to implementing DOE's "full range of counterintelligence activities and the use of polygraph testing."[7] The UC President's Council took a tactful but firm position on that issue. Polygraph testing, the report said, often yields false positives and is most useful as an investigative tool in specific cases and as a deterrent to security leaks to foreign nationals. Its widespread use, however, would undermine morale at the laboratories and discourage talented scientists and engineers from joining them.

A new security issue cropped up at Los Alamos the following spring. On June 1, 2000, lab officials learned that two computer hard drives with classified information had gone missing. The hard drives had disappeared sometime during the two-week period in which the Cerro Grande wildfire (a huge conflagration that burned through 43,000 acres in northern New Mexico, including 7,500 acres of LANL) forced the closure of the laboratory. This security mishap had potentially serious implications: the hard drives were part of a nuclear emergency tool kit and contained information that could be useful to existing or emerging nuclear powers. On June 16 the drives were discovered behind a copy machine, undamaged and apparently untouched. Richardson, criticized for not reporting the incident immediately to Congress, appointed a DOE panel to "address the serious shortcomings of the University of California contractor at our weapons laboratories."[8] A subsequent DOE proposal to relieve UC entirely of its security responsibilities at Los Alamos and Livermore got no support in Congress. But the University's argument that science and security were compatible, and that UC could handle both equally well, was being met with increasing skepticism.

MORE MANAGEMENT ISSUES

By summer 2002 rumors had begun to surface about business operations at Los Alamos, specifically its procurement practices. An Albuquerque reporter claimed he had received an anonymous thirty-pound box of laboratory documents that were said to reveal a variety of unauthorized charges, misuse of the lab-issued purchase cards, and other illegitimate business practices at LANL. In August the University engaged John Layton, a former DOE and Department of the Treasury Inspector General, to conduct an independent review of the purchase card system and LANL business practices generally.

The growing problems at Los Alamos prompted Atkinson to send a special review team there in November 2002, headed by Senior Vice President Bruce Darling. During lunch on the first day, the members of the review team learned that LANL management had fired two employees—potential whistle-blowers who had recently been in touch with the Department of Energy about alleged irregularities in the laboratory's business practices. It was an inauspicious beginning to a visit that also turned up evidence of lax controls of purchasing and a backlog of more than 250 audit recommendations that management had not acted on. After a second visit in December, the team concluded that "sweeping changes" were needed in the Los Alamos administration. Director Browne resigned at the end of that month. Seventeen LANL employees were fired, removed from management positions, or reassigned. Atkinson appointed a new director, retired Vice Admiral George P. Nanos, on January 2, 2003.

The administrative and business problems at Los Alamos were real, but their fiscal consequences were far less than they first appeared and were later portrayed in the press. Twelve months of audits covering 170,000 separate transactions stretching back over almost four years uncovered a few instances of employee fraud, a handful of purchases that were clearly unorthodox, and a certain degree of carelessness about business controls. In a purchasing budget of $120 million, the auditors found $3,000 in fraudulent purchases and $320,000 worth of costs that might not be allowed under DOE contract guidelines.[9] During the Cerro Grande wildfire, for example, laboratory funds paid for camping equipment, dog food, and a pair of oars. The dog food might have been for animals used in fighting the fire, but the camping supplies and the oars were harder to explain.

The strangest example—the one that became the bumper sticker for allegations of corrupt business practices at Los Alamos—was the Mustang incident, which illustrated both the importance and the impossibility of managing public perceptions of events at the laboratory. The media version was that an LANL employee had attempted to buy a customized black Mustang GT convertible with her laboratory purchase card. In reality she had placed an order for some laboratory equipment over the telephone without realizing the number she dialed, which had belonged to the laboratory's regular supplier, was now being used by an enterprising car salesman with a history of unorthodox business practices. He took advantage of her mistake to bill the laboratory $30,000 for a Mustang. No money, and no Mustang, ever changed hands. The University ultimately concluded that the employee and the laboratory were the innocent victims of fraud rather than its perpetrators. But UC was prohibited from doing an investigation until the FBI finished its own inquiry, and by that time it was far too late for the facts to catch up with the story.

In a less frantic political environment, the administrative stumbles at Los Alamos might have been considered more akin to a wake-up call than a crisis. UC auditor Pat Reed used a different metaphor. The barn door had been left open, he concluded, but it was a tribute to the people employed by the laboratory that by and large the horses were still inside.

FOR THE DEFENSE

The University's response to criticism of its management did not end with the audits. Atkinson approved a major revamping of the University's oversight mechanisms for the laboratories in spring 2003. The President's Council had devoted most of its attention to overseeing the quality and performance of the laboratories' scientific programs. The changes included a new external governance board and much broader internal oversight that incorporated UC's audit, business and finance, legal, and human resources expertise.

UC won some of the battles over the laboratory. The Los Alamos contract was not terminated early, ahead of its 2005 expiration date, as some members of Congress were demanding. But it became clear that UC had lost the competition issue when, at a celebration of LANL's sixtieth anniversary in April 2003, one of its staunchest friends announced he was endorsing an open competition for the 2005 Los Alamos contract. Senator Pete Domenici (R-NM) left no doubt about his position: "The evidence is clear that the Laboratory has not been managed well, particularly in the area of business systems," he said, adding that the time had come for the application of "tough love." Domenici's withdrawal of support made contract competition inevitable. It was an especially painful defeat because Domenici had been a champion of UC management through many public controversies and political storms.

DOE's undersecretary of energy, Linton Brooks, told the Regents in May 2003 that he had reviewed events at Los Alamos for Secretary Spencer Abraham, Richardson's successor. Brooks's conclusion was that DOE and the University shared responsibility for the shortcomings that had developed at the laboratory. Once those shortcomings surfaced, however, he considered the University's actions "broad, forceful, and effective. . . . It is difficult to see how any organization could have done more to deal with the problem than the University of California did."[10] His review, moreover, found that the quality of LANL's science was unaffected by the administrative missteps that led to DOE's decision to open the contract to competition.

There had been occasional murmurings of discontent about the University's management of the three DOE laboratories in earlier years, but in each case the threat of competition had not materialized. President David Gardner, on learning that DOE had plans to put the laboratory contracts up for competition in 1992, told Secretary of Energy James Watkins the University would not seek to win them; its stewardship of the laboratories was a public service undertaken at the request of the federal government. The Regents supported Gardner's decision.[11] DOE did not put the contracts out to bid.

The University of California had maintained for six decades that it managed the federal laboratories only as a public service. Did this preclude competition? In facing this question, Atkinson had no formal policy to guide him. What he and the Regents did have was sixty years of history.

AN EVOLVING RELATIONSHIP

When UC President Robert Gordon Sproul and the Regents agreed to contract with the US government in 1943 to create the world's first atomic bomb, Sproul considered the arrangement an act of wartime service that would end with the conflict itself. But there was to be nothing temporary about the University of California's involvement with nuclear weapons research. The army prevailed upon the University to continue its stewardship of Los Alamos until Congress passed legislation to establish the Atomic Energy Commission, which would assume civilian responsibility for all nuclear matters on behalf of the federal government. By the time the legislation passed several years later, the cold war had already begun, and Sproul and the Regents were persuaded to continue managing Los Alamos by Professor Ernest O. Lawrence, inventor of the cyclotron and UC's first Nobel Prize winner. The University ultimately agreed not only to run Los Alamos but also to establish a branch of Lawrence's Radiation Laboratory in 1952 to conduct nuclear research at Livermore, about thirty-five miles east of Berkeley. The Lawrence Livermore National Laboratory was a response to the Korean War and the Soviet Union's testing of a hydrogen bomb. In the postwar world, dominated by apocalyptic fears of nuclear catastrophe and a national policy of mutually assured destruction, the argument for two nuclear weapons laboratories rested on the logic of competition: Los Alamos and Livermore would ensure American nuclear dominance over the Soviet Union by vying with each other for the best people and the best programs.

The scientists and engineers who built the nation's nuclear arsenal thought of themselves not as "contractors"—the Department of Energy's term for the laboratories—but as the last line of defense for the United States and democracies everywhere. This perspective endured long after the Manhattan Project ended. In the 1980s a visiting auditor asked a Livermore nuclear weapons physicist for a description of the laboratory's customers. "The Free World!" was the reply. And consistent with this expansive view of the laboratories' mission, for at least three decades after the end of World War II the relationship between the University and DOE was predicated on the idea of mutuality—a temporary wartime alliance transformed into a permanent postwar partnership uniting national security and big science. The federal government, through DOE, defined the laboratories' priorities and programs and provided their budget. The University's responsibility was to produce outstanding scientific programs, monitored through rigorous peer review, principally but not entirely in the area of nuclear weapons.

"Mutuality" implied several things. Laboratory employees were UC employees and could not be fired by the Department of Energy. As long as the laboratories met the goals established by DOE, they had broad flexibility with regard to how to go about it; differences would be settled through discussion and agreement, including differences over the uncertain costs of producing cutting-edge science. All three DOE laboratories—the nonweapons Berkeley laboratory and Los Alamos and Livermore—regularly took on unprecedented scientific challenges, creating technologies and building machines no one had ever attempted before.[12] The University received a modest fixed payment for the costs it incurred running the laboratories. This last point was a highly symbolic declaration of independence: DOE might consider UC a government contractor, but the University saw itself as performing a public service.

There were disputes and power struggles between UC and the huge DOE bureaucracy, an early example of which was the federal government's imperious appointment of LANL's first postwar director without consulting the University. But in the era of mutuality, the balance of power was largely on the University's side. The laboratories were the single most important barrier between the nation and the threat of nuclear conflict in a dangerous world. Laboratory directors were respected in Washington and listened to when they testified about nuclear weapons and national security before congressional committees. Friends and defenders in Congress saw that money flowed to the weapons laboratories, and money meant independence.

From the beginning, however, there were those who were troubled by an ethical question—the apparent contradiction between traditional academic openness and secret research on weapons of mass destruction. Justifying this seeming paradox was to be one of the larger challenges of managing the laboratories. The administrations of David Saxon (1975–83) and David Gardner (1983–92) were marked by recurring protests, public demonstrations, political controversy, and faculty admonitions to exercise stronger administrative oversight of the laboratories. Both Saxon and Gardner defended the University's involvement with the laboratories by an appeal to principle. It was the job of the US president and Congress to decide whether the design and development of nuclear weapons were essential to the defense of the United States. With that assumption, the University had two important contributions to make. First, UC could ensure the laboratories' scientific independence and intellectual freedom and offer the Congress and the president of the United States unbiased advice on vital nuclear issues. Second, as long as the federal government's policy was to build and maintain nuclear weapons in the national defense, the University of California rendered an important public service in managing the laboratories at Los Alamos and Livermore.

The question this rationale left unanswered was exactly how the weapons laboratories fit within the larger organization of UC as an academic institution. The University had accepted more or less permanent responsibility for two organizations that were direct instruments of national policy. They served multiple masters—Congress and the Department of Energy as well as the University—and were highly vulnerable to shifts in the political landscape. And like other complex organizations, over time the weapons laboratories developed their own culture and inner logic, their own trajectory of growth, and their own pattern of responding to pressures from within and without. The University's managerial role was an accident of history, but like many such accidents it had unforeseen consequences and ramifications.

It was the faculty who, through the Academic Senate, periodically raised the question of the ethics of UC's involvement with nuclear weapons. The first of a series of Academic Senate reports on the subject—the 1970 Zinner report, named after the committee chair, UC Davis professor of political science Paul Zinner—laid out with remarkable clarity the major reservations about UC's nuclear connection that were to surface again and again over the next thirty years. Mixing sober analysis with the heady moral rhetoric of the Vietnam era, Zinner and his colleagues argued that making sense of UC's relationship with all three of its national laboratories would require the University to define its role in the new era of big science, when it would be called upon to help society adapt to the massive changes—overpopulation and environmental pollution among them—created by scientific progress of all kinds. Their complaint was that the laboratories were not being used to their full potential or sufficiently connected to the campuses.

All but one member of the Zinner committee agreed that the University's relationship with Los Alamos and Livermore was "in principle not inappropriate" while at the same time leaving "much to be desired in practice." But it offered a stern assessment of the University's management, describing it as "nominal," the President's Office as adopting a "hands-off policy," the role of the Board of Regents as "largely ornamental," and the University itself as a "benevolent absentee landlord. . . . The laboratories, therefore, exist in a world of their own, isolated from the academic community of the University and to some extent from each other as well."[13]

Given the portentous tone of the discussion, the report's recommendations to improve the University's management were for the most part surprisingly modest.[14] Two dealt with the status of the Livermore laboratory. The committee argued for severing the administrative relationship between Berkeley and Livermore, making the Livermore laboratory independent—which the Regents ultimately did—and for considering, at some unspecified future date, the option of transforming Livermore into a UC campus.

Nothing came of this last recommendation, but it touched on a central issue nonetheless: the anomalous organizational status of the laboratories within the University of California. The Zinner committee saw them as annexed to the larger institution but unincorporated, neither truly part of it nor entirely separate but suspended somewhere on the periphery. UC's oversight was too episodic and haphazard, and the University itself followed the government's nuclear weapons policy without voicing the objections it was an academic institution's obligation to make. The proportion of nuclear weapons research should decline, Zinner and his colleagues argued, to be replaced by research on pressing national problems like the environment, energy, and disease. Finally, UC's institutional involvement in nuclear weapons should continue only if oversight were strengthened and expanded. The Regents agreed with this recommendation and appointed two advisory committees, one for the weapons laboratories and one for the Berkeley lab, with "experience relevant to the Laboratories' programs" to advise the laboratory directors and the president on the breadth and quality of the laboratories' research.[15]

The straight line leading from morality to management was the Zinner report's solution to the contradiction between the University's role as an academic institution and its role as a contractor for laboratories devoted to the design of nuclear weapons. It was the integrity and rigor of UC's stewardship that removed the moral taint of involvement with nuclear weapons: "We consider the University's failure to assume leadership over [the laboratories], shape their policies, guide their development and tap their resources more troubling than either the actual or the fancied liabilities incurred by sponsorship of nuclear weapons research." Zinner and his colleagues recognized their recommendations would pose organizational challenges. "The laboratories are too big to be treated as ordinary organized research units located on the campuses," the report concluded. "They are veritable campuses in their own right. Yet they lack the essential attributes of a campus."

The committee's call for closer ties between the laboratories and the University was therefore easier to prescribe than to accomplish. The classified nature of most work conducted at the laboratories is a major obstacle in and of itself. The mission-oriented character of research at the weapons laboratories, even unclassified research, means that their budgets and their programs are enmeshed in the constantly shifting politics of Congress and the administrative bureaucracy of the Department of Energy. It was virtually impossible for any UC president, including physicist David Saxon, to understand the laboratories as well or as deeply as he understood the campuses. There were times when this fact gave the laboratories an autonomy the campuses did not have.

The laboratories were constantly faced with organized groups of citizens and students opposed to their inclusion within UC and, in some cases, to their very existence.[16] These groups naturally used controversies surrounding the laboratories to push their case for converting or closing them. Clashes over the laboratories were even more likely than campus imbroglios to be trumpeted by the national media and amplified by national politics, drawing the president or the Regents into the line of fire.

Security, mission, and institutional culture all pointed up the difficulty of seeing the laboratories as proto-campuses. The idea that there was an organizational and management solution to the moral issue of managing weapons laboratories held an enduring appeal nonetheless. Of the various faculty reports on UC's management, only one—a 1994 report by a committee headed by Professor Malcolm Jendresen of UC San Francisco—called on the University to withdraw entirely from work on nuclear weapons and the laboratories that produced them. The others consistently echoed the essential message of the Zinner report: more oversight, more opportunities for faculty and graduate students to engage in research at the laboratories, closer scrutiny by the Office of the President and the Regents. The years since Zinner and his colleagues rebuked the University as an absentee landlord have been marked by successive UC attempts at more, and more sophisticated, oversight of the DOE laboratories.

PERFORMANCE-BASED MANAGEMENT

While the forces behind the Zinner committee were nuclear protest and faculty qualms about involvement in nuclear weapons, most of the later oversight changes were driven by a very different force: the US Department of Energy. In the 1980s, fading cold war tensions brought a sharper focus on environmental issues at all DOE laboratories. Secretary of Energy Watkins, appointed in 1989 by President George H. W. Bush, was determined to bring a stricter and more disciplined spirit to DOE's relations with its contractors. The secretary, whose uninhibited vigor in expressing his views had earned him the nickname "Radio Free Watkins," sent in teams of outside contractors, called Tiger Teams, to report on ES&H—environ-mental safety and health—procedures at all DOE facilities. The three UC-managed laboratories found the Tiger Teams imperious and punitive in their approach. The 1990–91 DOE inspection at the Lawrence Berkeley Laboratory lasted five weeks, involved sixty-one Tiger Team members, and resulted in a seven-hundred-page report. It turned up no serious ES&H violations but left the laboratory with much remaining work to comply with regulations.[17] A 1995 government report subse-quently found that "the degree to which the government is specifying how these [ES&H] issues are to be handled is beginning to absorb virtually as much funds as funds remaining for science."[18]

The Tiger Teams represented a disturbing new venture into micromanagement by DOE. The agency was also contemplating the introduction of an "incentiviza-tion process" in its contracts as a way to gain more direct control over laboratories' operations; in other words, DOE wanted to pay a larger fee to gain leverage over UC and other contractors. This concept was at odds with the idea of laboratory management as a public service. On the contrary, as the Regents were told in May 1991, it "characterizes a defense contractor relationship but does not describe the University's traditional relationship with the government in its management of the laboratories."[19]

It was becoming increasingly difficult to call on powerful allies in Congress to serve as a buffer between the University and DOE's more burdensome microman-agement. DOE was starting to renegotiate contracts in a way that required all of its national laboratories to shoulder more financial risk.[20] DOE also made it clear to the University that it would need to know what management improvements the University planned to make before it could make its own decision about whether to open the 1992 contracts to other competitors.

The University wanted to shift the conversation to outcomes, not procedures and regulations. Former UC senior vice president for administration, Ronald Brady, describes this position in his 1998 oral history:

> We don't decide to build nuclear weapons. They [the Department of Defense] decide to build nuclear weapons, OK. Now, there comes a point when the scientists say, "OK, DOE, you said you want the following weapons built, now get out of our hair and we'll build them for you." And DOE says, "Oh, no. We want to task you. We want to tell Professor X (called Scientist X in the laboratories, but they're just like profes-sors) to do the following things on Monday, and the next things on Tuesday, and the following things on Wednesday." And our position is "Not us. That's not the way we do business."[21]

Brady was the University's chief negotiator for the 1992 contracts. He was highly skilled at bureaucratic combat and was to dominate the negotiations for those contracts.

The Academic Senate polled the faculty on whether they supported renewal of the University's contracts; the response was decisively negative, with 64 percent of the faculty opposed and 39 percent in favor. The administration's strategy was to give DOE and the critics what they claimed to want: more oversight and accountability on the part of the University. Gardner disbanded the small advisory committees for the laboratories in favor of a much larger and more comprehensive oversight body, the UC President's Council on the National Laboratories, composed of distinguished representatives drawn from the faculty, the Regents' oversight committee, the Office of the President, government, and private industry. Its job was to advise the president and the laboratory directors not just on the quality of science at the labs, but on all aspects of their operation and management, reporting annually to the president and the Regents.

But the heart of the University's new approach was measuring performance— establishing a set of standards that would provide objective metrics of its major activities, from designing nuclear weapons to enforcing safety procedures. The existing management fee would be replaced by a larger one based on how well UC met the criteria and taking into account the greater level of risk UC was accepting under the new arrangements. UC would define the operational standards by which it would be judged, but the President's Council and DOE would have to agree. And so performance-based management was born.

The University administration was specific about the principles guiding its negotiations. Three spoke directly to its history as a contractor: the principle of mutuality—"a key element of the philosophy underlying the contract being negotiated"; the no gain/no loss philosophy; and the academic atmosphere at the laboratories—the intellectual and scientific freedom of laboratory employees, including the ability of the directors and other officials to offer independent advice to Congress and the US president. This was a capsule description of the spirit of partnership with the federal government in the early days, a relationship that had long since begun to fray. Although Gardner told the Regents that the goal of the negotiations would be "to preserve the principle of mutuality on which the contracts have been based for nearly fifty years," the University's move to performance-based management was a tacit admission that the era of mutuality was over.[22]

A NEW WORLD

Looking back, Gardner felt laboratory issues absorbed a disproportionate amount of time and energy during his administration.[23] They were soaking up even more during the Atkinson administration. The 1992 contracts had only limited effect on righting what UC saw as a growing imbalance in its relationship with DOE. Performance-based management gave UC useful feedback on its stewardship, but in practice DOE often ignored any evaluation of University performance other than its own. The new regime was not inexpensive: laboratory administration in the Office of the President, which had been overseen by one scientist-manager assisted by a secretary, now employed more than twenty people. The turmoil that began with the Lee case piled on even greater expenditures of administrative time and effort; UC Auditor Pat Reed alone had made forty-two visits to Los Alamos in a single year.

For an allegedly absentee landlord, the University was investing enormous effort in the job. Probably no other University obligation had attracted more trouble, toil, and controversy. Was competition worth it? "One does not compete to perform a public service . . . ," a UC official in laboratory administration had written in 1991. "If the client thinks it can do better, it should by all means do so."[24]

Further, after the April 2003 decision to open the contract to competition, DOE made it clear that future contracts would not be like those of the past. Any future manager of Los Alamos or Livermore would have to come to the table with a partner to run the business side of the laboratories. The management fee was increased accordingly to attract private-sector firms. DOE intended to award the contracts without discussion or negotiation with any of the competitors—a rejection of the principle of mutuality. On the other side of the question were, first, the reluctance to walk away from an enterprise into which the University had poured increasing amounts of time and attention; second, the blow to institutional prestige that could be involved in public perceptions that UC had "lost" the laboratories; and third, the conviction that managing the laboratories was an important act of national public service.

The decision to compete for the Los Alamos and Livermore contracts was made during the administration of Atkinson's successor, Robert C. Dynes, in 2005. UC's bid included three private partners, Bechtel National, Babcock and Wilcox Technical Services Group, and the Washington Group International, which would be responsible for managing the business side of the laboratories. In 2004 the Academic Senate conducted a poll to determine faculty sentiment about whether UC should continue to manage the weapons laboratories. In striking contrast to 1990, this time the faculty endorsed UC's involvement by a three-to-one margin, although only about a quarter of the faculty supported sharing management responsibility with an industrial business partner.[25] The principal reasons supporters gave for their vote were the opportunities the laboratories offered for collaborative research between laboratory scientists and campus faculty and graduate and postdoctoral students; the high quality of the laboratories' unclassified research; and the view—held by nearly two-thirds of those responding—that UC's management was a "historic public service to the nation."[26]

Against huge odds and most expectations, UC and its partners were awarded the contracts for the weapons laboratories.[27] DOE's decision was an unexpected victory and a vindication of the scientific excellence that UC management, for all its recent difficulties, had brought to the laboratories.

The University's long history of conflict over the laboratories reflects the intrinsic difficulty of reconciling academic values and management style with service as a contractor in the design of nuclear weapons. A 1990 report from the president's advisory committee on the laboratories pointed out, "The University's role as manager of the entities that design nuclear weapons is . . . an outgrowth of history and not something that we believe the University would be likely to enter into *ab initio* today. Management of a laboratory predominantly devoted to the design of nuclear weapons is not a 'normal' activity for a university."[28]

Among the wider currents that shaped the crisis over the weapons laboratories was a long-standing dissatisfaction in Congress with the Department of Energy, which made UC's management stumbles seem part of a larger problem. UC was not alone in dealing with an overly directive DOE. In 1995 the Task Force on Alternative Futures for the Department of Energy National Laboratories summarized DOE's management philosophy for all the laboratories under its purview: "The laboratories are purported to be contractor operated. The system is titled Government-owned, Contractor-Operated or GOCO. The GOCO system was a promising concept. . . . [But] [n]umerous instances of poor DOE regulatory and management practices have come to the attention of all members of the Task Force during its investigation of the national laboratories. The system has been tried long enough; the evidence is in. Today, the system has evolved to a virtual GOGO—Government Owned, Government Operated, but certainly strongly government-dominated system."[29] The perception of DOE as a huge, impenetrable, micromanaging bureaucracy remains today.

In addition, the security controversy occurred at a time of transition in US security policy in the new international landscape of the post–cold war world. The laboratories, as Atkinson pointed out, did not set security policy or their own security budgets, and some of the University's requests for funds to strengthen security measures at the labs had been turned down by DOE. The persistent negative publicity surrounding the issue eclipsed the University's really important contribution to national security, the superb science the laboratories produced. Some UC officials regard the proliferation of security regulations at Los Alamos and Livermore, as a result of the Lee case and the hard drive incident, as an expensive impediment to that science, one that does not yield a compensatory benefit in safeguarding nuclear secrets.

In the broadest sense, the University's difficulties were—and continue to be—a reflection of the changed status of nuclear weapons in the new world order. The days when the laboratories were seen as the most important arsenal of democracy faded with the cold war. US nuclear policy has been in a state of flux since then, and without clear direction from Congress and the administration the laboratories face large difficulties planning for their future. As one former UC official put it, the nuclear weapons enterprise is getting old and showing some of the signs of a declining industry. The relationship between the University and the federal government has changed because the world itself has changed. The future direction of the laboratories depends on whether a national consensus on nuclear policy can be achieved.

Oddly enough, given the incredible array of sophisticated scientific talent and weapons expertise, the laboratories appear to have an image problem as institutions from a time when the most serious threats facing the United States came from nation-states, not terrorist groups. And in terms of perceptions and their influence, a major question is whether the laboratories will continue to be seen as places where the UC traditions of public service and scientific independence play a dominant role. The division of laboratory management into a scientific side, managed by the University, and a business side, run by private-sector corporate partners, is the profoundest organizational challenge UC has ever faced in its stewardship of the laboratories.

It is important to get the relationship right because the laboratories' extraordinary scientific capabilities matter for national security and much else. The laboratories have produced spectacular science and Nobel Prize winners, beginning with E. O. Lawrence. Los Alamos devotes more attention to experimental science and Livermore to modeling and computer simulation; both laboratories, however, cover the full spectrum of science, from basic research to applied technology. Long before the official end of the cold war, laboratory scientists were working on the national security implications of terrorism, biological and chemical weapons, and nuclear proliferation. Los Alamos trains nuclear weapons inspectors for the International Atomic Energy Agency; Livermore leads the world in computer modeling of climate and climate change.

In May 2003 Atkinson testified before the House Subcommittee on Oversight and Investigations about UC's management of the laboratories. Like several UC presidents before him, he recalled the University's long history with the laboratories, the demise of the era of mutuality, the divisive controversies, and the commitment to science the University of California had brought to its sixty years of stewardship. "We've carried a heavy burden in running these laboratories," he concluded. "We've done it as a matter of national service."[30] Both statements are still true. But what the next era of UC management will look like remains to be seen.

Presidents and Chancellors

Recent studies of universities, a familiar form of organized anarchy, suggest that such organizations can be viewed for some purposes as collections of choices looking for problems, issues and feelings looking for decision situations in which they might be aired, solutions looking for issues to which they might be an answer, and decision makers looking for work.

—MICHAEL D. COHEN, JAMES G. MARCH, AND JOHAN P. OLSEN, "A GARBAGE CAN MODEL OF ORGANIZATIONAL CHOICE," 1972

"It has been pointed out that I seem to have a knack for picking tumultuous times for my entrances and exits," Atkinson told the Board of Regents at his last meeting as University president in September 2003.[1] This was something of an understatement. Atkinson began his administration at the end of one budget crisis and was departing at the start of another. On the day he spoke, Gray Davis, who had been so instrumental to UC's financial recovery during the middle years of Atkinson's administration, was six weeks away from being swept out of office in a recall election won by an Austrian-born actor and former bodybuilder, Arnold Schwarzenegger.

With its various crises, its political twists and turns, its activist Regents and demonstrating students, divided faculty and competing agendas, there were times during the Atkinson years when the University of California appeared to be engaged in testing some administrative version of chaos theory. The nature of the issues made that inevitable. The admissions wars inaugurated by SP-1 took place at the contentious nexus of politics and principle. They could not be controlled— or concluded—by any single individual or group, including the president. They struck with too little warning to allow for a master strategy, or even real advance preparation, by either the faculty or the administration.

In conflicts like these, university presidents are often among the casualties. Atkinson survived the hazards of his position despite the early imbroglio over the implementation date of SP-1. This was due, in part, to the generous state budgets that prevailed during all but a year or so of his tenure, which spared him the internal battles that surface in hard times. The general prosperity of his tenure also made possible opportunities for action denied to less fiscally fortunate presidents. His background in cognitive science, psychometrics, and student learning proved unexpectedly useful, and not only with the SAT I. It helped in sorting out the complex questions of defining academic merit and the goals of admissions policy in the post–affirmative action era. The greatest threat to Atkinson's presidency might well have been the issue for which his background had least prepared him, the frustrating and politics-riddled controversy over managing the nuclear weapons laboratories at Los Alamos and Livermore. Ultimately the decision about whether to continue UC's management was made during the administration of his successor. His enthusiasm for building bridges to industry might have aroused controversy among those with a traditional view of the university, but that did not happen—perhaps because the University already offered sufficient controversies to occupy the public mind. And perhaps a little luck entered into his survival as well. Clark Kerr took a gloomy view of the likely fate of UC presidents. He accepted the job, he wrote in his memoirs, despite his knowledge that every one of his eleven predecessors had left under less than cordial circumstances.[2]

Atkinson had the good fortune to become president at a time when it was possible to do what he most wanted: pursue the kind of Terman-inspired institution building he had done in San Diego. His initiatives in expanding industry-university research and enrollments in engineering and computer science programs are examples. The California Digital Library, which he founded in 1997 and which is considered the best online research library in the country, is another. Intensive academic and physical planning for UC Merced, the first new campus established by the University of California in forty years, built on the work of earlier administrations and Academic Senates in laying the foundation for the campus's opening in 2005. Whatever the issue or objective, he used his staff, from vice presidents to analysts, to mediate, advance, and defend his initiatives. His collaboration with BOARS on admissions, with the governor on the California Institutes for Science and Innovation, with the Regents and the Academic Senate on rescinding SP-1— all were an exercise in applying the dictum that university governance is much more about influence than authority.

Not all his plans were realized. He would have liked to see University Extension integrated more closely into the academic life of the University through a program of professional and part-time degrees, designed with the involvement of regular faculty. The Academic Senate, historically unenthusiastic about part-time education, agreed to one such program, the Master of Advanced Study, but its impact has been modest and the larger aim is still unfulfilled. Another initiative was an experiment in digital publishing of scholarly and scientific journals by the University. It was essentially an act of resistance intended to fight back against the soaring costs of these journals and the monopoly power of a few large publishing companies. Although the project never reached critical mass, it ultimately became the foundation for UC's eScholarship Repository, which offers faculty and researchers opportunities for online publication of their work.

At the end of his administration, Atkinson worried most about two things. The first was the University's budget. Between 2001 and 2003 the University's net state-funded budget fell by 14 percent, at a time when enrollments continued to grow—a portent of worse to come. The second was the future of diversity at UC. Redefining admissions policy was the first imperative after the end of affirmative action, followed by outreach. Outreach—mandated in the language of SP-1—continues in much-diminished form since the cataclysmic plunge in state funding of the early 2000s. The top 4 percent plan, however—Eligibility in the Local Context—has succeeded in its goal of opening a new path to a UC education. Today, more than 75 percent of students eligible for ELC apply to the University, and of these more than 60 percent are accepted. Since the institution of comprehensive review, with its broader measures of student achievement and promise, the academic qualifications of applicants and students have risen and the University has been able to do a better job of taking into account the inequalities of California's K–12 schools, according to a 2010 assessment by the Academic Senate.[3]

But the goal of making UC a place that reflects the full diversity of the state remains unfulfilled. There is near-universal agreement that it will be virtually impossible to achieve without the renewal and revitalization of pre-collegiate education—the K–12 public schools. There is little evidence that the state is capable of mustering the money or the legislative will to get its arms around this challenge, especially in light of the initiative-dominated, tax-resistant, limited-government political culture that prevails today. Where education is concerned, California, with its outsized ambitions and golden dreams, has dwindled into a cautionary tale.

For UC, diversity remains a profound institutional and political problem. The University can make a strong case for the support of legislators and governors convinced that the state's high-tech economy must be fed with innovative research and excellent education. But the dilemma Atkinson and his colleagues struggled to resolve—how an elite public university can prosper without offering educational opportunity to the full spectrum of its constituencies—will continue to occupy the energies of UC presidents and chancellors well into the future.

THE CHANCELLOR'S PRESIDENT

Atkinson came to the presidency in 1995 convinced that the concept of one, possibly two, flagship campuses—Berkeley and UCLA—was inconsistent with the history and values of the UC system. The idea that UC's special character was to grow and develop as one university, its campuses charged with the same missions and expectations of quality, was a fundamental premise of its organizational philosophy. It was a concept that Atkinson simultaneously embraced and sought to reinterpret. In a 1996 discussion with UC's executive leadership, Atkinson described the University of California as "a collection of ten research universities—a single but not a monolithic institution of ten campuses. . . . Just as Princeton and the University of Michigan are both research universities but clearly different in size, in the array of academic disciplines, and in the makeup of their professional schools, so the University of California's campuses can be seen as variations on a single theme, each pursuing excellence in different ways."[4] Presidents from Robert Gordon Sproul on had made similar statements, but Atkinson's struck a different balance—more on the side of diversity than of unity. It was a statement of his dissent from the flagship campus idea, but it was also an expression of his position on the role of the chancellors in UC's multicampus system.

This orientation had a strong influence on how Atkinson conducted his presidency. Within the University, Atkinson could be described a chancellor's president, a systemwide leader who made a deliberate practice of fostering campus independence. The budgetary changes he introduced not only reshaped the budget process; they reshaped the architecture of UC governance. Control of the budget is one of the most powerful tools presidents have to influence campus decisions and development. In ceding to the chancellors an unprecedented degree of budgetary authority, Atkinson imposed strong limits on this presidential prerogative. It was not something many presidents would have done, but for Atkinson it was both a matter of conviction and an act of faith in the value of campus autonomy. Each of the ten chancellors, he felt, was similar in responsibility to the president of a private research university. The UC president, on the other hand, was not a chief executive officer in the traditional sense. His day-to-day responsibilities lay principally with the Regents, the governor, the legislature, the University-wide Academic Senate, and the federal government. In 1996 the Association of American Universities demurred on adding UC Davis and UC Irvine to its ranks because the University of California already had four member campuses besides the president, who had always represented the University system at AAU meetings. Atkinson resigned to open the way for Davis and Irvine, and the AAU admitted both. "I sought to give the chancellors as much independence and freedom as possible," he wrote in 2000.[5]

Much less inclined than Kerr or Gardner to view the president as a symbolic figure, he was not a unifying leader in the sense that they would have understood the term. He wavered over whether to have a presidential inauguration, briefly considered an online ceremony, and finally decided against it. He ended the long-standing practice of writing letters of thanks from the president to donors who had made gifts to the campuses; Atkinson felt it undermined public perceptions of the chancellors as important figures in their own territory. This was one reason that he was an infrequent participant in campus events or public ceremonies during his presidency. He assumed that the chancellors would prefer to be seen as the leaders of their own academic communities, and he had a certain amount of sympathy with occasional campus complaints about the ceremonial precedence given the president.

Behind these decisions was his personal experience as a chancellor in a multi-campus system. During his time at UCSD, he once received a visit from a constituent who pulled out a letter Atkinson had written him, pointed at the president's name at the top of the letterhead, and demanded to see that person, "the one who is really in charge." Incidents like this made him sensitive to the way in which minor matters of symbolism could undermine perceptions that chancellors were "really in charge" on their own campuses. When he became president, he ended the practice of including the president's name on campus correspondence.

Along with David Saxon (who also chose not to have an inauguration), Atkinson was regarded in some quarters as having diluted the power of the presidency. He saw his actions from the other side of the question, as giving due weight to the place of campuses and chancellors in the life of the University.

The Atkinsons returned to La Jolla and to the UCSD community when Atkinson stepped down as president in 2003. In addition to their campus-related activities, Atkinson has devoted much of his post-presidential life to the National Academy of Sciences. The Academy was established by Congress in 1863 to assist the government with reports "upon any subject of science or art" and today produces between 200 and 250 reports a year on topics from the future of the US economy to global warming. As chair of the advisory committee for the Division of Behavioral and Social Sciences and Education in recent years, Atkinson has been once again involved in national science policy and its implications for the American scientific enterprise.

In 2005 the San Diego campus recognized his long service on its behalf by naming a building in his honor—Atkinson Hall, the home of the California Institute for Telecommunications and Information Technology, Calit2. Calit2's mission of pursuing new and innovative ideas is reflected everywhere in the building's striking design.

From the easily reconfigured furniture to the state-of-the-art broadband communication, Atkinson Hall is intended to exemplify and honor change. It is an entirely appropriate tribute.

11

Epilogue

One University

We are building one great university in California. Let no small mind direct you along the paths of suspicion, distrust or jealousy.
—UC PRESIDENT ROBERT GORDON SPROUL TO THE STUDENTS OF UCLA, SEPTEMBER 27, 1932

Sproul's admonition to UCLA's students came at a sensitive moment in the history of the University of California. In 1932 the Los Angeles campus—long fought for by Southern California citizens and interest groups, long delayed by University leaders in the north, and only recently settled in the hills of Westwood where it stands today—had recently made UC the nation's first multicampus university.[1] UCLA was a fledgling institution at that point, very much in the shadow of its distinguished older sibling four hundred miles away at Berkeley. Sproul's remark was an attempt to lift morale and instill a sense of solidarity between north and south. The phrase he used—"one great university"—has come to symbolize the institutional identity of the University of California as a set of research university campuses united by a common mission and common standards for the admission of students, for promotion of faculty, and for high academic quality. This characteristic makes UC different from other American multicampus systems, most of which have been organized around existing and sometimes very different kinds of educational institutions. The one-university idea is widely regarded as a key organizational reason for UC's emergence as one of the world's most distinguished universities.

The second, equally powerful theme of UC's evolution into a multicampus system—the institutional preference for administrative decentralization—has led a sometimes uneasy coexistence with the one-university principle. Sproul recognized that the more decision making became local and the more campuses were seen as independent actors in their communities, the less loyalty would be channeled to the one great university California was in the process of building. The University of California might well fragment into a series of local institutions, he feared, without a strong centering force—the president and the University-wide administration. As articulated by Sproul, the one-university idea was more than an expression of institutional character. It was also an organizational framework, a means of containing the tensions of competing campuses, and a statement about the role of the president.

A quarter of a century after Sproul's ringing speech to the students of UCLA, President Clark Kerr and the Regents dismantled the highly centralized organizational edifice he had created. The University committed itself to an administrative enterprise governed by two values: authority at the center coupled with considerable independence everywhere else. Maintaining organizational equilibrium between these two values has been a major task of successive presidents. This task occurs entirely outside the purview of most faculty, and virtually all students, alumni, and members of the public. And why not? Students learn, faculty teach and discover, and the process of education goes on, whatever administrators do or whatever they think about the organizational philosophies that govern their work.

Yet the all-but-invisible struggle between authority at the center and independence on the campuses has become surprisingly public in recent years. An obvious contributor has been a steep budgetary downturn. State funding has gone from bad to worse to devastating in the wake of California's long-standing budget problems and the international economic cataclysm of 2008. The economist Gary Gorton has compared the public reaction to the meltdown on Wall Street to what happens after a massive electrical blackout: once the panic begins to subside, what follows is an intense upsurge of interest in understanding how the system works and what went wrong.[2] Something analogous has occurred within UC, raising fundamental questions not only about its fiscal strategies for survival but also about the integrity and efficiency of its organizational structure.[3]

This budgetary reversal of fortune is not the whole story, however. The University was already in a state of internal disequilibrium even before the worst of the financial storms hit. A much-publicized controversy over UC executive compensation in 2005 and 2006 made UCOP once again the object of public and legislative anger.[4] In 2008 the Regents cited the executive compensation disaster as "illustrative of a broader governance problem" in the Office of the President.[5]

The governance issue was also amplified by campus criticisms of UCOP management that had begun to catch the attention of the Board of Regents. Regents' chair Richard Blum was outspoken in characterizing the Office of the President as an "outmoded and dysfunctional" bureaucracy.[6] When he commissioned an external consulting firm, the Monitor Group, to assess the organization, effectiveness, and efficiency of the University's administrative and finance functions in 2007, its mandate was to begin with the Office of the President.[7] Blum criticized what

he saw as the absence of clear lines of authority as well as delays and other bureaucratic inefficiencies throughout the University's administration. The planned
restructuring of its central office, he announced, would make it "a model of transformation to efficiency and service" as a first step toward serial reform of UC's
administrative operations generally.[8]

The message of the 2007 Monitor Group report—an unremittingly negative
assessment of the organization, culture, and performance of the Office of the
President—was that UCOP was too large, too bureaucratic, and too opaque in its
decision making, imposing requirements on campuses instead of partnering with
them, and insufficiently oriented toward service. The Regents then set in motion
a fundamental restructuring that, as of May 2010, reduced UCOP's budget by $85
million ($30 million, or more than a third of this amount, is in the form of trans-
fers of UCOP functions and budgets to campuses, however) and its workforce by
28 percent, according to UCOP sources.[9] The cuts in the Office of the President
have been extraordinary, given that even the Monitor Group report noted that
costs within the Office of the President were relatively modest compared to those
of the system as a whole.[10] The loss of institutional memory and analytical skills
has been considerable. The chair of the Academic Council wrote President Mark
Yudof in 2009 about the difficulties the staff cutbacks presented for the work of the
University-wide Academic Senate.[11] A year later, an Academic Senate report recommended reducing campus staff, if necessary, rather than making further cuts
in UCOP personnel.[12]

An internal task force, chaired by UC Davis Chancellor Larry Vanderhoef and
charged with redefining the Office of the President's role in the new administrative framework, recommended that UCOP focus exclusively on policy, oversight, and other clearly executive functions.[13] Anything that could be defined as
"operational"—a continuing education program for attorneys and a study abroad
program for UC students, for example, both administered by UCOP—should be
removed from the Office of the President and reassigned to the campuses or managed elsewhere.

The Vanderhoef report was a strong reassertion of the decentralization principle that campuses manage programs and UCOP manages policy. In this respect,
it echoed the three major organizational reports of the past fifty years: the Cresap, McCormick, and Paget study of 1959; an analysis of the role of the Office of
the President and the campuses done in 1976; and a report on UC organization
commissioned by outgoing President Gardner and incoming President Peltason
in 1992. The consistency of their conclusions suggests that decentralization has
remained unfinished business. But while the message may be the same, today's
context and circumstances give it a very different import. To explain why, it is
necessary to take a closer look at the recurring debate over the role of the president and the Office of the President, the shifting balance of centralization and

decentralization in UC's multicampus system, and the origins and evolution of the one-university model.

ROBERT GORDON SPROUL AND ONE UNIVERSITY

The concept of one great university, so eloquently articulated by Sproul, began as a defensive tactic before it became an organizational philosophy. By the 1930s, at the beginning of Sproul's long presidency (1930–58), the University had campuses at Berkeley and UCLA, as well as the medical school in San Francisco, the University Farm at Davis, the Citrus Experiment Station at Riverside, Scripps Institution of Oceanography at San Diego, the Lick Observatory on Mount Hamilton (near San Jose), and a series of agricultural experiment stations throughout California; in 1944 it would add the state college at Santa Barbara. California's population had increased by two-thirds during the 1920s and demand for education along with it. The University was in competition for public funds with the seven state teachers' colleges and the thirty-four community colleges; the regional college movement was under way and the possibility of new state-funded institutions, created in response to local demand, was an ever-present threat.[14] There was much discussion in the legislature and elsewhere about the organization of higher education in California, including the question of whether UC should take over the state teachers' colleges. In this context, Sproul worried about two related matters.

The first was the constant struggle for money to meet the needs of the Berkeley campus. Initial opposition to a second campus in Southern California grew out of fears that it would drain resources away from the original northern campus. Sproul recognized the need for a Southern California presence but thought the state would balk at supporting two first-rate campuses. Under the pressures of population growth, local boosters, and Los Angeles business interests, UCLA might be split off to become a separate, regional university. This he was determined to oppose.[15]

The second issue was how to defend the University generally against similar political or regional threats. In 1923, before becoming president, Sproul had served on a legislative commission to study the organization of agricultural research in California and the nation. The impetus was a move by the state's powerful agriculture leaders to separate agricultural research from the University.[16] This was headed off by the commission's recommendation to develop the Davis campus as a center of agricultural research and thus leave it within UC. But the danger that agriculture or other functions of the University might be moved out of UC remained. At the same time, there was the possibility that the unsettled conditions of education in the state might mean that UC would be asked to absorb the state teachers' colleges. What form of organization could bring safety and coherence to an increasingly far-flung academic empire?

Sproul's strategy was to present the University as a single organic institution in which removal of any constituent part would damage the whole. Over time, this aspect of the one-university idea began to evolve. In the mid-1930s, according to Verne Stadtman,

> a subtle shift in the One University concept occurred. . . . Sproul and other admin- istrators began to speak not of just UCLA and Berkeley, but of "two great major campuses, and five others to be conducted as a single institution." The "five others"— Mount Hamilton, Scripps Institution of Oceanography, San Francisco, the Citrus Experiment Station at Riverside, and Davis—had been around before UCLA was established, but they were generally regarded as auxiliary facilities of the Berkeley campus and not as separate entities.[17]

Sproul dedicated himself to driving home this message to the legislature, the public, and the various economic and industrial interests in the state: the Univer- sity of California was a single institution. More, its founders had always intended it to be a single institution. As Sproul put it in one of many similar speeches:

> That we have today a truly great University on . . . campuses scattered over almost the whole length and breadth of California, is a direct result of the planting of fertile and right growing seeds by a handful of men who came to our State during the days of the Gold Rush. . . . These early leaders, it is interesting to note, had their troubles with sectionalism just as we do today; it was necessary for them to reiterate constantly that they were not interested in a University of San Francisco or a University of Sacra- mento, but in a University of California. . . . When we speak of maintaining the unity of the University of California, we are not referring to some recently coined slogan, manufactured as a matter of political expediency. Instead, we are talking about an ideal that has been part of the University ever since it was established, and which has been transmitted in strength and vigor to each new campus as it developed.[18]

At the same time, Sproul felt it essential to emphasize the symbolic meaning of his office, to make clear to faculty, students, and local campus communities that the University of California was a single university with a single leader—the president. And although his official home was on the Berkeley campus, he made it a practice beginning in 1936 to spend considerable time in residence at UCLA. When the Berkeley and UCLA football teams played each other, Sproul sat on one side for the first half and then took a ceremonial walk across the field to finish the game on the other. In a 1976 oral history his assistant, Agnes Roddy Robb, said that Sproul "envisaged the University ultimately, I think, as being somewhat like the British Empire, with a king or queen who would be the symbol of the singleness of the University, and the various campuses similar to the dominions of the Brit- ish Empire. He pretty closely followed that; he was the head, not a figure head, but definitely the symbol of the University."[19]

Sproul did not believe that the University could be unified on the basis of geography. It was too big and too scattered. In 1937 he presented the Regents with a report on the organization of UC and proposed three alternatives: a centralized administration with one president and "such vice presidents as are necessary"; a decentralized university, again with a number of vice presidents; and separation into two independent universities, one in the north and one in the south. Sproul reminded the Regents that in December 1935 he had recommended that the University follow the advice of a recent report on California higher education and agree to incorporate the state colleges, "believing that such a plan would be the best of all the possibilities open to the University." The Regents felt the existing campuses were more than enough responsibility, however, and rejected this idea. Of the three alternatives put before them, they approved the first: a centralized administration with strong presidential control of the details of campus decisions and operations.[20]

As Sproul considered the internal problem of uniting the university, he came to feel that the solution was to think of the organization not in terms of separate campuses but in terms of disciplines. Groups of related academic fields—letters, social sciences, natural sciences, and arts—at both Berkeley and UCLA would each report to a University-wide vice president, who would travel back and forth between the campuses to keep in touch with faculty and departmental needs. Sproul called this "the functional university," and the organizational model was agriculture. Just as agricultural programs at Davis, Berkeley, Riverside, and Los Angeles reported to a single statewide official, so, under Sproul's plan, would the various disciplinary fields throughout the University, whatever their location. Monroe Deutsch, Sproul's vice president at the Berkeley campus, wrote him a series of passionate, handwritten letters opposing the president's fixation on organizing UC along functional lines. A Latin professor turned administrator—in fact he had been Sproul's Latin teacher—Deutsch was especially disturbed by the prospect of a clutch of peripatetic vice presidents. "Each Vice President will presumably have to have an office—and a staff—on the Berkeley and Los Angeles campus. . . . When I think of the constant duplication of reports and letters for each office and the probability that not infrequently important correspondence will be in the other office—as has certainly been the case with the President—I feel that endless confusion will result."[21] Although Sproul's grand design was never fully realized, his approach led to centralizing authority over most key academic and administrative matters in the president or the comptroller, who at that time reported directly to the Regents.

The administrative contradictions and difficulties this organizational scheme engendered continued to mount, along with the burden on the president. None of this shook Sproul's belief in his vision of the functional university. In 1947 he was offered the presidency of Columbia University. He told the Regents that before he made a decision, he had two questions to ask them. Did they want him to stay? Would they pledge to safeguard the unity of the University? Yes, the Regents replied to both, adding that "the unity of the University shall be considered sacred."[22] Sproul stayed.

SEPARATING OUT

In 1948 a report on the University's organization conducted by the Public Administration Survey concluded that the problem was "inadequate delegation by the regents to the president; conflicting delegation with respect to business affairs and accounting; insufficient intermediate administrative posts to which the president might delegate; and inadequate major staff assistance to the president."[23] At that time, UC's enrollment was 48,000, with a faculty of 3,200 and an operating budget of $37 million.[24] Although Sproul himself recognized the need for administrative reform, he sat on the report for nine months before sending it to the Regents. It was to take three more years and regental pressure before the chancellorship was established at UCLA and Berkeley in 1951.[25]

Even so, Sproul managed to remain in charge, in fact if not in name. Clark Kerr, the first chancellor of the Berkeley campus, found himself decidedly underemployed during his time in office. Having suffered for years under Sproul's possessive presidential eye, Kerr was determined to make the chancellors masters in their own house when he became president in 1958. In the late fifties and early sixties, he initiated a wave of decentralization in which approximately three-fourths of the Office of the President's staff—750 of 1,025—were reassigned to the campuses.[26] Before the decision to decentralize, every transfer of funds from one account to another in the University of California had to be approved in the Office of the President; afterward, 80 percent of these transactions were handled on the campuses.[27] More than anyone else, Kerr was responsible for redefining the relationship between the Office of the President and the campuses, and in the process he transformed UC from an institution run by a few at the center to one of distributed power and responsibility. "In this administration, the burden of proof will always rest with the centralizers," he declared in his 1958 inaugural remarks at UCLA.[28]

This reorganization, Kerr later wrote in language suggestive of the struggles of early American federalism, changed the University from a "consolidated nation state" to a "federation of campuses" while saving it from disintegrating into a weak "confederation."[29] In the process, he thought he had solved all the problems caused by the extreme concentration of authority in the Sproul presidency. He soon had occasion to revisit that conclusion.

In 1960 he recruited Franklin Murphy, a physician-administrator from the University of Kansas, to be UCLA chancellor. Murphy had enjoyed a much freer rein in Kansas than he found in Los Angeles. He was a man whose sense of outrage was easily ignited, and he battled unceasingly with Kerr throughout much of the 1960s—about authority over tenure decisions, about who could talk to Regents, about whether the president or the chancellor had the right to lead in a UCLA academic procession, even about whether the president had an obligation to obtain permission from the chancellor before setting foot on campus. Murphy's anger must have come as something of a shock to Kerr, the master decentralizer; but in a way quite independent of Murphy as an individual, it represented UCLA's experience in the multicampus UC system. Skirmishes with Murphy over symbolic issues were especially bitter, centering on who should have precedence during campus ceremonial events, such as visits from foreign dignitaries. Kerr's experience with the UCLA chancellor, and several other clashes with chancellors, brought home the limits of any administrative reorganization, however well planned and orchestrated. By 1965, as he later wrote,

> the president had, and exercised, great influence but kept almost no final item-by-item authority over the campuses. Thus, I thought, the governance issue was settled for all time. . . . How wrong I was. What I came to realize only slowly was that to some chancellors use of the tools of authority meant use of all of its symbols as well; that nearly all chancellors would welcome both in their entirety; and that in micro-battles over power—which are everywhere and all the time—there is never a final solution.[30]

The president who had done so much to liberate chancellors had some retrospective doubts about the unprecedented authority he had delegated to them. Pondering the changes in UC governance over the previous half century in his 2001 memoirs, he perceived a gradual shift in the balance of power from the Office of the President to the campuses, from the president to the chancellors. "The reforms I largely led from 1952 to 1966," he said, "were directed too much, I now think, at empowering the chancellors and too little at building a Madisonian system of checks and balances. . . . I paid too little attention to how their [the chancellors'] aspirations might outrun reasonable attainments."[31]

ONE UNIVERSITY THEN AND NOW

This brief excursion into the struggle between two leaders is intended, first, to clarify not only what divided them but also what they had in common. They shared a belief in the one-university ideal and its organizational implications: a strong president with a symbolic role reinforcing internal and external awareness of UC as an indivisible institution and (despite Kerr's disclaimers of presidential power) an Office of the President with the professional staff and analytical capabilities to ensure campus compliance with policy and the president's ability to act in the interests of the University as a whole.[32] For both Sproul and Kerr, this meant a center strong enough to counter the centrifugal forces inherent in a huge multicampus system.

The second purpose of this discussion is to give some context for thinking about the very different world in which the one-university model now exists. Kerr's successful breakup of Sproul's empire was done in the service of creating a modern university about to grow into new areas of the state with three new campuses—Santa Cruz, Irvine, and San Diego—and thousands of new students. A major assignment of the Office of the President was to get these additional campuses started—an operational responsibility if ever there was one—and the state provided the money to do it. The guiding assumption of this expansion was the one-university idea that the young campuses would have the resources to begin the climb toward the academic standards of Berkeley and UCLA.

By 1975, President David Saxon believed, the University's campuses fell into two major categories: the mature campuses—Berkeley, Los Angeles, and, to a great extent, Davis and San Francisco—and the campuses in a state of "interrupted development" because of the University's budget problems at the time—Irvine, Riverside, San Diego, Santa Barbara, and Santa Cruz. The organizational report he commissioned in 1976, "Systemwide Leadership"—another call for greater decentralization—was intended to address what Saxon considered the Office of the President's tendency to veer between exercising too much or too little control, without taking sufficient account of each campus's unique circumstances and stage of development.[33]

Differences in quality among the campuses remain today, but these differences have shrunk over the decades since Saxon's time, as three National Research Council studies of graduate program quality have shown.[34] Davis, Irvine, Santa Barbara, and San Diego have joined Berkeley and UCLA as members of the Association of American Universities; no other university system comes close to UC's record-setting six AAU campuses. This steady improvement of academic quality systemwide is what the one-university model envisioned and striking evidence of its success. Although Kerr saw chancellorial ambition as the leading cause of a slow shift of power away from the Office of the President to the campuses, that phenomenon—if it has indeed occurred—can just as easily be seen as a reflection of growing campus size, distinction, and maturity. But does this campus evolution also work against a sense of common stake in the university as a whole? The entrepreneurial university, with its expanding ties to industry, its spinoffs, its emphasis on rewarding personal and campus initiative, may not be the most hospitable environment for the idea that the larger university matters more than the individual parts.

Certainly many would disagree with Kerr's assertion that chancellors and campuses have acquired too much independence. Atkinson is among them. The changes he made in how the Office of the President allocates enrollment and over-head reimbursement funds, salary and inflation increases, constituted a major transfer of budget authority to the campuses. His reservations about the ceremo-nial and symbolic aspect of the president's role, so important to Sproul and a num-ber of later presidents, led him to delegate more symbolic responsibility to the chancellors as well. Atkinson was a believer in the one-university paradigm, but his was a more open and fluid version of Kerr's federation, with a little more em-phasis on the variety than on the unity of the University. UC, he wrote in 1996, is "a collection of ten research universities . . . not all identical and not all moving toward the same template."[35]

The emphasis on removing operational activities from the Office of the Presi-dent, a major theme of the restructuring that began in 2007, is the latest manifesta-tion of the long decentralizing trend within UC. The complexities of administering a large research university system, however, do not slip easily into a neat division of responsibility between operational activities (campuses) and policy (UCOP). Historically, the Office of the President, along with its primary responsibility for University-wide policy, has taken on operational activities when that approach made fiscal, organizational, or managerial sense. One of the central administra-tion's most important and least recognized functions—acting as a buffer between the campuses and various external critics and agencies, including the state and federal governments—has operational as well as policy dimensions. In carrying out this role, the Office of the President has deflected many shocks that would otherwise reverberate on the campuses.

In the 1970s and 1980s the exuberant growth of state and federal reporting regulations and the passage of new collective bargaining laws created their own rationale for a central response in some areas to meet legal requirements or avoid duplication of effort on the campuses. Other UCOP operational activities were legacies of choices made long ago—the decision that the UC system would have its own retirement system, for example, and that the Office of the President would administer a program of benefits for all retired faculty and staff. Some programs were originally located in the Office of the President because of their University-wide character (student admissions and financial aid, for example, as well as re-search grant programs, mostly in the health sciences, for which various campuses compete). Even after the 2007 restructuring, 55 percent of UCOP's budget was dedicated to systemwide academic programs.[36]

The major theme of organizational studies, as noted earlier, has been the push for more decentralization and chancellorial discretion, not less. "Decentraliza-tion not only allows for more policy leadership at the executive and board levels," the Transition Team wrote in its 1993 report, "but it also puts decision-making closer to the operational level, where more informed choices can be made."[37] But even the Transition Team's recommendations for greater decentralization, many of them implemented during the administration of Jack Peltason (1992–95), co-existed with the practice of "earned delegation" from the Office of the President, whereby campuses were expected to demonstrate their ability to devote the necessary resources and expertise in areas such as technology transfer before they were delegated authority for them. As a 1991 report put it, "The principle of *selective centralization* is a corollary theme [along with the principle of decentralization] which has also guided the evolution of the Office of the President."[38] The division of labor and authority between the Office of the President and the campuses has reflected both administrative imperatives and a pragmatic willingness to cross the boundary between policy and operations when that was in the best interests of the University.

However organized, the Office of the President must have the standing and resources to represent the interests of the University of California as a whole. The institutional assumption has long been that these interests are best served by the one-university principle, for reasons that date back to Sproul and that have been explored here. California gains from the geographic distribution of high-quality university campuses, each with its own character but the same mission, throughout the state. The University itself is stronger as a unified system of campuses than as ten separate institutions vying for public support and government funds. New campuses find room for realizing their aspirations and a legacy of academic quality that acts as a magnet for talented faculty and students.

As every UC president who has lived through a budget crisis can attest, the most potent threat to the one-university idea is the politics of scarcity. It unleashes fierce competition for resources and the spirit of suspicion, distrust, and jealousy Sproul warned about long ago. Although his functional university was not the answer, his analysis of the problem remains relevant. Multicampus institutions must deal regularly with external threats and pressures that threaten their goals, their institutional integrity, and their future. Within the system, campuses compete with each other for students, faculty, facilities, money, and prestige. The one-university idea has been a way of moderating competition and encouraging cooperation.

Some of the proposals that have emerged in the wake of current budgetary stress underscore closer cooperation among campuses and the advantages of leveraging UC's potential as a system. Others—from a two-tier university with differential student fees to the request by the dean of a campus school of management to sever its financial link to UC and go private—suggest that in some parts of the University the temptation to go one's own way is considerable. Hard times offer campuses the opportunity to argue for greater independence from the system and less oversight. To date, the strongest statements of support for the one-university principle have come from the University-wide Academic Senate. The Senate has gone on record as opposing campus stratification and restating its "longstanding belief that UC's commitment to one University and to treatment of its ten campuses as inherently equal is responsible for California's uniquely great university."[39]

California's entrenched budget crisis has made it clear that a fundamental rethinking of all aspects of the University's organization and future path is inevitable—indeed it is already under way. A decision will have to be made about the appropriate balance between the University's historical values of authority at the center and independence on the campuses. The issue is not simply decentralization—the case for its utility was made long ago—but the future of the one-university model. The question is whether this paradigm still applies at this stage of the University's development and in today's environment of unprecedented financial turmoil.

If there were a new organizing idea to replace one university, what would it be? James G. March, a well-known scholar of organization theory, has written about the growing influence of markets on thinking about institutions, including universities, in the past twenty years. The fall of the Soviet Union in 1991, March says, seemed the definitive validation of market systems and private sector strategies. Business schools, rather than political science or sociology departments, have become the locus of much of the research on organizations in recent years.[40] In the California context, the likeliest candidate to replace the one-university idea is the entrepreneurial university, which offers a more comprehensive framework than the bottom-line business model approach but also embodies some of the same leading proclivities of our time—the still-potent deregulatory spirit and the emphasis on competition and individual achievement. And, it should be added, the conviction that research universities have a natural role in the marketplace.

The new University of California that emerges on the other side of today's fiscal and internal stress will be strongly influenced by these forces. They are likely to bring pressures to take decentralization far beyond anything envisioned by the one-university idea and make short work of the notion that all campuses are "inherently equal." Campuses and chancellors will have considerably more influence in the running of the UC system, the Office of the President less, with unknown implications for the role of future presidents. The trend has already begun. If it has dissenters, they have yet to be heard from.

The one-university idea has been a brilliant strategy for presenting a united front in an uncertain political world, a force for internal coherence and cohesion, an act of collective imagination that created a great university system. If its time has come and gone, the burden of proof rests with its critics.

Regents' Resolutions SP-1, SP-2, and RE-28

SP-1

Board of Regents
July 20, 1995
POLICY ENSURING EQUAL TREATMENT—ADMISSIONS

WHEREAS, Governor Pete Wilson, on June 1, 1995, issued Executive Order W 124–95 to "End Preferential Treatment and to Promote Individual Opportunity Based on Merit"; and

WHEREAS, paragraph seven of that order requests the University of California to "take all necessary action to comply with the intent and the requirements of this executive order"; and

WHEREAS, in January 1995, the University initiated a review of its policies and practices, the results of which support many of the findings and conclusions of Governor Wilson; and

WHEREAS, the University of California Board of Regents believes that it is in the best interest of the University to take relevant actions to develop and support programs which will have the effect of increasing the eligibility rate of groups which are "underrepresented" in the University's pool of applicants as compared to their percentages in California's graduating high school classes and to which reference is made in Section 4;

NOW, THEREFORE, BE IT RESOLVED AS FOLLOWS:

Section 1. The Chairman of the Board, with the consultation of the President, shall appoint a task force representative of the business community, students, the University, other segments of education, and organizations currently engaged in academic "outreach." The responsibility of this group shall be to develop proposals for new directions and increased funding for the Board of Regents to increase the eligibility rate of those currently identified in Section 4. The final report of this task force shall be presented to the Board of Regents within six months after its creation.

Section 2. Effective January 1, 1997, the University of California shall not use race, religion, sex, color, ethnicity, or national origin as criteria for admission to the University or to any program of study.

Section 3. Effective January 1, 1997, the University of California shall not use race, religion, sex, color, ethnicity, or national origin as criteria for "admissions in exception" to UC-eligibility requirements.

Section 4. The President shall confer with the Academic Senate of the University of California to develop supplemental criteria for consideration by the Board of Regents which shall be consistent with Section 2. In developing such criteria, which shall provide reasonable assurances that the applicant will successfully complete his or her course of study, consideration shall be given to individuals who, despite having suffered disadvantage economically or in terms of their social environment (such as an abusive or otherwise dysfunctional home or a neighborhood of unwholesome or antisocial influences), have nonetheless demonstrated sufficient character and determination in overcoming obstacles to warrant confidence that the applicant can pursue a course of study to successful completion, provided that any student admitted under this section must be academically eligible for admission.

Section 5. Effective January 1, 1997, not less than fifty (50) percent and not more than seventy-five (75) percent of any entering class on any campus shall be admitted solely on the basis of academic achievement.

Section 6. Nothing in Section 2 shall prohibit any action which is strictly necessary to establish or maintain eligibility for any federal or state program, where ineligibility would result in a loss of federal or state funds to the University.

Section 7. Nothing in Section 2 shall prohibit the University from taking appropriate action to remedy specific, documented cases of discrimination by the University, provided that such actions are expressly and specifically approved by the Board of Regents or taken pursuant to a final order of a court or administrative agency of competent jurisdiction. Nothing in this section shall interfere with the customary practices of the University with regard to the settlement of claims against the University relating to discrimination.

Section 8. The President of the University shall periodically report to the Board of Regents detailing progress to implement the provisions of this resolution.

Section 9. Believing California's diversity to be an asset, we adopt this statement: Because individual members of all of California's diverse races have the intelligence and capacity to succeed at the University of California, this policy will achieve a UC population that reflects this state's diversity through the preparation and empowerment of all students in this state to succeed rather than through a system of artificial preferences.

SP-2

Board of Regents
July 20, 1995
POLICY ENSURING EQUAL TREATMENT—EMPLOYMENT AND CONTRACTING
WHEREAS, Governor Pete Wilson, on June 1, 1995, issued Executive Order W 124-95 to "End Preferential Treatment and to Promote Individual Opportunity Based on Merit"; and

WHEREAS, paragraph seven of that order requests the University of California to "take all necessary action to comply with the intent and the requirements of this executive order"; and

WHEREAS, in January 1995, the University initiated a review of its policies and practices, the results of which support many of the findings and conclusions of Governor Wilson;

NOW, THEREFORE, BE IT RESOLVED AS FOLLOWS:

Section 1. Effective January 1, 1996, the University of California shall not use race, religion, sex, color, ethnicity, or national origin as criteria in its employment and contracting practices.

Section 2. The President of the University of California is directed to oversee a system-wide evaluation of the University's hiring and contracting practices to identify what actions need to be taken to ensure that all persons have equal access to job competitions, contracts, and other business and employment opportunities of the University. A report and recommendations to accomplish this objective shall be presented to the Board of Regents before December 31, 1996.

Section 3. Nothing in Section 1 shall prohibit any action which is strictly necessary to establish or maintain eligibility for any federal or state program, where ineligibility would result in a loss of federal or state funds to the University.

Section 4. Nothing in Section 1 shall prohibit the University from taking appropriate action to remedy specific, documented cases of discrimination by the University, provided that such actions are expressly and specifically approved by the Board of Regents or taken pursuant to a final order of a court or administrative agency of competent jurisdiction. Nothing in this section shall interfere with the customary practices of the University with regard to the settlement of claims against the University relating to discrimination.

Section 5. Believing California's diversity to be an asset, we adopt this statement: Because individual members of all of California's diverse races have the intelligence and capacity to succeed at the University of California, this policy will achieve a UC population that reflects this state's diversity through the preparation and empowerment of all students in this state to succeed rather than through a system of artificial preferences.

RE-28

Board of Regents
May 16, 2001
FUTURE ADMISSIONS, EMPLOYMENT, AND CONTRACTING POLICIES—RESO-LUTION RESCINDING SP-1 AND SP-2

WHEREAS, on July 20, 1995, The Regents of the University of California adopted SP-1, a resolution that prohibited the consideration of race, religion, sex, color, ethnicity, or national origin as criteria for admission to the University or to any program of study, and SP-2, a resolution that prohibited the consideration of the same attributes in the University's employment and contracting practices; and

WHEREAS, on November 6, 1996, the voters of California passed Proposition 209 which was incorporated into the California Constitution as Article 1, Section 31; and

WHEREAS, On February 15, 2001, President Atkinson requested that the Academic Senate conduct a comprehensive review of the University's admissions policies including, among other issues, the use of quantitative formulas, and provide recommendations to The Regents.

It is anticipated that the admissions review initiated by President Atkinson and currently under way by the Academic Senate, will be completed in calendar year 2001; and

WHEREAS, some individuals perceive that the University does not welcome their enrollment at its campuses;

NOW, THEREFORE, BE IT RESOLVED THAT SP-1 AND SP-2 ARE RESCINDED BY THIS RESOLUTION, AND

A. That the University has complied with and will be governed by Article 1, Section 31 of the California Constitution by treating all students equally in the admissions process without regard to their race, sex, color, ethnicity or national origin, and by treating employees and contractors similarly.

B. That the University shall seek out and enroll, on each of its campuses, a student body that demonstrates high academic achievement or exceptional personal talent and that encompasses the broad diversity of backgrounds characteristic of California. ·

C. In keeping with longstanding Regents' policy, The Regents reaffirm that the Academic Senate shall determine the conditions for admission to the University, subject to the approval of The Regents, as provided in Standing Order 105.2.

D. Pending any changes which The Regents might approve, the provisions for admission shall be those outlined in the Guidelines for Implementation of University Policy on Undergraduate Admissions, which were adopted in July 1996 and revised in May 2000.

E. That the University shall have programs available to assist in the retention of all students so as to assure that they successfully complete their education.

F. That the University's current commitment to outreach programs for California's public elementary and secondary school students shall be pursued on a long-term basis to improve the early educational preparation of students who will seek a college education in the future.

G. That the University shall undertake new initiatives to improve the transfer of academically prepared students from California's Community Colleges to the University.

Atkinson Presidency Timeline

Date	Event
Date	*Event*
Aug. 1995	The Regents appoint Richard C. Atkinson president of the University of California, effective October 1, 1995.
Oct. 1995	National Research Council releases "Research-Doctorate Programs in the United States," a comprehensive study of the quality of Ph.D. programs in American universities. More than half of UC's 229 graduate programs were ranked in the top twenty in the nation. When averages were computed for individual universities, Berkeley ranked first in the nation, San Diego tenth, and Los Angeles twelfth; the other nine institutions in the top twelve were all private universities.
Oct. 1995	Three UC faculty members awarded the Nobel Prize: Frederick Reines (Physics, Irvine); F. Sherwood Rowland (Chemistry, Irvine); Paul Crutzen (Chemistry, San Diego).
Oct. 1995	Inauguration of Henry Yang as fifth chancellor of UC Santa Barbara.
Jan. 1996	Industry-University Cooperative Research Program (IUCRP) established.
Mar. 1996	Regents authorize construction of new headquarters in Oakland for the Office of the President.
Apr. 1996	M. R. C. Greenwood appointed sixth chancellor of UC Santa Cruz.
Apr. 1996	Robert C. Dynes appointed sixth chancellor of UC San Diego.
June 1996	UC and the Los Alamos National Laboratory establish an office in northern New Mexico to strengthen relationships with regional communities.
Aug. 1996	President Atkinson announces a new methodology for allocating state funds to the campuses. Among the changes are the following: most allocations to the campuses to be made as a single block of funds; indirect cost reimbursements to be returned to the campuses on the basis of how the dollars are

generated; campuses to assume greater flexibility and responsibility for how funds are spent.

Aug. 1996   Commission on the Future of Medical Education appointed (Charles Wilson, M.D., chair).

Oct. 1996   Davis and Irvine campuses invited to join the Association of American Universities, bringing UC's membership to six campuses—the only university system in the nation with more than one AAU member.

Jan. 1997   The UC Flood and Emergency Resource Task Force established to assist the state in dealing with natural disasters.

Jan. 1997   President's Retreat on UC's Relationships with Industry in Research and Technology Transfer held at UCLA.

Mar. 1997   Robert M. Berdahl appointed eighth chancellor of UC Berkeley.

Mar. 1997   Albert Carnesale appointed fifth chancellor of UCLA.

Mar. 1997   All-University Conference on Teaching and Learning Technologies held at UCLA.

Apr. 1997   Haile T. Debas appointed seventh chancellor of UC San Francisco for 1997–98.

Apr. 1997   Establishment of the Board on Research and Economic Development, with representatives from the private sector, to advise on future directions of the Industry-University Cooperative Research Program.

May 1997   Regents approve Mission Bay site for major expansion of UC San Francisco.

May 1997   UC joins with the California State University, the California Institute of Technology, Stanford University, and the University of Southern California in establishing the Corporation for Education Network Initiatives in California (CENIC) to design and deploy CalREN-2, an advanced electronic superhighway to link California's universities to the national high-speed network.

May 1997   UC and its affiliated national laboratories produce more research leading to patented inventions than any other public or private research university or laboratory in the nation, according to a study by the National Science Foundation.

June 1997   Hugh Graham presentation to the Regents on his study (with Nancy Diamond), *The Rise of American Research Universities,* which found that the UC system leads the nation in high-quality research and productivity among public universities.

July 1997   Regents approve the Outreach Task Force report.

July 1997   UC and Mexico's National Council on Science and Technology (CONACYT) enter into the most comprehensive research and education collaboration ever established between a US university and Mexico.

Sept. 1997   Regents approve five-year extension of UC's contracts to manage the Department of Energy laboratories at Los Alamos, Livermore, and Berkeley.

Sept. 1997   Regents approve creation of UCSF Stanford Health Care, a merger of the clinical enterprises of UC San Francisco and Stanford University, to sustain the competitiveness of both in the changing health care marketplace.

Oct. 1997   Two UC faculty members awarded the Nobel Prize: Paul D. Boyer (Chemistry, UCLA) and Stanley Prusiner (Physiology or Medicine, UC San Francisco).

Oct. 1997   Report on UC academic planning, "Preparing for the Twenty-First Century."

Oct. 1997   John C. Browne appointed director of the Los Alamos National Laboratory.

Oct. 1997   UC Digital Library established, and Richard Lucier named University Librarian.

Nov. 1997   Pathways, UC's online undergraduate admission information and application network, begins accepting applications.

Nov. 1997   Faculty committee releases academic planning recommendations for UC's tenth campus.

Nov. 1997   Regents approve health benefits for domestic partners of UC faculty and staff.

Nov. 1997   Regents approve 1616 Rhode Island Avenue NW as the site for the UC Washington, DC, Center, to provide space for academic program and research activities and the Office of Federal Governmental Relations, as well as housing for 280 students studying and performing internships in Washington.

Dec. 1997   President Atkinson approves naming of tenth campus, "UC Merced."

Dec. 1997   UC Santa Barbara's School of Environmental Studies is renamed the Donald Bren School of Environmental Science and Management in recognition of a major gift from the Bren Foundation. The Bren gift supports establishment of the University's first program of environmental study integrating natural and social sciences, business, and law curricula.

Jan. 1998   Outreach Action Plan announced at meeting of the Regents.

Jan. 1998   Chancellor Emeritus Karl Pister appointed senior associate to the president (later vice president for outreach) to coordinate UC's systemwide response to the recommendations of the Outreach Task Force report.

Jan. 1998   For the third consecutive year, UC raises a record amount in contributions from alumni and friends, receiving $726 million in 1996–97.

Jan. 1998   Ralph J. Cicerone appointed fourth chancellor of UC Irvine.

Jan. 1998   UC announces applications from nearly 59,000 high school seniors for admission in fall 1998, an 8 percent increase from the previous year and the largest one-year jump in a decade.

Mar. 1998   President's Commission on Agriculture and Natural Resources, a group of agricultural, business, consumer, and governmental leaders, is established to advise the University on issues related to agriculture and natural resources.

Apr. 1998   J. Michael Bishop appointed eighth chancellor of UC San Francisco.

Apr. 1998   Carol Tomlinson-Keasey, vice provost for academic initiatives, is given additional appointment as senior associate to the president for UC Merced.

May 1998   UC Engineering Initiative established, with a goal of a 50 percent increase in the number of engineering and computer science students at UC by 2005.

May 1998   Office of the President relocates to 1111 Franklin Street, Oakland, near the site of UC's predecessor institution, the College of California, founded in 1853 as the Contra Costa Academy.

July 1998   The Master of Advanced Study, a new systemwide degree program offering advanced professional education and liberal studies for working adults, is established.

Oct. 1998   Two UC faculty members and one UC researcher awarded Nobel Prizes: Louis J. Ignarro (Physiology or Medicine, UCLA); Walter Kohn (Chemistry, UC Santa Barbara); Robert B. Laughlin (Physics, Livermore National Laboratory).

Nov. 1998   Governor-elect Gray Davis appoints President Atkinson to his Education Transition Group.

Nov. 1998   President Atkinson announces search for founding chancellor of UC Merced.

Jan. 1999   Governor Davis appoints President Atkinson a member of the governor's delegation to Mexico to strengthen relationships in commerce and education.

Mar. 1999   Regents approve Eligibility in the Local Context, which grants UC freshman eligibility to students in the top 4 percent of all California high schools.

Mar. 1999   California Studies Fellowship Program established at the University-wide Humanities Research Institute to support research and scholarship on the history of California.

Mar. 1999   California House, jointly sponsored by UC and the California Trade and Commerce Agency, established in London to stimulate academic and commercial exchange between the United Kingdom and California.

May 1999   Governor Davis approves a four-year partnership agreement with UC (1999–2000 through 2002–3), committing the state to a 4 percent annual increase in the State General Fund base for enrollment growth, along with budget increases in other areas for specific goals. The Office of the Secretary for Education and the Department of Finance are to assess annually UC's progress in achieving these goals.

May 1999   The University of California Commission on the Humanities is appointed to examine the challenges faced by the humanities and humanities scholars and to recommend ways to address them.

July 1999   Carol Tomlinson-Keasey appointed founding chancellor of UC Merced.

Oct. 1999   UC Medical Student Diversity Task Force created to examine short- and longer-term trends in the admission and enrollment of underrepresented minority students at UC medical schools.

Oct. 1999   Pierce's Disease Task Force established to mobilize the University's scientific and technical expertise to combat Pierce's disease, a threat to the state's wine and grape industries.

Oct. 1999   Stanford University President Gerhard Casper announces that Stanford will withdraw from UCSF Stanford Health Care.

Oct. 1999   At the request of Governor Davis, President Atkinson convenes and chairs the Advisory Group on Low-Level Radioactive Waste Disposal to advise the state of California on options for handling low-level radioactive material.

Nov. 1999   Regents authorize President Atkinson to take the necessary steps to dissolve UCSF Stanford Health Care.

Dec. 1999   Los Alamos National Laboratory scientist Wen Ho Lee arrested for allegedly mishandling nuclear weapons secrets.

Feb. 2000   Veterans Day (November 11) made an official University of California holiday.

May 2000   Cerro Grande fire near Los Alamos National Laboratory destroys over two hundred residential dwellings and forces closing of the laboratory from May 8 to May 22.

May 2000   Governor Davis and UC confirm a partnership agreement to provide the University with a 4 percent annual increase in state general funds, plus support for enrollment growth and other key areas.

June 2000   Missing hard drives found at Los Alamos National Laboratory.

June 2000   UC receives an 18 percent operating budget increase in the 2000–2001 state budget approved by Governor Davis. Capital budget includes $75 million to create three California Institutes for Science and Innovation, which will focus on scientific and engineering research and teaching in fields key to the future of the California economy.

July 2000   UC Institute for Labor and Employment established.

July 2000   Six finalists for California Institutes for Science and Inovation announced:

- Systems Biology (UC Irvine)
- Agricultural Genomics (UC Riverside, UC Davis, UC Berkeley)
- Communications and Information Technology (UC San Diego, UC Irvine)
- Nanosystems (UCLA, UC Santa Barbara)
- Information Technology in the Interest of Society (UC Berkeley, UC Santa Cruz, UC Davis, UC Merced)
- Bioengineering, Biotechnology, and Quantitative Biomedicine (UC San Francisco, UC Berkeley, UC Santa Cruz)

Sept. 2000   Regents approve mandatory student health insurance for undergraduates, making UC the first multicampus university system to adopt such a policy.

Oct. 2000   Three UC faculty members awarded Nobel Prizes: Alan J. Heeger (Chemistry, Santa Barbara); Herbert Kroemer (Physics, Santa Barbara); Daniel L. McFadden (Economics, Berkeley).

Dec. 2000   Governor Davis and President Atkinson announce creation of four California Institutes for Science and Innovation:

- California Institute for Telecommunications and Information Technology (UC San Diego, UC Irvine)
- California Institute for Quantitative Biomedical Sciences (UC San Francisco, UC Berkeley, UC Santa Cruz)

- California NanoSystems Institute (UCLA, UC Santa Barbara)
- California Institute for Information Technology Research in the Interest of Society (UC Berkeley, UC Davis, UC Merced, UC Santa Cruz)

Jan. 2001	Regents approve extension to 2005 of UC's contracts with the Department of Energy to manage the Los Alamos and Livermore National Laboratories.
Feb. 2001	In the Robert H. Atwell Distinguished Lecture at the annual meeting of the American Council on Education, President Atkinson announces two proposals he has asked the Academic Senate of the University of California to consider: (1) that UC eliminate aptitude tests as a requirement for admission and (2) that the University move away from its tiered system of admissions and toward procedures that look at applicants in a more comprehensive way.
Mar. 2001	Governor Davis, Mexico President Vicente Fox, and President Atkinson inaugurate the high-speed Internet2 link between California and Mexico.
May 2001	Regents unanimously approve RE-28, which rescinds SP-1 and SP-2 and reaffirms the University's commitment to a diverse student body and to shared governance in determining admissions criteria.
July 2001	In an address to the annual meeting at the Council for Advancement and Support of Education, President Atkinson discusses his proposals for change in UC admissions policies: Eligibility in the Local Context, Dual Admissions, and replacement of the SAT I with standardized tests tied to the high school curriculum.
Oct. 2001	Nobel Prize awarded to George Akerlof (Economics, Berkeley).
Oct. 2001	In response to Governor Davis's executive order following the September 11 terrorist attacks, UC provides an inventory of its research and expertise that could be useful to the state in combating terrorist threats.
Oct. 2001	Governor Davis asks all state-funded programs to consider options for cuts of up to 15 percent in light of California's economic downturn.
Nov. 2001	Regents approve admissions policy instituting comprehensive review of UC undergraduate applicants.
Nov. 2001	UC and the California State University agree to create a joint board to develop, fund, and expedite proposals for a joint doctorate in education (Ed.D.) program.
Dec. 2001	In follow-up to the 1997 UC-CONACYT agreement to foster educational and research cooperation, UC MEXUS and the California Council on Science and Technology present a workshop on technology transfer for representatives from Mexico's CONACYT and Mexican universities and industry.
Jan. 2002	UC's Commission on the Growth and Support of Graduate Education concludes that to serve California's needs, UC must increase graduate student enrollment by at least 11,000 students (a nearly 50 percent increase).
Jan. 2002	Board of Admissions and Relations with Schools issues discussion paper recommending the use of a core achievement examination in admissions covering mastery of the fundamental disciplines needed for University-level work.

Feb. 2002	The US District Court names UC as lead plaintiff in the shareholders' class-action lawsuit against senior executives of the Enron Corporation and the accounting firm of Arthur Andersen.
Apr. 2002	UC files a consolidated complaint in the US District Court, adding nine financial institutions, two law firms, and other new individual defendants in its lawsuit against senior executives of the Enron Corporation and Arthur Andersen.
Apr. 2002	UC recalls its Education Abroad Program students in Israel as a result of escalated violence in the Middle East.
Apr. 2002	France Cordova named seventh chancellor of UC Riverside.
Apr. 2002	Governor Davis signs legislation providing funding for the California Institutes for Science and Innovation and for construction of the first classroom building at UC Merced.
May 2002	UC Washington Center officially dedicated.
May 2002	University-wide Assembly of the Academic Senate votes 47–0 (with one abstention) to approve the Board of Admissions and Relations with Schools' recommendation to use a core achievement examination in admissions.
June 2002	Michael R. Anastasio appointed ninth director of the Lawrence Livermore National Laboratory.
June 2002	UC suspends its fall 2002 Education Abroad Program in India as a result of mounting tensions between India and Pakistan.
June 2002	Trustees of the College Board vote to develop a new SAT I that will be in accord with the specifications developed earlier in the year by UC's Board of Admissions and Relations with Schools.
June 2002	César Chávez Day in March officially designated a University-wide holiday to honor the leader of the United Farm Workers.
July 2002	UC and various sister institutions announce the creation of the Institute for Complex Adaptive Matter—an international multicampus organization to promote transdisciplinary collaborations between physical and biological scientists worldwide.
Aug. 2002	President Atkinson convenes a forum of experts to explore issues of academic standards and academic freedom, free speech, and constitutional law to guide the University on the subject of standards for course descriptions.
Sept. 2002	Lawrence Livermore National Laboratory marks fiftieth anniversary of its founding.
Sept. 2002	UC San Diego's Skaggs School of Pharmacy and Pharmaceutical Sciences welcomes its first class of twenty-five Doctor of Pharmacy students.
Oct. 2002	Carol Tomlinson-Keasey inaugurated as first chancellor of UC Merced.
Nov. 2002	President Atkinson announces his intention to retire in October 2003.
Nov. 2002	Board of Admissions and Relations with Schools issues a report concluding that comprehensive review of freshman applicants, begun in November 2001, was successfully implemented and maintains standards expected of students admitted to UC.

Dec. 2002   Governor Davis proposes $74 million in mid-year funding cuts for UC in response to a state budget deficit estimated at more than $21 billion.

Dec. 2002   A special review team appointed in November by President Atkinson recommends nine actions LANL should take regarding allegations of mishandling of government property and other business practice issues.

Dec. 2002   The Board of Regents adopts mid-year cuts in noninstructional areas of the University's budget and approves a $135-per-quarter student fee increase effective in the spring 2003 term, the first increase in mandatory systemwide student fees in eight years.

Jan. 2003   John C. Browne resigns as director of the Los Alamos National Laboratory. George P. Nanos appointed interim director.

Jan. 2003   Governor Davis proposes nearly $300 million in new state funding cuts for UC as part of his 2003–4 state budget proposal.

May 2003   President Atkinson, Senior Vice President Bruce Darling, Vice President Anne Broome, and University Auditor Patrick Reed testify before the House Energy and Commerce Committee's Subcommittee on Oversight and Investigations on issues related to the Los Alamos National Laboratory.

May 2003   The National Science Board selects President Atkinson to receive the Vannevar Bush Award for his contributions to the American scientific enterprise.

May 2003   Governor Davis's May revision proposes no additional cuts for the University of California beyond the $300 million imposed in January.

May 2003   The Board of Regents votes 15–3, with one abstention, to oppose a ballot initiative, Classification by Race, Ethnicity, Color, or National Origin, that would prohibit the use of racial classification by local governments and public entities. The initiative later fails at the polls.

June 2003   Regents appoint Robert C. Dynes as eighteenth president of the University.

July 2003   In the face of a deepening state budget crisis, the Regents vote to raise 2003–4 student fees by 25 percent and to authorize President Atkinson to raise them by 30 percent if the state's budget situation requires it.

July 2003   Regents approve amendment to the Faculty Code of Conduct prohibiting faculty from entering into consensual romantic or sexual relationships with any student for whom the faculty member has, or is likely to have, academic responsibility.

July 2003   Regents approve changes in the University's policy on admissions, effective in 2006, to align freshman admissions tests more closely to the high school curriculum.

July 2003   George P. Nanos appointed seventh director of the Los Alamos National Laboratory.

July 2003   California Legislature adopts a 2003–4 state budget that requires deep cuts in noninstructional programs at UC, a 30 percent student fee increase, a one-year delay in the opening of UC Merced, and no funding for salary increases for faculty and staff. The legislature also indicates that the state will not provide funding in 2004–5 for student enrollment growth, employee salary increases, or other inflationary cost increases at UC.

Aug. 2003   UC and Elias Technologies, Inc., win a verdict against Microsoft Corporation in a patent infringement suit and are awarded $520 million in damages.

Sept. 2003   The Board of Admissions and Relations with Schools issues a report indicating the measures of academic achievement have grown stronger under the comprehensive review policy. The proportion of students admitted to selective campuses from low-income families, families with no previous experience with college, low-performing schools, and rural areas is also higher than it was before the policy was implemented in 2001.

Oct. 2003   President Atkinson retires as seventeenth president of the University of California.

APPENDIX 3

University of California Indicators, 1995–2003

TABLE 1 Student and Faculty-Related Trends

	Undergradute and Graduate Enrollment	Undergraduate Tuition and Fees	Student Financial Aid (in millions)[a]	Outreach Funding (in millions)[b]	Faculty Salaries: Percentage of Market[c]
1995–96	154,198	$4,139	$484.7	$ 18.8	93.6
1996–97	155,387	$4,166	$513.3	$ 28.4	96.9
1997–98	157,811	$4,212	$533.2	$ 32.5	99.2
1998–99	161,400	$4,037	$569.5	$ 76.8	99.0
1999–2000	165,900	$3,903	$590.8	$ 98.5	99.0
2000–2001	171,245	$3,964	$647.7	$184.0	99.6
2001–2	185,304	$3,859	$730.0	$177.3	97.2
2002–3	196,188	$4,287	$789.7	$ 91.9	95.9
2003–4	201,896	$5,530	$976.0	$ 36.7	93.9

SOURCE: University of California Office of the President except as noted.

[a]Excludes student loans and work study.

[b]State and UC fund sources and all programs (student-centered and K–12 Professional Development programs). Excludes federal, foundation, and private funds.

[c]Figures from California Postsecondary Education Commission Faculty Salaries reports. Market represented by eight comparison institutions: Harvard University, MIT, Stanford University, State University of New York at Buffalo, University of Illinois, University of Michigan, University of Virginia, and Yale University.

TABLE 2 Budget and Revenue Trends

	Total Funding (in billions)	State General Funds (in billions)[a]	Federal Research Funds (in billions)[b]	DOE Labs (in billions)[c]	Capital Outlay (in millions)	Private Gifts (in millions)
1995–96	$10.4	$1.9	$1.1	$2.3	$ 509.5	$ 608.0
1996–97	$11.1	$2.1	$1.1	$2.5	$ 546.9	$ 695.8
1997–98	$11.6	$2.2	$1.2	$2.7	$ 583.9	$ 704.4
1998–99	$12.7	$2.5	$1.3	$3.0	$1,797.0	$ 829.3
1999–2000	$13.5	$2.7	$1.5	$2.0	$1,129.3	$ 954.9
2000–2001	$14.9	$3.2	$1.6	$3.1	$2,102.6	$1,022.5
2001–2	$16.1	$3.3	$1.7	$3.6	$1,813.5	$1,011.6
2002–3	$17.4	$3.2	$2.0	$4.1	$1,898.0	$1,115.0
2003–4	$18.1	$2.9	$2.2	$4.1	$1,005.5	$1,033.2

SOURCE: University of California Office of the President except as noted.

[a]Figures from governor's budgets.

[b]Includes indirect cost recovery funding.

[c]US Department of Energy Laboratories at Berkeley, Livermore, and Los Alamos.

TABLE 3 Underrepresented Minority (URM) Enrollment Trends

	Fall 1995	Fall 1996	Fall 1997	Fall 1998	Fall 1999	Fall 2000	Fall 2001	Fall 2002	Fall 2003
American Indian	1,240	1,234	1,201	1,155	1,046	920	908	936	908
African American	5,016	4,972	5,003	4,764	4,533	4,478	4,452	4,629	4,846
Chicano/Latino	17,024	17,281	17,195	16,978	17,052	17,402	18,633	20,048	21,634
Total URM	*23,280*	*23,487*	*23,399*	*22,897*	*22,631*	*22,800*	*23,993*	*25,613*	*27,388*
Total University[a]	*116,862*	*118,885*	*121,467*	*121,586*	*124,710*	*128,129*	*133,936*	*140,830*	*144,947*
American Indian	1.1%	1.0%	1.0%	0.9%	0.8%	0.7%	0.7%	0.7%	0.6%
African American	4.3%	4.2%	4.1%	3.9%	3.6%	3.5%	3.3%	3.3%	3.3%
Chicano/Latino	14.6%	14.5%	14.2%	14.0%	13.7%	13.6%	13.9%	14.2%	14.9%
Total URM	*19.9%*	*19.8%*	*19.3%*	*18.8%*	*18.1%*	*17.8%*	*17.9%*	*18.2%*	*18.9%*

SOURCE: University of California Office of the President.
[a]Excludes international students and students of unknown race/ethnicity.

NOTES

ABOUT THIS BOOK

1. Peter Schrag, *Paradise Lost: California's Experience, America's Future* (New York: New Press, 1998), p. 23.

2. Reprinted with permission of the publisher from *The Uses of the University*, Fifth Edition, by Clark Kerr, Cambridge, Mass.: Harvard University Press, Copyright © 1963, 1972, 1982, 1995, 2001 by the President and Fellows of Harvard College. Copyright © renewed 1991 by Clark Kerr.

3. Judith Iglehart, "Balancing the University of California's Academic Mission with Public and Private Research Needs: Presidential Decisions about Technology Transfer between 1992–2003" (Ph.D. diss., Mills College, Oakland, California, 2007).

CHAPTER 1

1. Mark Baldassare, *A California State of Mind: The Conflicted Voter in a Changing World* (Berkeley: University of California Press, 2002), p. 23.

2. "The University of California's Distinctive Freshman Admissions Process," White Paper Prepared by the Board of Admissions and Relations with Schools, Endorsed by the Academic Council on March 30, 2005.

3. "Comments by President David P. Gardner on the problems faced by the University of California in meeting the racial and ethnic balance in its student body as required by the state legislature," Regents' Meeting, San Francisco, May 17, 1990, University of California Office of the President.

4. Ward Connerly, *Creating Equal: My Fight against Racial Preferences* (San Francisco: Encounter Books, 2000), p. 120.

5. Connerly, *Creating Equal*, p. 124.

6. Remarks of Associate Dean Michael Drake, UC San Francisco School of Medicine, Regents' Meeting, November 17, 1994.

7. Minutes of the Committee on Educational Policy and the Special Committee on Affirmative Action, Regents' Meeting, November 17, 1994, p. 7.

8. Assistant Vice President Dennis Galligani, "Presentation on Undergraduate Admissions Policies and Practices," Regents' Meeting, May 17, 1995.

9. Vice Chancellor Winston Doby, "UCLA Undergraduate Admissions and Affirmative Action," presentation to the Board of Regents, May 17, 1995.

10. Early versions of the California Civil Rights initiative called for the elimination of "affirmative action." That language was deleted from the text of Proposition 209 when polling data showed voters responded more favorably to the phrase "racial and gender preferences." See Lydia Chavez, *The Color Bind* (Berkeley: University of California Press, 1998), p. 67.

11. Letter from Regent Ward Connerly to the Regents of the University of California, July 5, 1995, University of California Office of the President.

12. Brian Pusser, *Burning Down the House: Politics, Governance, and Affirmative Action at the University of California* (Albany: State University of New York Press, 2004), p. 141. Pusser's book provides an excellent and detailed analytical account of events leading up to the Regents' vote and its aftermath.

13. Governor Wilson's presidential campaign received a brief boost from the SP-1 and SP-2 votes, but by fall 1995 it had run out of funding, and media attention turned to other candidates. Chavez, *The Color Bind*, p. 69.

14. UC President David Gardner, asked for his views on the litigation in a 1986 interview with the *Los Angeles Times*, answered that the legal action was a matter for the courts to decide. His responsibility was to assess the effect of the lawsuit and the attendant negative publicity on Atkinson's performance as chancellor, and he had found strong support for him both on campus and in the San Diego community. See "UC President Gardner: A Study in Elusiveness," *Los Angeles Times*, August 15, 1986.

CHAPTER 2

1. Richard C. Atkinson, *The Pursuit of Knowledge: Speeches and Papers of Richard C. Atkinson*, ed. Patricia A. Pelfrey (Berkeley: University of California Press, 2007), pp. 11–14.

2. Gualtiero Piccinini, "The First Computational Theory of Mind and Brain: A Close Look at McCulloch and Pitts's 'Logical Calculus of Ideas Immanent in Nervous Activity,'" *Synthese* 141, no. 2 (2004): 175–215.

3. Richard C. Atkinson, "Remarks on Receiving the University of Chicago Alumni Medal," in *The Pursuit of Knowledge*, p. 13.

4. See Howard Gardner's *The Mind's New Science* (New York: Basic Books, 1987), pp. 10–16, on the significance of the Hixon Symposium to the development of the field of cognitive science.

5. It was also the beginning of a lifelong connection with the navy. During his time at Stanford he had long-term research funding from the Office of Naval Research and served as a consultant; while director of the National Science Foundation, he worked with the Department of the Navy on a number of projects. At UC San Diego he was a member of

NPS's advisory board and later served on the board of directors of the US Naval Academy Foundation.

6. C. Stewart Gillmor, *Fred Terman at Stanford: Building a Discipline, a University, and Silicon Valley* (Stanford: Stanford University Press, 2004), pp. 186–99.

7. Gillmor, *Fred Terman at Stanford*, p. 255.

8. Richard C. Atkinson, "20/20: Reflections on the Last 20 Years of the 20th Century," unpublished manuscript, August 2000, p. 11.

9. Gillmor, *Fred Terman at Stanford*, p. 404.

10. Bowker served as chancellor of UC Berkeley from 1971 to 1980 and later was a helpful adviser to Atkinson during his presidency.

11. The book, now titled *Atkinson and Hilgard's Introduction to Psychology*, is in its fourteenth edition and has been translated into French, German, Russian, Norwegian, Chinese, and several other languages. After the twelfth edition the Atkinsons chose not to continue as coauthors.

12. Ezra Bowen, "The Computer as a Tutor," *Life*, January 27, 1967, pp. 68–81.

13. R. C. Atkinson and H. A. Wilson, "Computer-Assisted Instruction," *Science* 162 (October 4, 1968): 73–77. See also R. C. Atkinson, "Adaptive Instructional Systems: Some Attempts to Optimize the Learning Process," in *Cognition and Instruction*, ed. D. Klahr (Hillside, NJ: Lawrence Erlbaum Associates, 1976).

14. Robert L. Solso, *Cognitive Psychology*, 2nd ed. (Boston: Allyn and Bacon, 1998), p. 128.

15. For a discussion of the Atkinson-Shiffrin model and its influence, see Chizuko Izawa, ed., *On Human Memory: Evolution, Progress, and Reflections on the 30th Anniversary of the Atkinson-Shiffrin Model* (Hillside, NJ: Lawrence Erlbaum Associates, 1999).

16. See Richard C. Atkinson, "The Golden Fleece, Science Education, and U.S. Science Policy," in *The Pursuit of Knowledge*, pp. 16–32.

17. Atkinson, *The Pursuit of Knowledge*, p. 22.

18. Diane Ravitch, *The Troubled Crusade: American Education, 1945–1980* (New York: Basic Books, 1983), p. 261.

19. NSF received no Golden Fleece Awards during Atkinson's three years as director (1977–80), although Proxmire bestowed several of them on the agency before and after Atkinson's tenure.

20. Stephen Cole, Leonard Rubin, and Jonathan R. Cole, "Peer Review and the Support of Science," *Scientific American*, October 1977, pp. 34–42. See also Stephen Cole, Jonathan R. Cole, and Gary A. Simon, "Chance and Consensus in Peer Review," *Science* 215, no. 4531 (November 1981): 344–48.

21. Atkinson, *The Pursuit of Knowledge*, p. 28.

22. David C. Mowery, "University-Industry Research Relationships: Historical and Policy Perspectives," in *The University of California's Relationships with Industry in Research and Technology Transfer*, Proceedings of the President's Retreat, UCLA, January 30–31, 1997, The Regents of the University of California, 1997. Mowery adds that in 1960, industry provided over 6 percent of university research funding, "a level that it would not regain until 1986" (p. 30).

23. "Competing Priorities," in *The National Science Board: A History in Highlights, 1950–2000,* available at www.nsf.gov/nsb/documents/2000/nsb00215/nsb50/1970/cmpt_priority .html.

24. For a critical view of the decision to eliminate RANN, see Richard J. Green and Wil Lepowski, "A Forgotten Model for Purposeful Science," *Issues in Science and Technology* (Winter 2006). Available at www.issues.org/22.2/green.html.

25. Richard C. Atkinson, "Recollection of Events Leading to the First Exchange of Students, Scholars, and Scientists between the United States and the People's Republic of China," December 14, 2006, available at www.rca.ucsd.edu/speeches/ChinaRecollections .pdf.

26. Daniel S. Greenberg, "Jarring Thoughts from a Scientist in the Know," *Washington Post,* July 1, 1980.

27. Atkinson, "20/20," pp. 4–6.

28. Nancy Scott Anderson, *An Improbable Venture: A History of the University of California, San Diego* (La Jolla: UCSD Press, 1993), p. 34.

29. Quoted in Anderson, *An Improbable Venture,* p. 37.

30. Letter from President David S. Saxon to Richard C. Atkinson, March 25, 1980, University of California Office of the President.

31. "William D. McElroy and the Illuminating Story of Bioluminescence," *Current Contents* 43 (October 25, 1982): 731–41.

32. The three academic vice chancellors during Atkinson's tenure were John Miles, mathematical geophysicist; Harold Ticho, physicist; and Marjorie Caserio, chemist.

33. Today six of UC's nine general campuses are members of the AAU. Only the State University of New York, with two campus members, comes close to this record.

34. William J. McGill, *Year of the Monkey: Revolt on Campus, 1968–69* (New York: McGraw-Hill, 1982), p. 244 n. 44.

35. Atkinson, *The Pursuit of Knowledge,* pp. 50–51.

36. "The University of California: A Multi-Campus System in the 1980s," Report of the Joint Planning Committee, ed. Patricia A. Pelfrey, Berkeley, September 1979.

37. See David S. Webster and Tad Skinner, "Rating Ph.D. Programs: What the NRC Study Says . . . and Doesn't Say," *Change* (May–June 1996): 24–44.

38. McGill, *Year of the Monkey,* p. 519.

CHAPTER 3

1. Senior Vice President William R. Frazer, Report to the Regents' Special Committee on Affirmative Action Policies, June 20, 1991.

2. "New Directions for Outreach: Report of the University of California Outreach Task Force," University of California Office of the President, July 1997, p. 8.

3. "Seeing Threat to Shared Governance, Faculty Group Prepares to Petition UC Regents," *Notice* (a publication of the University of California Academic Senate), October 1995.

4. The May 29, 1996, report of the AAUP's Commission on Governance and Affirmative Action Policy concluded that the Regents had the legal authority to pass SP-1 and SP-2 but that they nonetheless "violated the spirit, if not the letter, of shared governance" and that

their decision "involved no sustained consultation with faculty and administrators about the educational issues at stake" (p. 1). The commission's concluding recommendations were to urge the Regents, the administration, and the faculty to "reaffirm their commitment to the principles and practices of shared governance," to avoid both the appearance and the reality of "partisan political activity in deliberations about educational policy," and to postpone implementation of the ban on affirmative action until a joint task force of Regents, administrators, faculty, and students had completed a thorough review of the decision and its effects (p. 10). "Report of the AAUP Commission on Governance and Affirmative Action Policy," Washington, DC, May 29, 1996.

5. See John Aubrey Douglass, "Anatomy of a Conflict," *American Behavioral Scientist* 41, no. 7 (April 1998): 938–59.

6. On June 20, 1995, Simmons sent a letter to President Peltason conveying the statement and asking him to share it with the Regents.

7. Letter from General Counsel James E. Holst to Regent Ward Connerly, January 25, 1996, University of California Office of the President.

8. Letter from President Richard C. Atkinson to Academic Senate Chair Arnold Leiman, November 30, 1995, University of California Office of the President. The Academic Senate Task Force on Governance's Panel on Shared Governance produced several reports that presented a useful historical perspective on admissions as well as recommendations for repairing the breach over SP-1; see www.universityofcalifornia.edu/senate/reports/.

9. Letter from General Counsel James E. Holst to President Richard C. Atkinson, April 26, 1996, University of California Office of the President.

10. Richard C. Atkinson, "Statement on Shared Governance," Regents' Meeting, October 1996.

11. J. W. Peltason, "Political Scientist and Leader in Higher Education, 1947–1955: Sixteenth President of the University of California, Chancellor at UC Irvine and the University of Illinois," Regional Oral History Office, UC Berkeley, p. 598.

12. Letter from Regent Ward Connerly to Chairman Howard Leach and Members of the Board of Regents, December 21, 1993, University of California Office of the President.

13. Letter from President J. W. Peltason to Regent Ward Connerly, January 4, 1994, University of California Office of the President.

14. In her study of the political campaign surrounding the passage of Proposition 209, Lydia Chavez writes that before its passage less than one percent of California voters ranked affirmative action as a "pressing concern." Polling data revealed that many Californians supported affirmative action while expressing a dislike for "preferences." Many voters, she argues, were misled into supporting the measure because its ambiguous language did not make clear its goal of eliminating affirmative action programs. Lydia Chavez, *The Color Bind: California's Battle to End Affirmative Action* (Berkeley: University of California Press, 1998), p. 245.

15. The only litigation involving the University following the Regents' adoption of SP-1 and SP-2 was *Molloy v. Regents, et al.,* filed in February 1996 in Santa Barbara County Superior Court, almost seven months after the Regents' vote, alleging that unspecified Regents and Governor Wilson engaged in a series of telephone calls during the week leading up to the Regents' vote in which each agreed to vote in favor of SP-1 and SP-2, thus rendering

the action of the board, according to the allegation in the complaint, a mere formality. The plaintiffs—*Daily Nexus,* the Santa Barbara campus student newspaper, and Tim Molloy, one of its writers—alleged the telephone calls constituted a closed serial meeting prohibited by the Bagley-Keene Open Meeting Act and sought to nullify the Regents' action. The open-meeting law violation question was ultimately decided by a unanimous decision of the California Supreme Court (Regents v. Superior Court [1999] 20 Cal. 4th 509) holding that a right of an action under the act extended only to present and future actions and violations and not past ones; and that suits to void actions in violation of the act had to be brought within thirty days of the date the action was taken, regardless of when the public learned of the event. (Later in 1999 the legislature passed and Governor Davis signed a bill, AB 1234, amending the Bagley-Keene Act to allow lawsuits to be brought in the future that allege past violations of the act.)

CHAPTER 4

1. Quoted in Lauri Puchall, "Looking Down on Creation," *The Monthly,* November 2006.

2. Letter from UC Davis Chancellor Larry Vanderhoef to President Richard C. Atkinson, October 30, 1995, University of California Office of the President.

3. "A President for UC," *Sacramento Bee,* August 16, 1995.

4. "Initial Proposal for a Special University of California Commission," University of California Office of the President, May 31, 1994.

5. Richard C. Atkinson, "20/20: Reflections on the Last 20 Years of the 20th Century," unpublished manuscript, 2000, p. 27.

6. "1997–98 Budget for Current Operations," University of California Office of the President, October 1996, p. 22. Available at http://budget.ucop.edu/rbudget/199798/1997-98 budgetforcurrentoperations.pdf.

7. UC's projections included a commitment for a one-third increase in community college transfers by 2005. The projections also assumed that the University's graduate enrollment would remain constant at 18 percent of total enrollment.

8. Roger L. Geiger, *Knowledge and Money: Research Universities and the Paradox of the Marketplace* (Stanford: Stanford University Press, 2004), p. 149.

9. Hugh Davis Graham and Nancy Diamond, *The Rise of American Research Universities: Elites and Challengers in the Postwar Era* (Baltimore: Johns Hopkins University Press, 1997), pp. 149–50.

10. "Perspectives on the Economy and Demographics," in *Analysis of the 1997–98 Budget Bill, Perspectives and Issues Part II,* Legislative Analyst's Office, State of California, p. 2. Available at www.lao.ca.gov/analysis_1997part_2_econ_demographics_pi97.

11. Examples of state funding for UC at levels beyond the compact are offsets to student fee increases to hold fees down (and in two years the state provided funds to reduce fees), large allocations for student outreach programs and teacher professional development, and capital outlay money. The state provided well over $1 billion more than compact funding levels for three main areas: capital outlay funds for UC hospitals, the California Institutes

for Science and Innovation, and three buildings for the new campus in Merced. In addition, all operating funds devoted to starting UC Merced were above the compact.

12. "1998–99 Budget for Current Operations," October 1997, p. 81, University of California Office of the President. Available at http://budget.ucop.edu/rbudget/199899/1998–99 budgetforcurrentoperations.pdf.

CHAPTER 5

1. Letter from UC Davis Provost and Executive Vice Chancellor Robert D. Grey et al. to President-designate Richard C. Atkinson, September 20, 1995, University of California Office of the President.

2. Peter Schrag, *Paradise Lost: California's Experience, America's Future* (New York: New Press, 1998), p. 41.

3. Michael Kirst et al. "Conditions of Education in California, 1994–5," Policy Analysis for California Education, April 1995, p. 5. Available at http://pace.berkeley.edu/reports/Conditions_1994–95.pdf.

4. For an inventory of these programs, see "The Schools and UC: A Commitment to the Future of California," University of California Office of the President, 1995.

5. Charles Hitch, "The University of the Future: An Address to the Commonwealth Club of California," San Francisco, June 25, 1971.

6. Letter from General Counsel James E. Holst to President Richard C. Atkinson, January 9, 1996, University of California Office of the President.

7. Letter from Regent Ward Connerly to President Richard C. Atkinson, March 5, 1996, University of California Office of the President.

8. Regents' Policy 2102, Policy on Undergraduate Admissions, adopted May 20, 1998.

9. Regents' Resolution SP-1, Policy Ensuring Equal Treatment—Admissions, Adopted July 20, 1995.

10. See G. C. Hayward, B. G. Brandes, M. W. Kirst, and C. Mazzeo, "Higher Education Outreach Programs: A Synthesis of Evaluations," Policy Analysis for Higher Education, January 1997. Available at www.ucop.edu/sas/publish/pace/index.html.

11. "Educational disadvantage" as defined by the Outreach Task Force report also included such related factors as attending a school with little in the way of college-preparatory curricula and below-average SAT and ACT (American College Testing) examination scores, being the first family member to attend college, living in a community with low college-going rates, or belonging to a group with historically low attendance rates at UC campuses.

12. *A Nation at Risk: The Imperative for Educational Reform,* National Commission on Excellence in Education (Washington, DC: US Government Printing Office, April 1983), p. 5.

13. The report of the University-wide Committee on Student Preparation was chaired by UC Vice President–Academic Affairs William R. Frazer; former UCLA Graduate School of Education Dean John Goodlad chaired the report of the University-wide Program Review Committee for Education. Both reports were issued in 1984.

14. Hayward et al., "Higher Education Outreach Programs: A Synthesis of Evaluations," III, p. 2.

15. "New Directions for Outreach," Report of the University of California Outreach Task Force, University of California Office of the President, 1997, p. 11.

16. The fifteen-page minority report, written by former UC Regent Richard Russell, argued that the task force's analysis and recommendations fell short of answering the basic question of how to qualify more minority students for UC while ignoring the profound educational implications of race. The report expressed skepticism that a racially neutral approach to qualifying more minority students would yield big increases in minority applicants or do much to change the fact that in 1997 a meager 3.9 percent of Latino students, who were expected to make up 51 percent of public school students by 2005, qualified for UC. Among other things, the minority report argued for the imperative of racial targeting in outreach programs, "an honest and realistic discussion" of how much the outreach plan would cost, and the hurdles UC would encounter in recruiting minority students without attention to race. "Minority Report of the University of California Outreach Task Force," no date.

17. The total breaks down into five categories of expenditures: $27,200,000 for school-centered outreach; $17,900,000 for academic development; $7,900,000 for informational outreach; $1,550,000 for University research and evaluation; and $6,000,000 for infrastructure needs.

18. The task force decided that 1998–99 would serve as a baseline for measurement, so that the fifth year would be 2003–4.

19. "Forging California's Future through Educational Partnerships: Redefining Educational Outreach," Final Report of the Strategic Review Panel on UC Educational Outreach to the President of the University of California, February 2003, pp. 27–29.

20. "Forging California's Future through Educational Partnerships," p. 34.

21. Personal interview, January 16, 2009.

CHAPTER 6

1. Both SP-1 and SP-2, which dealt with employment and contracting, stipulated that UC could take any action "strictly necessary to establish or maintain eligibility for any federal or state program, where ineligibility would result in a loss of federal or state funds to the University." President Peltason explained in a statement issued a few days after the Regents' July 1995 vote that—unlike SP-1—implementation of SP-2 would involve "few significant changes . . . because UC's employment and contracting programs are governed by State and federal laws, regulations, executive orders, and the U.S. Constitution, and our practices historically have been and will continue to be in compliance with these various laws and requirements."

2. Minutes of the Committee on Educational Policy, Regents' Meeting, January 15, 1998. Available at www.universityofcalifornia.edu/regents/minutes/minarch.html.

3. I am indebted to Bruce Darling for information essential to this account of the steps leading to the May 2001 meeting and the rescission vote, and the to former Regents Judith Hopkinson and John Davies for their comments on an earlier version of this chapter.

4. "UC Regents Near Affirmative Action Compromise," *Sacramento Bee,* May 15, 2001.

5. Atkinson's letter read as follows:

> Dear Lieutenant Governor and Mr. Speaker,
>
> On February 15, 2001, I wrote to Michael Cowan, Chair of the University of California's Academic Council, requesting that the Academic Senate conduct a thorough review of the University's admissions policies including, among other issues, the use of quantitative formulas, and amend the admissions policies to require that all campuses employ comprehensive, unitary review processes.
>
> I am writing to confirm that any changes that The Regents may adopt to the University of California's undergraduate admissions criteria, following timely recommendations by the President and the Academic Senate, will be effective for students who matriculate in Fall 2002. I will put the matter on The Regents' agenda in time to affect students who will be admitted in the Fall 2002 admissions process. I have conferred with the University's General Counsel on this matter.
>
> Sincerely,
>
> Richard C. Atkinson
>
> President
>
> cc: Academic Council Chair Cowan
>
> Senior Vice President and Provost King
>
> Senior Vice President Darling

6. "Report of the Task Force on Undergraduate Admissions Criteria," University of California Office of the President, December 1995, p. 9.

7. "Report of the Task Force on Undergraduate Admissions Criteria," p. 6.

8. Letter from Assistant Vice President—Student Academic Services Dennis Galligani to Provost C. Judson King, June 13, 1997.

9. The 1868 Organic Act required the University to admit students from throughout California: "It shall be the duty of the Regents, according to population, to so apportion the representation of students, when necessary, that all portions of the State shall enjoy equal privilege therein." A 1974 legislative resolution called upon UC to admit a student body that approximates the racial and ethnic diversity of the state.

10. See John Douglass, "Setting the Conditions of Undergraduate Admissions: Part II," pp. 1–3 (available at http://ishi.lib.berkeley.edu/cshe/jdouglass/pub/part2.html); and "Report of the Task Force on Undergraduate Admissions Criteria," p. 3.

11. Richard C. Atkinson, "Diversity: Not There Yet," *Washington Post,* April 20, 2003.

12. Martin Trow, a UC Berkeley scholar of comparative higher education, observes in a paper analyzing UC governance, "Indeed, it has been the habit and strategy of the University of California, almost from its beginning, to take its operations out of the political arena in every way possible." Martin Trow, "Governance in the University of California: The Transformation of Politics into Administration," paper prepared for a German-American conference, "The University in Transition," Berkeley, CA, March 17–21, 1997, p. 7.

13. Brian Pusser, *Burning Down the House: Politics, Governance, and Affirmative Action at the University of California* (Albany: State University of New York Press, 2004), pp. 211–27.

CHAPTER 7

1. Personal interview, May 19, 2008.

2. Richard C. Atkinson, Foreword to C. Stewart Gillmor, *Fred Terman at Stanford: Building a Discipline, a University, and Silicon Valley* (Stanford: Stanford University Press, 2004), p. ix.

3. G. Pascal Gregory, *Endless Frontier: Vannevar Bush, Engineer of the American Century* (Cambridge, MA: MIT Press, 1999), p. 4.

4. Quoted in AnnaLee Saxenian, *Regional Advantage: Culture and Competition in Silicon Valley and Route 128* (Cambridge, MA: Harvard University Press, 1994), p. 22.

5. An exception was applied research in support of US defense.

6. Congress established the National Science Foundation in 1950 to serve as an independent federal agency devoted to supporting basic research and education in all scientific and engineering disciplines. Today NSF supplies about 20 percent of all federally supported basic research in American colleges and universities. Many other federal agencies and departments sponsor scientific research as well, among them the National Institutes of Health, which supports fundamental research in biology, medicine, and health.

7. Clark Kerr, "The Federal Grant University," in *The Uses of the University,* 5th ed. (Cambridge, MA: Harvard University Press, 1963), p. 53.

8. Jeffrey Madrick, *The End of Affluence* (New York: Random House, 1995), p. 42.

9. David C. Mowery and Nathan Rosenberg, *Technology and the Pursuit of Economic Growth* (Cambridge: Cambridge University Press, 1989), p. 218.

10. Mowery and Rosenberg, *Technology and the Pursuit of Economic Growth,* p. 220.

11. Richard C. Atkinson, *The Pursuit of Knowledge: Speeches and Papers of Richard C. Atkinson,* ed. Patricia A. Pelfrey (Berkeley: University of California Press, 2007), p. 17.

12. Governor Edmund G. Brown Jr., Executive Order B-91–81, November 17, 1981. The executive order established a state agency to foster California's competitiveness. The California Commission on Industrial Innovation was active during Brown's administration but not thereafter.

13. Other members of the commission were William C. Demers of the Communication Workers of America; Don Gevirtz, chairman of the Foothill Group; Regis McKenna, chairman of Regis McKenna, Inc.; Leland Prussia, chairman of the board of Bank of America; Jim Quillin of the California Conference of Machinists; Lynn Schenk of the California Business, Transportation and Housing Agency; Don Vial, director of the California Department of Industrial Relations; Jerry Whipple, regional director of the United Auto Workers; David Commons, consultant; Robert P. Marr of Operating Engineers Local #3; G. Rip Ridley, President of WAMS, Inc.; and E. Allison Thomas, the Commission's executive director.

14. "Winning Technologies: A New Industrial Strategy for California and the Nation," Report of the California Commission on Industrial Innovation, Office of the Governor, Sacramento, September 1982.

15. CONNECT, now an independent, nonprofit agency and a national model for creating entrepreneurial businesses, has helped launch hundreds of successful start-ups in the San Diego area. CONNECT start-ups are known for their high survival rate of about 60 percent.

16. Raymond Smilor, Niall O'Donnell, Gregory Stein, and Robert S. Welborn III, "The Research University and the Development of High-Technology Centers in the United States," *Economic Development Quarterly* 21, no. 3 (August 2007): 216. Available at http://edq.sagepub.com/cgi/content/abstract/21/3/203.

17. This was due, at least in part, to a study on engineering supply and demand headed by Fred Terman in the early 1960s. Terman's analysis concluded that California's schools were turning out enough engineers to meet its needs well into the future. UC, although in the midst of building three new campuses, shelved any plans for new engineering programs as a result of Terman's report, "A Study of Engineering Education in California" (Coordinating Council for Higher Education, Sacramento, March 1968). The Council, a California state agency, is now known as the California Postsecondary Education Commission.

18. Richard C. Atkinson, "20/20: Reflections on the Last 20 Years of the 20th Century," unpublished manuscript, 2000, pp. 32–33.

19. Smilor et al., "The Research University," p. 217.

20. "Developing High-Technology Communities: San Diego," p. 33.

21. Smilor et al., "The Research University," p. 203. See also Douglas Henton, Jon Melville, and Kimberly Walesh, "Collaboration and Innovation: The State of American Regions," *Industry and Higher Education* (February 2002): 9–17; and Mary Walshok, *Knowledge without Boundaries: What America's Research Universities Can Do for the Economy, the Workplace, and the Community* (San Francisco: Jossey-Bass, 1995).

22. Richard C. Atkinson, "The Future of the University of California: A Personal View," in *The Pursuit of Knowledge*, p. 39.

23. David Warsh, *Knowledge and the Wealth of Nations* (New York: W.W. Norton, 2006), p. 371.

24. Tapan Munroe, "What's New in the New Economy," June 18, 1999; and "Continued Prosperity in 2000; The New e-CONOMY Makes It Possible," December 27, 1999. Both available at www.tapanmunroe.com/columns.html.

25. The Council of Economic Advisers, "Supporting Research and Development to Promote Economic Growth: The Federal Government's Role," October 1995. Available at www.clintonlibrary.gov/archivesearch.html.

26. Paul Romer, "Endogenous Technological Change," *Journal of Political Economy* 98, no. 5, pt. 2 (October 1990): S71–S102.

27. Romer, "Endogenous Technological Change," p. S99.

28. Edwin Mansfield, John Rapoport, Anthony Romeo, Samuel Wagner, and George Beardsley, "Social and Private Rates of Return from Industrial Innovations," *Quarterly Journal of Economics* 91, no. 2 (May 1977): 221–40.

29. Edwin Mansfield, "Academic Research Underlying Industrial Innovations: Sources, Characteristics, and Financing," *Review of Economics and Statistics* 77, no. 1 (February 1995): 55.

30. Lynne G. Zucker and Michael R. Darby, "Star Scientists and Institutional Transformation: Patterns of Invention and Innovation in the Formation of the Biotechnology Industry," *Proceedings of the National Academy of Sciences* 93 (November 1996): 12709–16. Zucker and Darby conclude that a firm's collaboration with star scientists is a strong predictor of its success: "for an average firm, 5 articles coauthored by an academic star and the

firm's scientists result in about 5 more products in development, 3.5 more products on the market, and 860 more employees" (p. 12709).

31. UC exceeded this goal, with enrollments in both disciplines topping 27,000 by 2003.

32. Edward E. Penhoet and Richard C. Atkinson, "Town and Gown Join Forces to Boost State," *Los Angeles Times,* December 31, 1996.

33. Christophe Lecuyer, Bettina Horne-Muller, and Cherisa Yarkin, "Contributions by University of California Scientists to the State's Electronics Manufacturing Industry," Working Paper 07–03, Industry-University Cooperative Research Program, August 1, 2007.

34. Cherisa Yarkin, Andrew Murray, and Christina Chang, "Understanding the Economic Impact of Public Investment in Industry-University Research Partnerships: Phase II, Corporate Assessment of Economic Impact, Private Sponsor Survey, Grants Initiated in Years 1996 through 2000," Working Paper 02–1. Economic Research and Assessment Unit of the Industry-University Cooperative Research Program, January 23, 2002.

35. They were later renamed the Governor Gray Davis Institutes for Science and Innovation in recognition of Davis's contributions.

36. Quoted in Robert M. Rosenzweig, "The Pajaro Dunes Conference," in *Partners in the Research Enterprise: University-Corporate Relations in Science and Technology,* ed. Thomas W. Langfitt, Sheldon Hackney, Alfred P. Fishman, and Albert V. Glowasky (Philadelphia: University of Pennsylvania Press, 1983), p. 34.

37. Rosenzweig, "The Pajaro Dunes Conference," p. 36.

38. "Report of the University-Industry Relations Project," Systemwide Administration, and "Report of the Committee on Rights to Intellectual Property," both dated October 1982, University of California Office of the President.

39. Report of the Ad Hoc Technology Transfer Committee, March 8, 1994, p. 1.

40. "The University of California's Relationship with Industry in Research and Technology Transfer," Proceedings of the President's Retreat, UCLA, January 30–31, 1997, The Regents of the University of California, June 1997.

41. "The University of California's Relationship with Industry," pp. 217–18.

42. Former Harvard President Derek Bok warns about the imperative for active oversight: "Unless the system of governance has safeguards and methods of accountability that encourage university officials to act appropriately, the lure of making money will gradually erode the institution's standards and draw it into more and more questionable practices." Derek Bok, *Universities in the Marketplace: The Commercialization of Higher Education* (Princeton: Princeton University Press, 2003), p. 185. In *Knowledge and Money: Research Universities and the Paradox of the Marketplace* (Stanford: Stanford University Press, 2004), Roger L. Geiger analyzes the influence of market forces in shaping research universities since the 1980s.

43. "Overview, Industry-University Cooperative Research Program, 1996–2002," University of California Office of the President, 2002.

CHAPTER 8

1. "Call to Eliminate SAT Requirement May Reshape Debate on Affirmative Action," *Chronicle of Higher Education,* March 2, 2001.

2. Nicholas Lemann, *The Big Test: The Secret History of the American Meritocracy* (Farrar, Straus and Giroux, 1999), pp. 62–63.

3. "Achievement versus Aptitude Tests in College Admissions," *Issues in Science and Technology* (Winter 2001–2). Available at www.issues.org/18.2/atkinson.html.

4. Quoted in Stephen Jay Gould, *The Mismeasure of Man* (New York: W. W. Norton [1981] 1996), p. 181.

5. Gould, *The Mismeasure of Man,* pp. 181–82.

6. Gould, *The Mismeasure of Man,* p. 60.

7. James Crouse and Dale Trusheim, *The Case against the SAT* (Chicago: University of Chicago Press, 1988), p. 22.

8. Rebecca Zwick, ed., *Rethinking the SAT: The Future of Standardized Testing in University Admissions* (New York: Routledge Falmer, 2004), p. xi.

9. Jerome Karabel, *The Chosen: The Hidden History of Admission and Exclusion at Harvard, Yale, and Princeton* (Boston: Houghton Mifflin, 2005), pp. 175–76.

10. James Bryant Conant, *My Several Lives: Memoirs of a Social Inventor* (New York: Harper and Row, 1970), p. 131.

11. Conant, *My Several Lives,* pp. 130–31.

12. Conant, *My Several Lives,* p. 134.

13. "Call to Eliminate SAT Requirement May Reshape Debate on Affirmative Action," *Chronicle of Higher Education,* March 2, 2001.

14. Richard C. Atkinson, "College Admissions and the SAT: A Personal View," in *The Pursuit of Knowledge: Speeches and Papers of Richard C. Atkinson,* ed. Patricia A. Pelfrey (Berkeley: University of California Press, 2007), pp. 166–67.

15. "Latinos and Affirmative Action," from the Trial Transcript of Dr. Eugene Garcia, Expert Witness for the Student Defendant-Intervenors in the University of Michigan Law School Affirmative Action Trial: *Grutter v. Bollinger, et al.,* the Coalition to Defend Affirmative Action & Integration and Fight for Equality by Any Means Necessary (BAMN), February 8–9, 2001, p. 1.

16. This 3.8 percent figure compares to 2.8 percent for African Americans, 12.7 percent for whites, and 30 percent for Asian Americans. Percentages from the California Postsecondary Education Commission 1997 Eligibility Study.

17. Minutes, Educational Policy Committee, Board of Regents' Meeting, September 18, 1997, pp. 6–8.

18. September 18, 1997, Educational Policy Committee minutes, pp. 8–9.

19. Atkinson, "College Admissions and the SAT," pp. 168–69.

20. Crouse and Trusheim, *The Case against the SAT,* pp. 40–71.

21. Atkinson, "College Admissions and the SAT," p. 169.

22. Minutes of the Regents of the University, Committee on Educational Policy, February 19, 1998.

23. Numbers from interviews with Wayne Camara of the College Board and John Katzman of Princeton Review on the PBS series *Frontline,* "Secrets of the SAT," October 4, 1999.

24. National Research Council, "Myths and Tradeoffs: The Role of Tests in Undergraduate Admissions," ed. Alexandra Beatty, M. R. C. Greenwood, and Robert C. Linn, Steering

Committee for the Workshop on Higher Education Admissions, National Research Council, 1999, p. vii.

25. National Research Council, "Myths and Tradeoffs," pp. 22–24.

26. Michael W. Kirst, "Admissions Testing in a Disconnected K-16 System," in Zwick, *Rethinking the SAT*, p. 95.

27. Letter from President Richard C. Atkinson to Academic Council Chair Michael Cowan, February 15, 2001, University of California Office of the President.

28. Bob Laird, *The Case for Affirmative Action in University Admissions* (Berkeley: Bay Tree Publishing, 2005), p. 205 Atkinson's speech proposed using the SAT II subject examinations in lieu of the SAT I while the faculty explored other options.

29. "The SAT's Greatest Test," *Chronicle of Higher Education*, October 26, 2001.

30. Atkinson, *The Pursuit of Knowledge*, pp. 176–77.

31. David Owen, *None of the Above: Behind the Myth of Scholastic Aptitude* (Boston: Houghton Mifflin, 1985).

32. Peter Sacks, *Standardized Minds: The High Price of America's Testing Culture and What We Can Do about It* (Cambridge, MA: Perseus Books, 1999).

33. Karabel, *The Chosen*, p. 547.

34. Lemann, *The Big Test*, p. 350.

35. S. Geiser and M. V. Santelices, "The Role of Advanced Placement and Honors Courses in College Admissions," in *Expanding Opportunity in Higher Education: Leveraging Promise*, ed. Patricia C. Gandara, Gary Orfield, and Catherine L. Horn (Albany: State University of New York Press, 2006); S. Geiser and M. V. Santelices, "Validity of High-School Grades in Predicting Student Success beyond the Freshman Year: High-School Record vs. Standardized Tests as Indicators of Four-Year College Outcomes," Research and Occasional Paper Series, Center for Studies in Higher Education, UC Berkeley, 2007 (available at http://cshe.berkeley.edu/publications/publications.php?id = 265); and S. Geiser, "Back to Basics: In Defense of Achievement (and Achievement Tests) in College Admissions," *Change* 41, no. 1 (January–February 2009): 16–23.

36. William G. Bowen, Matthew M. Chingos, and Michael S. McPherson, *Crossing the Finish Line: Completing College at America's Public Universities* (Princeton: Princeton University Press, 2009).

37. Richard C. Atkinson and Saul Geiser, "Reflections on a Century of College Admissions Tests," *Educational Researcher* 38, no. 9 (2009): 665–76.

38. Atkinson and Geiser, "Reflections," p. 667.

39. "Admissions Tests and UC Principles for Admissions Testing," Report from the Board of Admissions and Relations with Schools (BOARS), December 2009, p. 4. Available at www.universityofcalifornia.edu/senate/reports/hp2mgy_boars-testing_010609.pdf.

CHAPTER 9

1. Testimony of John C. Browne at the Hearing of the Subcommittee on Military Procurement of the Committee on National Security, US House of Representatives, October 6, 1998.

2. "U.S. Fires Scientist Suspected of Giving China Bomb Data," *New York Times*, March 9, 1999.

3. The Rudman report recommended insulating the weapons laboratories from a dysfunctional DOE by carving out a separate management entity for them called the National Nuclear Security Administration (NNSA), with responsibility for America's nuclear weapons, nuclear proliferation, and naval reactors. DOE Secretary Bill Richardson successfully opposed making the NNSA an entirely independent agency; it remains within DOE.

4. *Science at Its Best, Security at Its Worst: A Report on Security Problems at the U.S. Department of Energy*, President's Foreign Intelligence Advisory Board, Special Investigative Panel, June 1999, p. 2. Available at www.fas.org/sgp/library/pfiab/index.html.

5. "Richardson Announces Results of Inquiries Related to Espionage Investigation," press release, US Department of Energy, Office of Public Affairs, Washington, DC, August 12, 1999.

6. The stalemate was resolved when Atkinson appointed an independent panel to advise him on appropriate disciplinary action for the three UC individuals cited in the Inspector General's report. The panel was not convinced that the employees in question were guilty of serious dereliction and recommended fairly mild penalties. The disciplinary actions Atkinson imposed, which ranged from formal letters of reprimand to restrictions on employment or job assignment, were in each case more severe than those the panel suggested.

7. Letter from the Honorable Bill Richardson to President Richard C. Atkinson, July 30, 1999, University of California Office of the President.

8. "Secretary Richardson Announces Changes with University of California Contract," press release, US Department of Energy, Office of Public Affairs, Washington, DC, June 30, 2000.

9. "Update on Los Alamos National Laboratory," Senior Vice President, University Affairs and Interim Vice President, Laboratory Management Bruce B. Darling, Regents' Meeting, April 3, 2003.

10. Minutes of the Committee on Oversight of the Department of Energy Laboratories, Regents' Meeting, May 15, 2003.

11. The chair of the Committee on Oversight, Regent Dean Watkins, made a statement for the record at the board's June 1991 meeting:

> The Regents welcome the report of the President concerning negotiations between the U.S. Department of Energy and the University of California regarding UC's management of DOE laboratories, and affirm the Board's earlier stated intention to renew the management contracts if mutually agreeable terms can be negotiated. The Regents also endorse the stated position of the President that such negotiations be actively pursued once the DOE decides to extend the contracts rather than to award them by competitive bidding.

This statement was the closest the Regents had ever come to a formal policy position on whether the University would compete to manage the laboratories.

12. The Lawrence Berkeley National Laboratory was not designated an unclassified laboratory until the early 1980s. During World War II it was deeply involved in nuclear research and production to support the war effort.

13. Report of the Special Committee on University Research at Livermore and Los Alamos, University of California Academic Senate, 1970, p. 12. The members of the committee were Paul E. Zinner, chairman, Thomas L. Allen, August C. Helmholz, Addison A. Mueller, Francis A. Sooy, Randolph T. Wedding, and George W. Wetherill.

14. In addition to the two relating to Livermore, the principal recommendations were as follows: directors and their principal staff should be regularly included in Regents' meetings and meetings with the president and the chancellors; the laboratories should prepare annual development plans; like organized research units throughout the University, their missions should be reviewed every five years by a faculty committee; employees should enjoy the same advantages as any University employee; and easing of classification and security procedures should be combined with an increase in graduate training.

15. "Response by The Regents to the Recommendations of the Academic Senate's Special Committee on University Research at Livermore and Los Alamos ("Zinner Committee")," Regents' Committee on Special Research Projects, April 15, 1971.

16. One of the earliest of such groups was the UC Nuclear Weapons Labs Conversion Project, established in 1976. There are many others, including Tri-Valley CAREs and the Project on Government Oversight.

17. Minutes of the Committee on Oversight of the Department of Energy Laboratories, March 14, 1991.

18. "Alternative Futures for the Department of Energy Laboratories," Secretary of Energy Advisory Board Task Force on Alternative Futures for the Department of Energy National Laboratories, February 1995, p. A-3. The report of the task force, chaired by Robert Galvin, chairman of Motorola, is available at www.lbl.gov/LBL-PID/Galvin-Report/Galvin-Report.html.

19. Minutes of the meeting of the Regents' Committee on Oversight of the Department of Energy Laboratories, May 16, 1991.

20. There are eleven multiprogram Department of Energy National Laboratories: Brookhaven National Laboratory (New York), Argonne National Laboratory (Illinois), Oak Ridge National Laboratory (Tennessee), National Renewable Energy Laboratory (Colorado), Los Alamos National Laboratory and Sandia National Laboratory (both in New Mexico), Idaho National Engineering Laboratory, Pacific Northwest Laboratory (Washington), Lawrence Berkeley National Laboratory, Lawrence Livermore National Laboratory, and SLAC National Accelerator Laboratory (all three in California). Nuclear weapons design and testing are done at Los Alamos and Livermore; weapons electronics are designed and built at Sandia.

21. "The University of California Office of the President and Its Constituencies, 1983–1995," Vol. 1: The Office of the President, Regional Oral History Office, UC Berkeley, 2002, p. 155.

22. Quotation is from the minutes of the Regents' Committee on Oversight of the Department of Energy Laboratories, September 20, 1990.

23. See Gardner's oral history, "A Life in Higher Education: Fifteenth President of the University of California, 1983–1992," Regional Oral History Office, UC Berkeley, 1997, pp. 365–75.

24. Letter from Special Assistant James S. Kane to Professor Emeritus Herbert F. York, chair of the Scientific and Academic Advisory Committee, June 26, 1991.

25. The faculty also voted in favor of UC's management in a 1996 poll by a margin of 61 to 39 percent.

26. Minutes of the Committee on Oversight of the Department of Energy Laboratories, May 19, 2004.

27. UC also won the competition for the Lawrence Berkeley National Laboratory, for which no business partner was required.

28. "On Renewal of the University of California Contracts with the Department of Energy for Management of the Livermore and Los Alamos National Laboratories," report by the Scientific and Academic Advisory Committee, May 18, 1990, p. 5.

29. "Alternative Futures for the Department of Energy Laboratories," p. 53.

30. Statement by University of California President Richard C. Atkinson before the Subcommittee on Oversight and Investigations of the Committee on Energy and Commerce, U.S. House of Representatives, 108th Cong., 1st sess., May 1, 2003, Serial no. 108-14.

CHAPTER 10

1. Richard C. Atkinson, "Farewell Remarks to the Board of Regents," in *The Pursuit of Knowledge: Speeches and Papers of Richard C. Atkinson,* ed. Patricia A. Pelfrey (Berkeley: University of California Press, 2007), p. 180.

2. "I . . . knew from reading history, from accounts by older faculty members, and from my own observations that no president of the university, and there had been eleven, had ever left the presidency under entirely friendly conditions—all had been in one kind of trouble or another, including Daniel Coit Gilman, Benjamin Ide Wheeler, and Robert Gordon Sproul. I also knew that, while college and university presidents are appointed ostensibly for life, they serve at the pleasure of several constituencies—and that pleasure comes and goes." Clark Kerr, *The Gold and the Blue: A Personal Memoir of the University of California, 1949–1967,* 2 vols. (Berkeley: University of California Press, 2001), vol. 1, p. 167.

3. "Comprehensive Review in Freshman Admissions at the University of California 2003–2009," Board of Admissions and Relations with Schools, Systemwide Academic Senate, University of California, May 2010, p. 4.

4. Richard C. Atkinson, "The University of California: A Personal View," in *The Pursuit of Knowledge,* p. 43.

5. Richard C. Atkinson, "20/20: Reflections on the Last 20 Years of the 20th Century," unpublished manuscript, pp. 65–66.

CHAPTER 11

1. On February 1, 1927, the Regents officially designated the campus—which had been known simply as the Southern Branch since its beginnings in 1919—the University of California at Los Angeles. Today its official designation is University of California, Los Angeles.

2. Gary Gorton, *Slapped by the Invisible Hand: The Panic of 2007* (Oxford: Oxford University Press, 2010), pp. 7–8.

3. See, for example, the Academic Senate's "Futures" report and its criticisms of the long-standing UC budget strategy of alliances with governors and reliance on the partnership agreements with the state: "Current Budget Trends and the Future of the University of California," University Committee on Planning and Budget, May 2006. Available at www.universityofcalifornia.edu/senate/reports/futures.report.0706.pdf.

4. For a description and analysis of the 2005–6 executive compensation controversy, see Patricia A. Pelfrey, "Executive Compensation at the University of California: An Alternative View," Research and Occasional Paper Series, Center for Studies in Higher Education, Berkeley, May 2008. Available at http://cshe.berkeley.edu/publications/publications.php?id=309.

5. Letter from Regent Sherry Lansing, Regent Russell Gould, President Robert C. Dynes, and Provost Wyatt R. Hume to President and Executive Director Ralph Wolff, Western Association of Schools and Colleges, January 18, 2008, University of California Office of the President.

6. Quoted in "Mark Yudof's Impossible Fix," *San Francisco Magazine,* February 2010. Available at www.sanfranmag.com/print/node/9834.

7. See "Monitor Group Report to the Regents: University of California Organizational Restructuring Effort," September 2007.

8. Richard Blum, "We Need to Be More Strategically Dynamic," August 22, 2007; available at www.universityofcalifornia.edu/future/blumpaper0807.pdf. See also "UC's Top Regent Bashes System," *San Francisco Chronicle,* August 23, 2007.

9. Minutes of the meeting of the Regents' Committee on Finance, May 19, 2010.

10. "Monitor Group Report to the Regents: University of California Organizational Restructuring Effort," September 12, 2007, p. 2: "UCOP's administrative spending for both personnel and non-personnel is $127 million, whereas the combined campus expenditure on administrative personnel alone is estimated to be between $650 million and $750 million." The University's own analysis comparing the growth of academic and nonacademic employees in 1997–98 and 2008–9 concluded that "increases in employee FTE have been driven primarily by expansion in Teaching Hospitals, Research and Auxiliary Enterprises," which includes "thousands of nurses, doctors, custodians, food service workers, and other staff who provide direct services to students, faculty and the public" ("The University of California Academic and Non-Academic Personnel Growth FY 1997–98 to FY 2008–09," Executive Summary, UCOP Institutional Research, March 5, 2010, p. 1).

11. "The Senate relies on the institutional memory and analytical strength of key UCOP staff to support its analyses and recommendations. [The Academic] Council's increasing concern arises from the departure or reassignment of long-time colleagues, as well as the move of unique analytical functions in specific subject areas to centralized units." Letter from Academic Council Chair Mary Croughan to President Mark Yudof, March 11, 2009.

12. "The Choices Report," Submitted by the University Committee on Planning and Budget, Systemwide Academic Senate, University of California, March 2010, p. 4.

13. "Report of the Working Group on the Roles of the Office of the President," Governance Committee of the Board of Regents, January 8, 2008. Available at www.universityofcalifornia.edu/future/roleofOPrpt.pdf.

14. Verne Stadtman, *The University of California, 1868–1968: A Centennial Publication of the University of California* (New York: McGraw-Hill, 1970), p. 261 ff.

15. Agnes Roddy Robb, "Robert Gordon Sproul and the University of California: A Memoir by Agnes Roddy Robb," introduction by Garff Wilson, Regional Oral History Office, UC Berkeley, 1976, p. 13.

16. Robb, "Robert Gordon Sproul and the University of California," p. 9a.

17. Stadtman, *The University of California, 1868–1968*, p. 270.

18. Speech to the California Club, 1948, quoted in Robb, "Robert Gordon Sproul and the University of California," pp. 14–15.

19. Robb, "Robert Gordon Sproul and the University of California," p. 13.

20. Minutes of the meeting of the Committee on Educational Policy, Board of Regents, February 11, 1937.

21. Letter from Vice President Monroe Deutsch to President Robert Gordon Sproul, April 26, 1941, University Archives, Berkeley, CA.

22. Minutes of the Board of Regents, January 24, 1947. Quoted in Eugene C. Lee, *The Origins of the Chancellorship: The Buried Report of 1948*, Chapters in the History of the University of California, no. 3 (Berkeley: Center for Studies in Higher Education, 1995), p. 16.

23. Lee, *The Origins of the Chancellorship*, p. 28.

24. Lee, *The Origins of the Chancellorship*, p. 3.

25. Lee, *The Origins of the Chancellorship*, p. 56. Provosts at UC Riverside, UC Santa Barbara, and UC Davis were designated chancellors in 1958; at UC San Francisco, the title was first used in 1964.

26. Clark Kerr, *The Gold and the Blue: A Personal Memoir of the University of California, 1949–1967*, 2 vols. (Berkeley: University of California Press, 2001), vol. 1, p. 198.

27. "The Role of the Office of the President in the Management of the University of California," Office of Educational Relations, Office of the President, August 1991, p. 28.

28. Quoted in Kerr, *The Gold and the Blue*, vol. 1, p. 160.

29. Kerr, *The Gold and the Blue*, vol. 1, p. 219.

30. Kerr, *The Gold and the Blue*, vol. 1, p. 206.

31. Kerr, *The Gold and the Blue*, vol. 1, pp. 224–26.

32. Martin Trow, who knew Kerr personally, wrote that Kerr's various descriptions of the multicampus university head as a "coordinator rather than a creative leader," "an expert executive, a tactful moderator," but "mostly a mediator" failed to reflect not only the demands of academic leadership in the United States but also Kerr's own performance. Both as chancellor and as president, Trow writes, Kerr "had an enormous impact on the institutions that he led." Martin Trow, "The University Presidency: Comparative Reflections on Leadership," Ninth David D. Henry Lecture, University of Illinois, Urbana-Champaign, October 31–November 1, 1984, pp. 29–30.

33. A major goal of his administration, Saxon said, was to "retain and to extend and develop endemic excellence ... throughout the University of California." David S. Saxon, "The Endemic Excellence of the University of California," Address to the Academic Senate, fall 1975.

34. National Research Council, "An Assessment of Research-Doctorate Programs in the United States," 1982; "Research Doctorate Programs in the United States: Continuity

and Change," 1995; and "A Data-Based Assessment of Research Doctorate Programs in the United States," 2010. Available at http://search.nap.edu/nap-cgi/de.cgi?term=Assessment+of+Doctoral+Programs&x=0&y=0.

35. Richard C. Atkinson, "The Future of the University of California: A Personal View," in *The Pursuit of Knowledge: Speeches and Papers of Richard C. Atkinson,* ed. Patricia A. Pelfrey (Berkeley: University of California Press, 2007), pp. 39–53.

36. Minutes of the Regents' Committee on Finance, May 19, 2010.

37. "The University of California Transition Team Final Report," vol. 1, September 1993, p. 6.

38. "The Role of the Office of the President in the Management of the University of California," p. 30.

39. Letter from Academic Council Chair Mary Croughan to President Mark Yudof, August 6, 2009.

40. James G. March, "The Study of Organizations and Organizing since 1945," *Organization Studies* 28, no. 9 (2007): 15–18.

SELECT BIBLIOGRAPHY

American Association of University Professors. "Report of the AAUP Commission on Governance and Affirmative Action." Washington, DC, May 29, 1996.

Anderson, Nancy Scott. *An Improbable Venture: A History of the University of California, San Diego.* La Jolla, CA: UCSD Press, 1993.

Atkinson, Richard C. "Adaptive Instructional Systems: Some Attempts to Optimize the Learning Process." In *Cognition and Instruction,* edited by D. Klahr. Hillside, NJ: Lawrence Erlbaum Associates, 1976.

———. "20/20: Reflections on the Last 20 Years of the 20th Century." Unpublished manuscript, 2000.

———. *The Pursuit of Knowledge: Speeches and Papers of Richard C. Atkinson.* Edited by Patricia A. Pelfrey. Berkeley: University of California Press, 2007.

———. "Recollection of Events Leading to the First Exchange of Students, Scholars, and Scientists between the United States and the People's Republic of China." December 14, 2006. www.rca.ucsd.edu/speeches/ChinaRecollections.pdf.

Atkinson, Richard C., and Saul Geiser. "Reflections on a Century of College Admissions Tests." *Educational Researcher* 38, no. 9 (2009): 665–76.

Atkinson, R. C., and H. A. Wilson. "Computer-Assisted Instruction." *Science* 162 (October 4, 1968): 73–77.

Baars, Bernard J. *The Cognitive Revolution in Psychology.* New York: Guilford Press, 1986.

Baldassare, Mark. *A California State of Mind: The Conflicted Voter in a Changing World.* Berkeley: University of California Press, 2002.

Bok, Derek. *Universities in the Marketplace: The Commercialization of American Higher Education.* Princeton: Princeton University Press, 2003.

Bowen, Ezra. "The Computer as a Tutor." *Life,* January 27, 1967.

Bowen, William G., Matthew M. Chingos, and Michael S. McPherson. *Crossing the Finish Line: Completing College at America's Public Universities*. Princeton: Princeton University Press, 2009.

Chavez, Lydia. *The Color Bind: California's Battle to End Affirmative Action*. Berkeley: University of California Press, 1998.

Cohen, Michael D., James G. March, and Johan P. Olsen. "A Garbage Can Model of Organizational Choice." *Administrative Science Quarterly* 17, no. 1 (March 1972): 1–25.

Cole, Stephen, Jonathan R. Cole, and Gary A. Simon. "Chance and Consensus in Peer Review." *Science* 215, no. 4531 (November 1981): 344–48.

Cole, Stephen, Leonard Rubin, and Jonathan R. Cole. "Peer Review and the Support of Science." *Scientific American*, October 1977, 34–42.

"Competing Priorities." In *The National Science Board: A History in Highlights, 1950–2000*. Available at www.nsf.gov/nsb/documents/2000/nsb00215/nsb50/1970/cmpt_priority .html.

Conant, James Bryant. *My Several Lives: Memoirs of a Social Inventor*. New York: Harper and Row, 1970.

Connerly, Ward. *Creating Equal: My Fight against Racial Preferences*. San Francisco: Encounter Books, 2000.

Crouse, James, and Dale Trusheim. *The Case against the SAT*. Chicago: University of Chicago Press, 1988.

Douglass, John Aubrey. "Anatomy of a Conflict." *American Behavioral Scientist* 41, no. 7 (April 1998): 938–59.

———. *The Conditions for Admission: Access, Equity, and the Social Contract of American Universities*. Stanford: Stanford University Press, 2007.

Furtado, Loren M. *Budget Reform and Administrative Decentralization in the University of California*. Berkeley: Berkeley Public Policy Press, Institute of Governmental Studies, 2002.

Gardner, David P. *Earning My Degree: Memoirs of an American University President*. Berkeley: University of California Press, 2005.

———. "A Life in Higher Education: Fifteenth President of the University of California, 1983–1992." Regional Oral History Office, UC Berkeley, 1997.

Gardner, Howard. *The Mind's New Science*. New York: Basic Books, 1987.

Geiger, Roger L. *Knowledge and Money: Research Universities and the Paradox of the Marketplace*. Stanford: Stanford University Press, 2004.

Geiser, S. "Back to Basics: In Defense of Achievement (and Achievement Tests) in College Admissions." *Change* 41, no. 1 (January–February 2009): 16–23.

Geiser, S., and M. V. Santelices. "The Role of Advanced Placement and Honors Courses in College Admissions." In *Expanding Opportunity in Higher Education: Leveraging Promise*, edited by Patricia C. Gandara, Gary Orfield, and Catherine L. Horn. Albany: State University of New York Press, 2006.

———. "Validity of High-School Grades in Predicting Student Success beyond the Freshman Year: High-School Record vs. Standardized Tests as Indicators of Four-Year College Outcomes." Research and Occasional Paper Series. Center for Studies in Higher Education, UC Berkeley, 2007.

Gillmor, C. Stewart. *Fred Terman at Stanford: Building a Discipline, a University, and Silicon Valley.* Stanford: Stanford University Press, 2004.

Goodlad, John I. *A Place Called School: Prospects for the Future.* New York: McGraw-Hill, 1984.

Gorton, Gary. *Slapped by the Invisible Hand: The Panic of 2007.* Oxford: Oxford University Press, 2010.

Gould, Stephen Jay. *The Mismeasure of Man.* New York: W. W. Norton, [1981] 1996.

Graham, Hugh Davis, and Nancy Diamond. *The Rise of American Research Universities: Elites and Challengers in the Postwar Era.* Baltimore: Johns Hopkins University Press, 1997.

Green, Richard J., and Wil Lepowski. "A Forgotten Model for Purposeful Science." *Issues in Science and Technology* (Winter 2006). www.issues.org/22.2/green.html.

Greenberg, Daniel S. "Jarring Thoughts from a Scientist in the Know." *Washington Post,* July 1, 1980.

Gregory, G. Pascal. *Endless Frontier: Vannevar Bush, Engineer of the American Century.* Cambridge, MA: MIT Press, 1999.

Hayward, G. C., B. G. Brandes, M. W. Kirst, and C. Mazzeo. "Higher Education Outreach Programs: A Synthesis of Evaluations." Policy Analysis for California Education, January 1977. Available at www.ucop.edu/sas/publish/pace/index.html.

Henton, Douglas, Jon Melville, and Kimberly Walesh. "Collaboration and Innovation: The State of American Regions." *Industry and Higher Education* (February 2002): 9–17.

Izawa, Chizuko, ed. *On Human Memory: Evolution, Progress, and Reflections on the 30th Anniversary of the Atkinson-Shiffrin Model.* Hillside, NJ: Lawrence Erlbaum Associates, 1999.

Karabel, Jerome. *The Chosen: The Hidden History of Admission and Exclusion at Harvard, Yale, and Princeton.* Boston: Houghton Mifflin, 2005.

Kennedy, V. Wayne. "University of California Senior Vice President for Business and Finance, 1993–2000—UC San Diego Vice Chancellor, Administration, 1985–1993." Berkeley: University of California Regional History Office, 2007.

Kerr, Clark. *The Gold and the Blue: A Personal Memoir of the University of California, 1949–1967.* 2 vols. Berkeley: University of California Press, 2001.

———. *The Uses of the University.* 5th ed. Cambridge, MA: Harvard University Press, 2001.

Kirp, David L., and Patrick S. Roberts. "Mr. Jefferson's University Breaks Up." *Public Interest,* no. 148 (Summer 2002): 70–84.

Laird, Bob. *The Case for Affirmative Action in University Admissions.* Berkeley: Bay Tree Publishing, 2005.

Landes, David S., Joel Mokyr, and William J. Baumol. *The Invention of Enterprise: Entrepreneurship from Ancient Mesopotamia to Modern Times.* Princeton: Princeton University Press, 2010.

Langfitt, Thomas W., Sheldon Hackney, Alfred P. Fishman, and Albert V. Glowasky, eds. *Partners in the Research Enterprise: University-Corporate Relations in Science and Technology.* Philadelphia: University of Pennsylvania Press, 1983.

Lecuyer, Christophe, Bettina Horne-Muller, and Cherisa Yarkin. "Contributions by University of California Scientists to the State's Electronics Manufacturing Industry." Working

Paper 07–03. University of California Industry-University Cooperative Research Program, August 1, 2007.

Lee, Eugene C. *The Origins of the Chancellorship: The Buried Report of 1948*. Chapters in the History of the University of California, no. 3. Berkeley: Center for Studies in Higher Education, 1995.

Lee, Wen Ho. *My Country versus Me: The First-Hand Account by the Los Alamos Scientist Who Was Falsely Accused of Being a Spy*. New York: Hyperion, 2001.

Lemann, Nicholas. *The Big Test: The Secret History of the American Meritocracy*. New York: Farrar, Straus and Giroux, 1999.

Lohman, David E. "Aptitude for College: The Importance of Reasoning Tests for Minority Admissions." In *Rethinking the SAT: The Future of Standardized Testing in University Admissions*, edited by Rebecca Zwick. New York: Routledge Falmer, 2004.

Madrick, Jeffrey. *The End of Affluence*. New York: Random House, 1995.

Mandler, George. *A History of Modern Experimental Psychology from James and Wundt to Cognitive Science*. Cambridge, MA: MIT Press, 2007.

Mansfield, Edwin. "Academic Research Underlying Industrial Innovations: Sources, Characteristics, and Financing." *Review of Economics and Statistics* 77, no. 1 (1995): 55–65.

Mansfield, Edwin, John Rapoport, Anthony Romeo, Samuel Wagner, and George Beardsley. "Social and Private Rates of Return from Industrial Innovations." *Quarterly Journal of Economics* 91, no. 2 (1977): 221–40.

March, James G. "The Study of Organizations and Organizing since 1945." *Organization Studies* 28, no. 9 (2007): 15–18.

McGill, William J. *Year of the Monkey: Revolt on Campus, 1968–69*. New York: McGraw-Hill, 1982.

Mokyr, Joel. *The Gifts of Athena: Historical Origins of the Knowledge Economy*. Princeton: Princeton University Press, 2002.

Mowery, David C. "University-Industry Research Relationships: History and Policy Perspectives." In *The University of California's Relationships with Industry in Research and Technology Transfer*. Proceedings of the President's Retreat, UCLA, January 30–31, 1997. The Regents of the University of California, June 1997.

Mowery, David C., and Nathan Rosenberg. *Technology and the Pursuit of Economic Growth*. Cambridge: Cambridge University Press, 1989.

Murphy, Franklin D. *My UCLA Chancellorship: An Utterly Candid View*. Los Angeles: UCLA Oral History Program, 1976.

A Nation at Risk: The Imperative for Educational Reform. National Commission on Excellence in Education. Washington, DC: US Government Printing Office, 1983.

National Research Council. "An Assessment of Research-Doctorate Programs in the United States," 1982; "Research Doctorate Programs in the United States: Continuity and Change," 1995; "A Data-Based Assessment of Research Doctorate Programs in the United States," 2010. http://search.nap.edu/nap-cgi/de.cgi?term=Assessment+of+Doctoral+Programs&x = o&y = o.

———. "Myths and Tradeoffs: The Role of Tests in Undergraduate Admissions." Ed. Alexandra Beatty, M. R. C. Greenwood, and Robert C. Linn. Steering Committee for the Workshop on Higher Education Admissions, National Research Council, 1999.

"New Directions for Outreach." Report of the University of California Outreach Task Force. University of California Office of the President, 1997.

Owen, David. *None of the Above: Behind the Myth of Scholastic Aptitude*. Boston: Houghton Mifflin, 1985.

Pelfrey, Patricia A. "Executive Compensation at the University of California: An Alternative View." Research and Occasional Paper Series. Center for Studies in Higher Education, Berkeley, 2008.

————. "Origins of the Principles for Review of Executive Compensation." Research and Occasional Paper Series. Center for Studies in Higher Education, Berkeley, 2008.

Peltason, J. W. "Political Scientist and Leader in Higher Education, 1947–1995: Sixteenth President of the University of California, Chancellor at UC Irvine and the University of Illinois." Regional Oral History Office, UC Berkeley, 2001.

Piccinini, Gualtiero. "The First Computational Theory of Mind and Brain: A Close Look at McCulloch and Pitts's 'Logical Calculus of Ideas Immanent in Nervous Activity.'" *Synthese* 141, no. 2 (2004): 175–215.

Pusser, Brian. *Burning Down the House: Politics, Governance, and Affirmative Action at the University of California*. Albany: State University of New York Press, 2004.

Ravitch, Diane. *The Troubled Crusade: American Education, 1945–1980* (New York: Basic Books, 1983), p. 261.

"Report of the Special Committee on University Research at Livermore and Los Alamos." University of California Academic Senate, 1970.

"Report of the Task Force on Undergraduate Admissions Criteria." University of California Office of the President, December 1995.

Robb, Agnes Roddy. "Robert Gordon Sproul and the University of California: A Memoir by Agnes Roddy Robb." Regional Oral History Office, UC Berkeley, 1976.

"The Role of the Office of the President in the Management of the University of California." Office of Educational Relations, University of California Office of the President, 1991.

Romer, Paul. "Endogenous Technological Change." *Journal of Political Economy* 98, no. 5 (1990): S71–S102.

Sacks, Peter. *Standardized Minds: The High Price of America's Testing Culture and What We Can Do about It*. Cambridge, MA: Perseus Books, 1999.

Saxenian, AnnaLee. *Regional Advantage: Culture and Competition in Silicon Valley and Route 128*. Cambridge, MA: Harvard University Press, 1996.

"The Schools and UC: A Commitment to the Future of California. A Guide to the University of California's Pre-Collegiate Programs." University of California Office of the President, 1995.

Schrag, Peter. *Paradise Lost: California's Experience, America's Future*. New York: New Press, 1998.

Science at Its Best, Security at Its Worst: A Report on Security Problems at the U.S. Department of Energy. President's Foreign Intelligence Advisory Board, Special Investigative Panel, June 1999. Available at www.fas.org/sgp/library/pfiab/index.html.

Sinsheimer, Robert. *The Strands of a Life*. Berkeley: University of California Press, 1994.

Smilor, Raymond, Niall O'Donnell, Gregory Stein, and Robert S. Welborn III. "The

Research University and the Development of High-Technology Centers in the United States." *Economic Development Quarterly* 21, no. 3 (2007): 203–22.

Solso, Robert L. *Cognitive Psychology.* 2nd ed. Boston: Allyn and Bacon, 1998.

Stadtman, Verne. *The University of California, 1868–1968: A Centennial Publication of the University of California.* New York: McGraw-Hill, 1970.

Stober, Dan, and Ian Hoffman. *A Convenient Spy: Wen Ho Lee and the Politics of Nuclear Espionage.* New York: Simon & Schuster, 2001.

"Supporting Research and Development to Promote Economic Growth: The Federal Government's Role." Council of Economic Advisers, Washington, DC, 1995.

Trow, Martin. "The University Presidency: Comparative Reflections on Leadership." Ninth David D. Henry Lecture, University of Illinois, Urbana-Champaign, October 31–November 1, 1984.

"The University of California: A Multi-Campus System in the 1980s." Report of the University of California Joint Planning Committee. Edited by Patricia A. Pelfrey. Berkeley, September 1979.

"The University of California Office of the President and Its Constituencies, 1983–1995." Vol. 1: The Office of the President. Regional Oral History Office, UC Berkeley, 2002.

Walshok, Mary Lindenstein. *Knowledge without Boundaries: What America's Research Universities Can Do for the Economy, the Workplace, and the Community.* San Francisco: Jossey-Bass, 1995.

Warsh, David. *Knowledge and the Wealth of Nations.* New York: W.W. Norton, 2006.

Webster, David S., and Tad Skinner. "Rating Ph.D. Programs: What the NRC Study Says . . . and Doesn't Say." *Change* (May–June 1996): 24–44.

"William D. McElroy and the Illuminating Story of Bioluminescence." *Current Contents* 43 (1982): 731–41.

"Winning Technologies: A New Industrial Strategy for California and the Nation." Report of the California Commission on Industrial Innovation. Sacramento: Office of the Governor, 1982.

Yarkin, Cherisa, Andrew Murray, and Christina Chang. "Understanding the Economic Impact of Public Investment in Industry-University Research Partnerships: Phase II, Corporate Assessment of Economic Impact, Private Sponsor Survey, Grants Initiated in Years 1996 through 2000." Working Paper 02-1. University of California Industry-University Cooperative Research Program, January 23, 2002.

Younger, Stephen M. *The Bomb: A New History.* New York: HarperCollins, 2009.

Zucker, Lynne G., and Michael R. Darby. "Star Scientists and Institutional Transformation: Patterns of Invention and Innovation in the Formation of the Biotechnology Industry." *Proceedings of the National Academy of Sciences* 93 (November 1996): 12709–16.

Zwick, Rebecca, ed. *Rethinking the SAT: The Future of Standardized Testing in University Admissions.* New York: Routledge Falmer, 2004.

INDEX

ABC, 9, 116

Abraham, Spencer, 145–46

Academic Senate: Academic Council, 130, 163; admission policy, ix, 7, 40, 47–48, 88–98, 115–16, 124–26, 130–34, 137–38, 176, 193n8, 197n5; for affirmative action, 1, 41, 50; Assembly, 130, 183; and Atkinson at UCSD, 31–32; Berkeley division, 47; campus academic senates, 40, 134; comprehensive review, 87, 89, 90–91, 97–98, 116, 158, 176, 183, 185, 197n5; Cowan as Chair, 90, 130, 197n5; and defense laboratories, 148–50, 152, 153; domestic partner benefits, 66; Leiman as Chair, 46; Master of Advanced Study, 157; one-university concept, 171–72; Pister as Chair, 31–32, 79; President Atkinson's relations with, 56–57; Simmons as Chair, 40, 41; and SP-1, 38, 40, 42, 47, 50, 173, 193n8; TA collective bargaining, 68; and tests, 98, 116, 124–26, 130–34, 137–38, 182, 183; UC Merced, 157; and UCOP staff cutbacks, 163, 206n11; UC-state budgetary partnerships, 206n3; Zinner report (1970), 148–49, 150. *See also* Board of Admissions and Relations with Schools (BOARS)

accountability: General Accounting Office (GAO) critiques, 25, 140; industry-university collaborations, 113, 200n35; outreach programs in K–12 public schools, 83–84

achievement: admissions based on, 40, 93, 116, 120, 136, 182, 183; gap, 38–39, 84–85; tests, 120, 121, 123, 127–31, 133–34, 137–38, 182, 183

ACT, Inc., 132, 134

ACT with Writing, 134

Adams, Ansel, 55

Adams, Bob, 29

Adler, Mortimer, viii, 16

admissions, 2–3, 6–9, 115–16, 184; achievement-based, 40, 93, 116, 120, 136, 182, 183; and Advanced Placement courses, 96–97, 124; affirmative action, 1–12, 14, 38; Atkinson presidency and, 42–48, 51–53, 57–58, 60, 86–95, 98, 156, 157, 176, 182; campus of choice, 95–96; Director of Admissions Research Geiser, 94; division of responsibility among Regents, faculty, and administration, 47, 50; Dual Admissions Plan, 115–16, 182; ELC, 94–95, 96–97, 115–16, 158, 180, 182; faculty/ Academic Senate authority over, ix, 7, 40–41, 47–48, 87–98, 115–16, 124–26, 130–34, 137–38, 176, 193n8, 197n5; and grades, 93, 97, 124, 128, 138; and honors, 96–97; income-based, 39, 50, 185; K–12 public schools and, 71, 115–16, 129, 158; Master Plan and, 2, 39, 50, 52–53, 94, 121; medical school, 5–6; "opportunity to learn" factors, 92–93; Pathways online admission, 179; RE-28, 89–92, 175–76, 182; after SP-1, 60, 92–99, 125, 126, 127, 158;

215

admissions (*continued*)
    "supplemental criteria," 92–93; Task Force on
    Undergraduate Admissions Criteria, 94, 96,
    97; and tests, ix, 89–93, 97–98, 115–26, 128,
    130–34, 136–38, 182, 183; two-tier system, 87,
    96, 171, 182; zero-sum, 3, 11, 38, 50, 94. *See
    also* comprehensive review; enrollments;
    SP-1 (anti-affirmative action for admissions);
    UC diversity policy
Advisory Committee on the University's
    Relations with the Department of Energy
    Laboratories, 139
Advisory Group on Low-Level Radioactive
    Waste Disposal, 181
affirmative action, xiii–xiv, 6, 196n1; Academic
    Senate for, 1, 41, 50; admissions, 1–12, 14, 38;
    case establishing, 1–2; employment, 1, 6, 8;
    Hayashi and, 127; post-affirmative action
    age, vii, 85, 157; Regents discussing, 3–12, 43,
    48–49, 193n6. *See also* anti-affirmative action
African Americans: and SAT, 121; UC enroll-
    ments, 84
agricultural programs: agricultural experi-
    ment stations, 164; Agricultural Genomics
    institute, 181; Davis University Farm, 164, 165;
    President's Commission on Agriculture and
    Natural Resources, 179; research, 164; UC
    organization proposal modeled after, 166. *See
    also* UC Davis
Akerlof, George, 182
All-University Conference on Teaching and
    Learning Technologies (March 1997), 178
aluminum, Kaiser, 54–55
American Association of University Professors
    (AAUP), 40–41, 46, 192–93n4
American Civil Liberties Union (ACLU), 52
American Council on Education (ACE), 11;
    Atkinson's "Standardized Tests and Access
    to American Universities" (Atwell Lecture,
    February 2001), 115, 116–17, 126–31, 134–35,
    182, 202n28
analogies, test, 123, 124, 131, 134
Anastasio, Michael R., 183
anti-affirmative action: Connerly, 4–9, 11, 43–45,
    48–52, 59; Cooks, 3–4, 11; faculty, 41; fairness,
    9, 97, 125–26; growing national debate, 125;
    Proposition 209, 7, 52, 88, 190n10, 193n14;
    Wilson, 2–11, 43–45, 48, 49, 58, 66, 79, 173,
    174, 190n13, 193–94n15. *See also* SP-1 (anti-
    affirmative action for admissions); SP-2
    (anti-affirmative action for employment)

anti-immigrant sentiment, 2; Proposition 187,
    2, 4–5
Apple Computer, 104
aptitude tests, 115–23, 128–31, 136–37, 182;
    "Aptitude for College: The Importance of
    Reasoning Tests for Minority Admissions"
    (Lohman, 2004), 115
army: Atkinson, 18; IQ tests, 118–19
Arthur Andersen accounting firm, 182
Asians: K–12 public schools, 70; outreach
    programs and, 74, 76; testing, 121, 127; UC
    admissions and, 4, 5, 8, 9, 11, 38–39, 74, 127.
    See also China; Japan
Assembly, Academic Senate, 130, 183
Associated Press, 116
Association of American Universities (AAU),
    159, 169, 178, 192n33; UCSD, 33, 169
Atkinson, Lynn (daughter), 18, 23, 30, 123
Atkinson, Richard C., xv; China trip, 27–28;
    Computer Curriculum Corporation, 21,
    102; Indiana University, 18; *Introduction
    to Psychology* with Hilgard, 20, 191n11;
    lawsuit involving extramarital affair, 13, 57,
    190n14; man of action, viii–ix; manage-
    rial style, viii, 37, 58–59; *Markov Learning
    Models for Multi-person Interactions* (with
    Suppes), 20; mathematics, viii, 16–17, 18–23,
    121; post-presidential life, 160; presidential
    search committee and, 12–13; *Principles of
    Psychology,* 21–22; Stanford, viii, x, 19–23,
    22*fig. 3,* 101–2, 103, 121, 190n5; testing studies,
    15–16; UCLA, 19, 30; University of Chicago,
    viii, 15–18, 101, 117, 121; Vannevar Bush
    Award, 184; writing as a social scientist and
    administrator, 16
Atkinson, Richard C.—NSF director (1977–80),
    viii, 19, 23–29, 59, 101; Vannevar Bush influ-
    ence, x, 102; Golden Fleece Awards, 191n19;
    initiatives, 103; managerial style, viii, 37; navy
    connection, 190n5
Atkinson, Richard C.—UC presidency
    (1995–2003), viii, xiii, 156–60, 177–85; ad-
    ministrative organization, 56, 59, 156, 169–70;
    admission policies, 42–48, 51–53, 57–58,
    60, 86–95, 98, 156, 157, 176, 182; agenda, 61;
    appointment, 12–13, 13*fig. 2,* 37, 177; Atwell
    Lecture ("Standardized Tests and Access to
    American Universities," February 2001), 115,
    116–17, 126–31, 134–35, 182, 202n28; Bowker
    as helpful adviser, 191n10; chancellor's
    president, 159; chaos, 59, 156; characteristic,

134–35; collective bargaining, 67–68; defense laboratories, 143, 144, 145, 146, 152–53, 155, 157, 184, 203n6; domestic partner benefits, 66–67; first day, 54–55; goals, 60–65; inauguration declined, 159; industry-university collaborations, 108–14, 157; initiatives, 106–9, 112–14; managerial style, viii, 58–59; name on campus correspondence, 160; Oakland apartment, 45; official residence in Kensington, 45; outreach in K–12 public schools, 69–85; "peculiar set of events," 43–46; Pelfrey work with, xiii; Pister on, vii, viii–x; relations with internal constituencies, 56–60; retirement, 156, 160, 183, 185; shared governance, ix, 46–48, 60, 98; SP-1 implementation, 42–48, 51–52, 57–58, 156; SP-1 rescinding, 86–92, 157; speediness valued, 58; and tests, 115, 116–17, 121–23, 126–37, 157, 182, 202n28; thank you notes to donors, 159; Tidal Wave II, 60–61, 64, 65; UC budget, 60–65, 156, 158, 159, 177–78

Atkinson, Richard C.—UCSD chancellorship (1980–95), viii–ix, 12–13, 29–37, 59; and chancellor authority, 160; and chancellor relations as president, 57; Gardner assessment, 190n14; Roosevelt College dedication, 36fig. 4; University of Chicago and, 15; university-industry collaboration, x, 101, 103–6, 157

Atkinson, Rita Lloyd (wife): Indiana University, 18; Introduction to Psychology with Richard and Hilgard, 20; New York Public Library presidency, 35–36; NSF move, 23; post-presidential life, 160; UC presidency, 13fig. 2; UCSD, 30

Atkinson and Hilgard's Introduction to Psychology, 191n11

Atkinson Hall, 160

Atkinson-Shiffrin model of memory, 23

atomic bomb, 15, 141, 146

Atomic Energy Commission, 146

Atwell Distinguished Lecture (ACE, February 2001), "Standardized Tests and Access to American Universities" (Atkinson), 115, 116–17, 126–31, 134–35, 182, 202n28

Babcock and Wilcox Technical Services Group, 153

Bagley, Bill, 45, 49, 86, 87

Bagley-Keene Open Meeting Act, 194n15

Bakke, Allan/Bakke case, 1–2, 7–8, 9

Bank of America Foundation, 81

Bauman, Robert, 24–25

Bay Area Writing Project, 80

Bayh-Dole Act (1980), 26, 103, 112

Bechtel National, 153

behaviorism, 17, 18

Bell Laboratories, 110

Bender, Wilbur J., 119–20

benefits: domestic partner, 66–67, 179; UC employee, 12, 170

Bentham, Jeremy, 16

Berdahl, Robert, 131, 178

Berkeley. See UC Berkeley

"Berkeley: Today and Tomorrow" (Heyns), 38

Beyond Prediction (Commission on New Possibilities for the Admissions Testing Program), 127

The Big Test (Lemann), 135, 136

Biller, Les, 84

Binet, Alfred, 118, 121

biological determinism, IQ testing and, 118

biotechnology, 108, 110, 112, 114

Bishop, J. Michael, 179

Blake, William, xiii

Bloom, Allan, 16, 35

Blum, Richard, 162–63

Board of Admissions and Relations with Schools (BOARS): Atkinson relations, 93–95, 98, 132, 133, 157; and comprehensive review, 97–98, 183, 185; diversity policy, 93–95; and testing, 124–26, 130–34, 137–38, 182, 183; UC Santa Barbara conference (November 2001), 132

Board of Regents: and administrative organization, 55–56, 162, 163, 166–67, 206n10; affirmative action discussions, 3–12, 43, 48–49, 193n6; Atkinson retirement, 156; Bakke case, 1–2, 7–8, 9; vs. ballot initiative Classification by Race, Ethnicity, Color, or National Origin (2003), 184; budget cuts, 184; and comprehensive review, 90–91, 96, 176, 182, 197n5; Gray Davis nominees, 86; and decentralization, 162; and defense laboratories, 146, 149–52, 178, 182, 203n11; diversity policy, 7, 88, 173, 175–76; divisions, viii, 13–14, 43, 57, 86; domestic partner benefits, 66–67; and ELC, 96–97, 180; executive compensation debacle, 2, 11, 59, 162; fee increases, 184; Latino Eligibility Task Force, 122; Oakland headquarters for UCOP, 177; and outreach, 79, 82–83, 87, 88, 176, 178, 179; President Atkinson's relations with, ix, 57, 59–60; and presidential authority, ix, 59–60, 166;

Board of Regents (*continued*)
RE-28, 89–92, 175–76, 182; Sproul presidency,
166–67; Standing Order 105.2 delegating
admissions policy to faculty, 40, 41; and tests,
117, 130, 134, 135, 184; UC Merced site selec-
tion, 60–61. *See also* SP-1 (anti-affirmative
action for admissions); SP-2 (anti-affirmative
action for employment)
Board on Research and Economic Development,
178
Board on Testing and Assessment (BOTA), Na-
tional Academy of Sciences, 122, 123, 125
BOARS. *See* Board of Admissions and Relations
with Schools (BOARS)
Bok, Derek, 127, 200n42
Boston, Route 128, 101
Bowker, Albert H., 20, 191n10
Boyer, Paul D., 179
Brady, Ronald, 151
Bren Foundation, 179
Brentwood Elementary School, East Palo Alto, 21
Brigham, Carl, 115, 118–20
Broder, David, 16
Brooks, Linton, 145–46
Broome, Anne, 184
Brophy, Roy, 12, 49
Brown, Edmund G. Jr., 198n12
Brown, Jerry, 65, 103–4
Brown, Willie, 9
Browne, John, 139–40, 142, 144, 179, 184
Bruner, Jerome, 24–25
budgets: IUCRP, 109–10; science, 24, 28; Scripps,
29. *See also* funding; UC budget
Burgener, Clair, 4, 5
Burning Down the House (Pusser), 98–99, 190n12
Burton, John, 68
Bush, George H. W., 150
Bush, George W., 67, 117, 142
Bush, Jeb, 125
Bush, Vannevar, x, 101, 102–3, 111
Bustamante, Cruz, 82–83, 87, 90–91

California: constitutional autonomy of UC,
91–92, 98–99; defense and aerospace industries collapse, 2; Department of Education,
73, 82, 83, 180; Department of Finance, 60,
64, 180; economy, 62, 65, 80, 103–4, 108, 114,
158, 172, 182, 184; history (research and scholarship on), 180; huge investment in public
services and public infrastructure (1950s and
1960s), 69; industry-university-government

collaborations, x, 109–12, 114; Internet2 link
with Mexico, 182; IUCRP funding, 109;
job loss population, 2; K–12 expenditures,
69–70; population expansion (1920s), 164;
Schrag on, xiv, 69; technology sector, 62,
65, 108, 109–11, 158; unemployment rate, 2;
United Kingdom academic and commercial
exchange, 180. *See also* California funding of
UC budget; California legislature; governors;
K–12 public schools; Master Plan for Higher
Education; UC
California Association of Scholars, 41
California Civil Rights initiative. *See* Proposition 209
California Commission on Children and Families, 81
California Commission on Industrial Innovation
(CCII), 104, 110, 198n12
California Council on Science and Technology,
182
California funding of UC budget, xi, 187, 194n11;
allocation of funds to campuses, 63–65,
177–78; California Institutes for Science
and Innovation, 110, 111, 181, 183, 194–95n11;
compact, x, 60, 62, 194–95n11; cuts and
downturns, 2, 158, 162, 182, 184; generosity and increases, 65, 156–57, 180, 181; SP-1
inspiring legislative threats to, 39–40, 89, 92;
UC competition with state and community
colleges, 164; UC Merced, 65, 183; UC-state
partnership, 62, 180, 181, 206n3
California House, 180
California Institute for Information Technology
Research in Interest of Society (CITRIS),
110–11, 181, 182
California Institute for Quantitative Biomedical
Sciences (QB3), 110–11, 181
California Institutes for Science and Innovation,
109, 110–12; Calit2, 110–11, 160, 181; CITRIS,
110–11, 181, 182; CNSI, 110–11, 181, 182; Gray
Davis and, x, 110–11, 157, 181–82, 183, 200n35;
funding, 110, 111, 181, 183, 194–95n11; QB3,
110–11, 181
California Institute of Technology (Caltech),
29; Consortium for Education Network
Initiatives in California (CENIC), 178; Hixon
Symposium, 17; industry-university research,
112
California Institute for Telecommunications and
Information Technology (Calit2), 110–11,
160, 181

California Labor Code, 67
California Labor Federation, 68
California legislature, 66–68; affirmative action policies, 3, 39–40, 41; California Subject Matter Projects bill (1988), 80; diversity policy, 7, 83, 93–94, 98, 197n9; and K–12 public schools, 158; and outreach, 82–83, 85; Public School Accountability Act (1999), 80; RE-28, 89–92; Senate Education Committee, 80; tests for admission, 117; UC admissions practices, 93–94, 117; UC's constitutional autonomy from, 91–92, 98–99. *See also* California funding of UC budget
California NanoSystems Institute (CNSI), 110–11, 181, 182
California Postsecondary Education Commission (CPEC), 60, 73, 94
California Professional Development Institutes, 83
California state teachers' colleges: UC competition for funding with, 164; UC incorporation proposal, 166
California State University (CSU): admission practices, 94; allocation of enrollment money, 64; California Subject Matter Projects (CSMPs), 80–81; collective bargaining, 68; Consortium for Education Network Initiatives in California (CENIC), 178; Institute for Education Reform at Sacramento State University, 80; Master Plan, 39; outreach programs, 73, 80–81, 83; proportion of public high school graduates, 70; UC joint doctorate in education (Ed.D.) agreement, 182
California Studies Fellowship Program, UC, 180
California Subject Matter Projects (CSMPs), 80–81, 83
California Trade and Commerce Agency, 180
Calit2 (California Institute for Telecommunications and Information Technology), 110–11, 160, 181
CalREN-2, 178
Caltech. *See* California Institute of Technology (Caltech)
Camara, Wayne, 131
Campbell, Glenn, 59
Caperton, Gaston, 117, 130–32, 134
Carnesale, Albert, 178
Carter, Jimmy, 26, 27
"The Case for Not Scrapping the SAT" (Laird), 131

The Case against the SAT (Crouse and Trusheim), 123, 135
Casper, Gerhard, 180
CBS, 9, 116
CCII (California Commission on Industrial Innovation), 104, 110, 198n12
Cerro Grande wildfire, 143, 144, 181
César Chávez Day, official UC holiday, 183
chancellors: Atkinson presidency and, ix, 56–57, 159–60, 170; Berdahl (UC Berkeley), 131, 178; Bishop (UCSF), 179; Bowker (UC Berkeley), 191n10; budgetary authority, 159; Carnesale (UCLA), 178; Cicerone (UC Irvine), 179; Cordova (UC Riverside), 183; Debas (UCSF), 178; decentralization and, 159, 167–68, 170–71; Dynes (UCSD), 177; Greenwood (UC Santa Cruz), 177; Heyman (UC Berkeley), 104, 112; Heyns (UC Berkeley), 38, 52; Kerr presidency and, 168–70; McElroy (UCSD), 30–31, 32, 34, 37; McGill (UCSD), 30, 33–34; Murphy (UCLA), 167–68; outreach programs, 79; and patents, 113; Peltason (UC Irvine), 11; Pister as Chancellor Emeritus (UC Santa Cruz), 79, 179; salaries, 65; Sinsheimer (UC Santa Cruz), 54, 112; Tomlinson-Keasey (UC Merced), 180, 183; UC Berkeley establishing, 167; UCLA establishing, 167; UC Merced, 180; Vanderhoef (UC Davis), 55, 163; Yang (UC Santa Barbara), 177. *See also* Atkinson, Richard C.—UCSD chancellorship
chaos theory, 17, 156
Chauncey, Henry, 119–20
Chávez, César, 183
Chavez, Lydia, 193n14
Chicago Tribune, 24
China, 27–28, 141
Chiron Company, 108
Chronicle of Higher Education, 115–16, 131
Cicerone, Ralph J., 179
CITRIS (California Institute for Information Technology Research in Interest of Society), 110–11, 181, 182
Citrus Experiment Station, Riverside, 164, 165
civil rights movement (1960s), 41
Clark, Frank, 59
Clarke, Richard, 73–76, 78–79, 83
Clinton, Bill, 9, 107, 140, 142
Clinton, Hillary, 36*fig.* 4
The Closing of the American Mind (Bloom), 16
CNN, 116

CNSI (California NanoSystems Institute), 110–11, 181, 182
Coalition to Defend Affirmative Action by Any Means Necessary, 87
Cohen, Michael D., 156
cold war, 142, 146, 150, 155
Cole, Jonathan R., 25–26
Cole, Stephen, 25–26
collective bargaining, 67–68, 170
College Board: Commission on New Possibilities for the Admissions Testing Program, 127; ETS, 116–17, 119, 120, 122–23; tests, 116–27, 129, 130–37, 183
College Entrance Examination Board, 118
College of California, 180
Columbia University, 166–67
Commission on New Possibilities for the Admissions Testing Program, College Board, 127
Commission on the Future of Medical Education, 178
Commission on the Growth and Support of Graduate Education, UC, 182
Commission on the Humanities, UC, 180
Committee on Student Preparation, UC, 195n13
community colleges: funding competition with UC, 164; Master Plan, 39; outreach programs, 78, 81, 176; student transfer to UC from, 88, 184, 194n7
compensation policies and practices: deferred compensation, 12; executive compensation debacle, 2, 11, 59, 162. See also benefits; income; salaries
comprehensive review, 95–96, 129, 197n5; Academic Senate and, 87, 89, 90–91, 97–98, 116, 158, 176, 183, 185, 197n5
Comprehensive Test Ban Treaty, 140
Computer Curriculum Corporation, 21, 102
computers: computer-assisted instruction, 20–21, 72, 101; defense laboratories, 140; early stage of development, 18. See also Internet
computer science enrollments, 108, 179
Conant, James B., 119
Congress. See US Congress
Conlan, John, 24–25
CONNECT, 198n15; UCSD, x, 105, 111
Connerly, Ward: anti-affirmative action, 4–9, 11, 43–45, 48–52, 59, 98; Coalition to Defend Affirmative Action by Any Means Necessary protesting, 87; division of responsibility between Regents and administration, 51–52; domestic partner benefits, 67; outreach

programs in K–12 public schools, 70, 74; SAT proposal, 130; SP-1 and SP-2 repeal, 88, 89–90, 90fig. 5
Consortium for Education Network Initiatives in California (CENIC), 178
Constitution, California, 91–92, 98–99
Contra Costa Academy, 180
Cook, Mr. and Mrs. Jerry and son James, 3–4, 6, 11
copyright, 113. See also patents
Cordova, France, 183
Council for Advancement and Support of Education, 182
Council of Economic Advisers, President Clinton's, 107
counterintelligence, defense laboratories, 140, 142, 143
Cowan, Michael, 90, 130, 197n5
Cresap, McCormick, and Paget study (1959), 163
crisis management, Atkinson at NSF, 23–24, 25–26
Crouse, James, 123, 135
Crutzen, Paul, 177
cybersecurity, 142

Daily Nexus, 194n15
Darby, Michael R., 199–200n30
Darling, Bruce, xv, 88–91, 144, 184
Davies, John, 8, 43, 44, 45, 87, 97
Davis: University Farm, 164, 165. See also UC Davis
Davis, Angela, 33
Davis, Gray, 65, 108; Advisory Group on Low-Level Radioactive Waste Disposal, 181; Bagley-Keene Act amendment, 194n15; Brown's chief of staff, 65, 103–4; California Institutes for Science and Innovation, x, 110–11, 157, 181–82, 183, 200n35; Education Transition Group, 80, 180; and ELC, 97; Internet2 link between California and Mexico, 182; K–12 school reform, 65, 80–82, 129; RE-28, 91; recall election, 156; Regent nominees, 86; UC funding, 180, 181, 184; UC partnership agreement, 62, 180, 181; union support, 67
Debas, Haile T., 178
decentralization, UC organization, 159, 162–72
defense and aerospace industries, collapse, 2
defense laboratories, 139–55, 204n20; Advisory Committee on the University's Relations with the Department of Energy Laboratories,

139; competition for contracts, x, 145–47, 151–54, 205n27; Congress and, x, 139–40, 142, 143, 145, 148, 150, 151, 154, 155, 184; contracts, x, 145–47, 151–54, 178, 182, 203n11, 205n27; counterintelligence, 140, 142, 143; DOE-UC mutuality, 147, 152–53; faculty and, x, 148–50, 152, 153; funding, 147, 187; GOCO (Government-owned, Contractor-Operated), 154; GOGO (Government Owned, Government Operated), 154; House Subcommittee on Oversight and Investigations, 139, 155, 184; management issues, 141–55, 157, 181, 203nn3,6; National Nuclear Security Administration (NNSA), 203n3; Regents' Committee on Oversight, 152, 203n11; Rudman report, 141, 203n3; scientists, x, 140–41, 146, 147, 155, 180; security, 139–44, 154; UC management as public service, 146, 147, 148, 151, 153, 155; UC Nuclear Weapons Labs Conversion Project, 204n16. *See also* Lawrence Berkeley National Laboratory (LBNL); Lawrence Livermore National Laboratory (LLNL); Los Alamos National Laboratory (LANL)

Deng Xiaoping, 27

Department of Psychology: Stanford University, 19, 20; UC San Diego (UCSD), 34

Deukmejian, George, 11, 49

Deutsch, Monroe, 166

Diamond, Nancy, 178

Digital Library, UC, 157, 179

diversity policy: California legislature, 7, 83, 93–94, 98, 197n9; testing and, 128; Wilson, 8. *See also* race and ethnicity; UC diversity policy

DOE. *See* US Department of Energy

Domenici, Pete, 145

domestic partner benefits, 66–67, 179

Donald Bren School of Environmental Science and Management, UC Santa Barbara, 179

Douglass, John Aubrey, 41

Drake, Michael, 5–6

Drucker, Peter, 107

Dual Admissions Plan, 115–16, 182

Dynes, Robert C., 153, 177, 184

Early Academic Outreach Program (EAOP), 78

earthquakes, UCSD lab, 36–37

Ebbinghaus, Hermann, 21

economics: admission policies and, 39, 50; financial aid programs, 170, 186; research grant

programs, 170. *See also* budgets; economy; funding; income; markets; salaries

economy: California, 62, 65, 80, 103–4, 108, 114, 158, 172, 182, 184; international cataclysm (2008), 162; Japan, 103; knowledge, 107; New Economy, 107; prosperity (1990s), 65; R&D role, 103, 108; reinventing, 100–114; San Diego, 34, 37, 100–101, 104; technology sector, 34, 37, 62, 65, 100–101, 107–11, 158; US (1970s), 103; US recession (1980s), 104, 106; US recession (1990s), 106; US since World War II, 107. *See also* industry

Education Abroad Program: India, 183; Israel, 183

educational disadvantage, ix, 75–76, 85, 97, 195n11

Educational Testing Service (ETS), 116–17, 119, 120, 122–23

Education Transition Group, Gray Davis's, 80, 180

ELC (Eligibility in Local Context), 94–97, 115–16, 158, 180, 182

electronics industry: California, 109; CalREN-2, 178; and copyright, 113. *See also* computers

Elias Technologies, Inc., 185

Eligibility in Local Context (ELC), 94–97, 115–16, 158, 180, 182

employment: affirmative action, 1, 6, 8; RE-28, 89–92, 175–76; UC Institute for Labor and Employment, 181. *See also* jobs; labor relations issues; SP-2 (anti-affirmative action for employment)

"Endogenous Technological Change" (Romer), 107–8

engineering: Atkinson presidency, 108, 179; foundational discipline for technical enterprises, 105; MESA (Mathematics, Engineering, Science, Achievement), 78; National Academies of Science and Engineering and the Institute of Medicine, 125; NSF and, 27; Terman study on supply and demand (1960s), 199n17; UC Engineering Initiative, 179

English Language Development Professional Institutes, 81

enrollments, UC, 186, 194n7; allocation of funding to campuses, 63–65; budget and, 35, 63–64, 158; minorities, 7–8, 11, 38, 39, 84, 95, 98, 122, 188; outreach programs and, 82–83, 84; Sproul era (1948), 167; Tidal Wave I (1960s), 60; Tidal Wave II (1998–99), 60–61, 64, 65, 179; UCSD, 35, 37. *See also* admissions

Enron Corporation, 183

entrepreneurship, xiv; academic, 102, 103–6, 109–12, 113–14, 169, 172; CONNECT, x, 105, 111, 198n15; IUCRP spurring, 109. *See also* industry

environmental issues: DOE and, 150–51; UC program, 179

eScholarship Repository, UC, 158

espionage, defense laboratories, x, 140–41

Estes, William K., 18, 19, 20

ETS. *See* Educational Testing Service

executive compensation debacle, 11, 59, 162

Extension, UC, 157; UCSD, 100, 104–5

faculty: admission policies, ix, 7, 40–41, 47–48, 87–98, 115–16, 124–26, 130–34, 137–38, 176, 193n8, 197n5; American Association of University Professors (AAUP), 40–41, 46, 192–93n4; anti-affirmative action opinion poll, 41; campus academic senates, 40, 134; and defense laboratories, x, 148–50, 152, 153; Faculty Code of Conduct, 184; industry collaboration policies, 113–14; Nobel Laureates, 62, 177, 179, 180, 181, 182; outreach involvement, 72, 79, 85; salaries, 65, 186; Sproul era (1948), 167; Task Force on Undergraduate Admissions Criteria, 94; and tests, 98, 116, 120, 124, 130–35, 137–38, 182, 202n28. *See also* Academic Senate

Faculty Committee to Rescind SP-1 and SP-2 (FCRS P), 40

fairness: anti-affirmative action, 9, 97, 125–26; testing, 125–26, 129

FairTest, 132

Fang Yi, 27–28

Federal Bureau of Investigation (FBI), and defense laboratories, 140–41, 142, 143, 145

federal funding: National Institutes of Health, 65; science and research, 20, 24–27, 102–3, 187; Scripps, 29

federal government: and defense laboratories, 139; UC Office of Federal Governmental Relations, 179. *See also* defense laboratories; federal funding; US

federalism, UC organization modeled after, 167

fees, UC students, 3, 184, 186, 194n11

"felicific calculus," 16

finance. *See* economics; income

financial aid programs, 170, 186

Fong, Justin, 87, 91

Ford, Gerald, 26

Fort Ord, California, 18

Fox, Vicente, 182

Frazer, William R., 31, 195n13

funding: defense laboratories, 147, 187; industry funding research, 105–6, 191n22; IUCRP, 109; MESA, 78; NSF, 24–27, 28, 65; outreach programs, 78–85, 158, 186; research, 20, 24–27, 65, 102, 105–6, 108, 110, 111, 187, 191n22; UCSD, 35, 105; Wilson presidential campaign, 190n13. *See also* budgets; California funding of UC budget; federal funding

Galligani, Dennis, 75–76, 95–96

"A Garbage Can Model of Organizational Choice" (Cohen, March, and Olsen), 156

Garcia, Eugene, 121–22

Gardner, David P., 58, 159; and affirmative action, xiii–xiv, 2, 3; and Atkinson lawsuit, 190n14; Commission on New Possibilities for the Admissions Testing Program, 127; and defense laboratories, 146, 148, 152; and executive compensation debacle, 2; first Regents' meeting, 57; indirect cost funds to campuses, 63; Pelfrey work with, xiii; school improvement outreach, 76–77; South African stock divestment, 11; and UC organization, 163

Gee, Gordon, 12

Geiser, Saul, xv, 94, 127–28, 132–33, 134, 137

General Accounting Office (GAO): and defense laboratories, 140; and NSF, 25

Gilman, Daniel Coit, viii, 205n2

Golden Fleece Awards, 23–24, 191n19

Golden State examination, 122

The Gold and the Blue (Kerr), 38, 54, 205n2

Gomez, Edward, 43

Gómez, Manuel, 83, 84–85

Goodlad, John, 195n13

Gore, Al, 117, 142

Gorton, Gary, 162

Gould, Stephen Jay, 118

governors, California, 66–68; Jerry Brown, 65, 103–4; Edmund G. Brown, 198n12; Deukmejian, 11, 49; Republican, 49; Schwarzenegger, 59, 156; UC's constitutional autonomy and, 99. *See also* Davis, Gray; Wilson, Pete

grades: admission policies and SP-1 and, 93, 97, 124, 128, 138; tests and, 122–23, 127–28, 132–33, 136

Graham, Hugh, 178

Gratz v. Bollinger, 125

Greenspan, Alan, 107

Greenwood, M. R. C., 177

Grutter v. Bollinger, 125
Guidelines on University Industry Relations
    (1989), 113

Hackerman, Norm, 23
happiness, quantifying, 16
Hart, Gary, 80–82
Harvard: Harvard/MIT Radio Research Labora-
    tory, 19, 101; industry-university research,
    112; President Bok, 127, 200n42; President
    Conant, 119–20; tests, 119–20, 121
Hayashi, Pat, xv, 126–27, 134
health benefits: domestic partner, 66, 179; man-
    datory insurance for students, 181
health care marketplace, xiv, 178, 180, 181
health sciences: research grant programs, 170.
    See also medical schools, UC
Hecker, Siegfried, 142
Heeger, Alan J., 181
Hershman, Larry, xv, 82
Hertzberg, Bob, 90–91
Hewlett Packard, 104
Heyman, Ira Michael, 104, 112
Heyns, Roger, 38, 52
Higher Education Employer-Employee Relations
    Act (1979), 68
Hilgard, Ernest, 20, 191n11
Hitch, Charles J., xiii, 71
Hixon Symposium, 17
holidays, UC, 181, 183
Holst, James, xv, 45, 47, 67, 74
Hopkinson, Judith, 88, 92
Hopwood v. Texas, 125
Hughes, Teresa, 93–94, 97
humanities: Commission on the Humanities,
    180; Humanities Research Institute, UC, 180
"Human Memory: A Proposed System and Its
    Control Processes" (Atkinson and Shiffrin),
    23
HumRRO (Human Resources Research Organi-
    zation), 18
Hutchins, Robert Maynard, viii, 16
Hybritech, Inc., 106

IBM, 21
Iglehart, Judith, xv
Ignarro, Louis J., 180
immigrants: anti-immigrant sentiment, 2, 4–5;
    Atkinson parents, 15; K–12 minorities, 70;
    Proposition 187, 2, 4–5
inauguration, presidential, declined, 159, 160

income: academically poorest schools, 76;
    admissions based on, 39, 50, 185. *See also*
    compensation policies and practices; salaries
India, Education Abroad Program, 183
Indiana University, 18
individualism, San Diego, 100
industry: CCII, 104, 110, 198n12; defense and
    aerospace industries, 2; funding research,
    105–6, 191n22; "Winning Technologies: A
    New Industrial Strategy for California and
    the Nation" (CCII), 104. *See also* entrepre-
    neurship; technology
industry-university collaborations, 108–14,
    157; accountability, 113, 200n35; Board on
    Research and Economic Development, 178;
    compliance to policies, 114; and government
    collaboration, x, 109–12, 114; Guidelines on
    University Industry Relations (1989), 113;
    Industry-University Cooperative Research
    Program (IUCRP), 109–10, 111, 114, 177, 178;
    Mexico-UC programs, 182; NSF, 26–27, 109;
    one-university concept and, 169; policy
    framework, 112–14; President's Retreat
    on UC's Relationships with Industry in
    Research and Technology Transfer (UCLA,
    January 1997), 113, 178; Stanford/Fred Ter-
    man, x, 37, 100, 101–2, 103, 106, 157; "star"
    scientists, 108, 199–200n30; UCSD, x, 101,
    103–6, 111, 157. *See also* technology
Institute for Complex Adaptive Matter, 183
Institute for Education Reform, Sacramento
    State University, 80
Institute for Labor and Employment, UC, 181
Institute of Medicine, 125
intellectual property rights, 113
intelligence testing, 20, 117–20, 121, 123, 137
International Atomic Energy Agency, 155
Internet, 111, 113; Digital Library, 157, 179;
    eScholarship Repository, 158; Internet2
    link between California and Mexico, 182;
    Pathways, 179
Introduction to Psychology (Atkinsons and Hil-
    gard), 20, 191n11
IQ tests, 20, 117–20, 121, 123, 137
Irvine. *See* UC Irvine
Israel, Education Abroad Program, 183
IUCRP (Industry-University Cooperative Re-
    search Program), 109–10, 111, 114, 177, 178

Jackson, Jesse, 9–10, 10*fig. 1*
James, William, 21–22

Japan, 103, 104, 109
Jendresen, Malcolm, 150
Jernigan, Ruth, 104
Jews, Harvard enrollment, 119
jobs: California, 2, 62. *See also* employment;
    labor relations issues
Jobs, Steve, 104
Johnson, Odessa, 92
Johnson, Sue, 117

K-12 public schools, California, ix, 69-85, 158;
    crisis, 69-70; ELC, 94-95, 96-97, 115-16, 158,
    180, 182; "initiative fatigue," 77; minorities,
    39, 49-50, 70; partnerships with individual
    campuses, 76-84; reform programs, 65,
    79-85, 129; state's educational hierarchy over,
    83; UC admissions policies and, 71, 115-16,
    129, 158. *See also* outreach programs in K-12
    public schools
Kaiser, Henry J., 54-55
Kaiser Center, 54-55
Kennedy, Bobby, 26
Kennedy, Donald, 112
Kennedy, Ted, 26
Kennedy, V. Wayne, xv, 32, 113
Kennedy family, 26, 29
Kerr, Clark, xiv, 31-32, 57, 159, 207n32; de-
    centralization, 162-70; firing, 99; Godkin
    Lectures, 102; *The Gold and the Blue*, 38,
    54, 205n2; inauguration at UCLA (1958),
    167; one-university concept, x-xi, 168-69;
    shared governance, 46; Tidal Wave I, 60; UC
    Berkeley chancellorship, 167, 207n32; UC
    presidents leaving under less than friendly
    circumstances, 157, 205n2; *The Uses of the
    University*, xiv
Khachigian, Meredith, 79
Kindred Spirit, FBI, 141
King, C. Judson, xv, 73-76, 78-79, 94, 95-96
knowledge, role in contemporary life, 106-7
Kohn, Walter, 180
Korean War, 146
Koret Foundation, xv
Kroemer, Herbert, 181
Kuckuck, Robert, xv

labor relations issues: UC, 68. *See also* collective
    bargaining; employment; jobs; unionization
Laird, Bob, 131
Lashley, Karl, 17

Latinos: Latino Caucus, 87, 90; Latino Eligibil-
    ity Task Force, 122; Puente Program starting
    with, 78; and SAT, 90, 121-22, 132; vs. SP-1,
    87; UC admission figures, 39, 84
Laughlin, Robert B., 180
Lawrence, Ernest O., 146, 155
Lawrence Berkeley National Laboratory
    (LBNL), 141, 147; contract, 178, 205n27;
    Tiger Team inspection, 151; World War II,
    203n12
Lawrence Livermore National Laboratory
    (LLNL), vii, x, 99, 139-40, 146-49, 157,
    204n20; Anastasio as director, 183; contract,
    153, 178, 182; fiftieth anniversary, 183; model-
    ing and computer simulation, 155; Nobel for
    scientists, 180; security, 143, 154
Layton, John, 144
learning process: mathematical models of, 18-23;
    technologies, 178; tests and, 121
Lee, Wen Ho, x, 140-41, 142, 153, 181
legislatures: Assembly of the Academic Senate,
    130, 183. *See also* California legislature; US
    Congress
Leiman, Arnold, 46
Lemann, Nicholas, 135, 136
Lerner, Richard, 110
Levin, Judith, 43
libraries: New York Public Library, 35-36; UC
    Digital Library, 157, 179; UC Librarian, 179;
    UCSD Library Walk, 33
Lick Observatory, Mount Hamilton, 164, 165
Life magazine, 21
Livermore lab. *See* Lawrence Livermore National
    Laboratory (LLNL)
Lohman, David E., 115
Loma Prieta temblor (1989), 37
Los Alamos National Laboratory (LANL), vii, x,
    99, 142, 146-49, 157, 177, 204n20; Atkinson-
    appointed special review team (2002), 144,
    184; Cerro Grande wildfire closure, 143, 144,
    181; contract, 145-46, 153, 178, 182; Director
    George P. Nanos, 144, 184; Director John
    Browne, 139-40, 142, 144, 179, 184; experi-
    mental science, 155; Lee case, x, 140-41, 142,
    181; missing hard drives, 143, 181; Mustang
    incident, 144-45; procurement practices,
    144-45; Reed visits, 153; security, 142-44,
    154; sixtieth anniversary (April 2003), 145;
    X Division, 140
Los Angeles. *See* UCLA

Los Angeles Times: Atkinson speech vs. SAT, 116; Gardner on Atkinson lawsuit, 190n14; Pelta-son retirement, 12; presidential search committee, 29; Regents' meeting on affirmative action (July 1995), 10*fig. 1;* SP-1 implementation, 44–45; SP-1 rescinding (2001), 90*fig. 5,* 91*fig. 6;* "UC Regents Defy Wilson, OK Gay Partner Benefits," 67; Wilson on diversity, 8
loyalty oath controversy, UC, 99
Lucier, Richard, 179
Lytle, Cecil, 79

Man: A Course of Study (MACOS), 24–25
Manhattan Project, 71, 147
Mansfield, Edwin, 108
Mao Zedong, 27
March, James G., 156, 172
Marcuse, Herbert, 33, 34
markets: health care, xiv, 178, 180, 181; and institutions, 172; technology, 107–8. *See also* economics
Markov Learning Models for Multi-person Inter-actions (Atkinson and Suppes), 20
Massey, Walter, 1, 12
Master of Advanced Study, 157, 180
Master Plan for Higher Education (1960), 55, 124; admission policies, 2, 39, 50, 52–53, 94, 121, 124
"mathematical biophysics," Atkinson theory, 16–17
mathematics: Atkinson, viii, 16–17, 18–23, 121; Indiana University, 18; MESA (Mathematics, Engineering, Science, Achievement), 78; in psychology, 19–23; Stanford, viii, 19; tests, 123, 131, 134, 136, 137; University of Chicago, 16–17
McCulloch, Warren, 17
McElroy, Bill, 30–31, 32, 34, 37
McFadden, Daniel L., 181
McGill, Bill, 30, 33–34, 37
McNealy, Scott, 117
McPherson, Rene, 104
medical schools, UC: anti-affirmative action, 4–5; Commission on the Future of Medical Education, 178; Davis, 1, 5; health care marketplace, xiv, 178, 180, 181; Medical Student Diversity Task Force, 180; minorities, 4–6, 180; San Diego, 4. *See also* UC San Francisco (UCSF)
Mellichamp, Duncan, 66

memory, human, Atkinson's mathematical models, 21–23
Merced. *See* UC Merced
MESA (Mathematics, Engineering, Science, Achievement), 78
Mexico: California commerce and education relations, 180; Internet2 link with California, 182; National Council on Science and Technology (CONACYT), 178, 182
MICRO, 109
Microelectronics and Computer Consortium, 104
Microsoft Corporation, 184
minorities: academically poorest schools, 75–76; achievement gap, 38–39; Brentwood Elementary School, 21; California population, 1–2; California's K–12 public schools, 39, 49–50, 70; Cooks' data, 4; Eligibility in Local Context (ELC), 95; enrollments, 7–8, 11, 38, 39, 84, 95, 98, 122, 188; population expansion statewide, 98; and tests, 90, 121–22, 128, 132–33; UC medical schools, 4–6, 180; and UC public image for anti-affirmative action, 42. *See also* affirmative action; diversity policy; Latinos; outreach programs in K–12 public schools; race and ethnicity
The Mismeasure of Man (Gould), 118
MIT: industry-university research, 112; NRC ranking, 61; Fred Terman and MIT/Harvard Radio Research Laboratory, 19, 101
Molloy, Tim, 194n15
Monitor Group, 162–63, 206n10
Montoya, Velma, 59, 67
Moores, John, 110
Morrison, Gary, 5
Morrison, Robert, 90*fig. 5*
Mount Hamilton, Lick Observatory, 164, 165
Mowery, David C., 191n22
Murphy, Franklin, 167–68
Mustang incident, LANL, 144–45
"Myths and Tradeoffs: the Role of Tests in Undergraduate Admissions" (NRC, 1999), 115, 125, 128

Nanos, George P., 144, 184
National Academies of Science and Engineering and the Institute of Medicine, 125
National Academy of Sciences, 19–20, 21, 126; Atkinson post-presidential life, 160; Board

National Academy of Sciences (*continued*)
on Testing and Assessment (BOTA), 122, 123, 125; defense laboratories security, 143; Division of Behavioral and Social Sciences and Education, 160
National Assessment of Educational Progress, 70
National Association for College Admissions Counseling, 137
National Council on Science and Technology (CONACYT), UC and Mexico, 178, 182
National Institutes of Health, 65
National Nuclear Security Administration (NNSA), 203n3
National Research Council (NRC): studies of graduate program quality, 36, 61–62, 169, 177; studies of testing, 115, 125–26, 128
National Scholarship Program, 119–20
National Science Board, 23, 26, 27, 30, 184
National Science Foundation (NSF), 198n6; basic research, 26, 30–31; funding, 24–27, 28, 65; Golden Fleece Awards, 23–24, 191n19; and patents, 26–27, 178; peer review, 25–26, 28; physics community and, 25, 26, 29; R&D role in economy, 108; science education curricula, 24, 25; UCSD and, 30, 105; university-industry collaboration, 26–27, 109. *See also* Atkinson, Richard C.—NSF director (1977–80)
National Semiconductor Corporation, 104
National Writing Project (NWP), 80
A Nation at Risk, 76–77
navy: Atkinson association, 18, 190–91n5; Naval Postgraduate School (NPS), 18, 190–91n5; San Diego, 34
NBC, 9
Neumann, John von, 17
New Economy, 107
New Growth Theory, 107–8
Newsweek, 117
New York Public Library, presidency, 35–36
New York Times, x, 116, 140–41
Nierenberg, Bill, 30
9/11 (2001), 132, 182
Nixon, Richard, 27, 28
Nobel Laureates: scientists at defense laboratories, x, 146, 155, 180; UC faculty, 62, 177, 179, 180, 181, 182; Watson, 16
None of the Above (Owen), 135
Norman, D. A., 23
NRC. *See* National Research Council

nuclear weapons, 140, 204n20; atomic bomb, 15, 141, 146; Comprehensive Test Ban Treaty, 140; declining industry, 154–55; Lee work with, 140–41, 181; security, 139–44; UC involvement with, 142, 146–47, 149, 150, 151, 152, 154. *See also* defense laboratories

Oakland: Atkinson apartment, 45; Oakland Technical High School, 78; UCOP, 54, 177
Obama administration, DOE, 155
Obley, Debora, xv
Office of Federal Governmental Relations, 179
Office of President. *See* presidency, UC; UC Office of President (UCOP)
Ohio State University, Gee, 12
Olsen, Johan P., 156
one-university concept, x–xi, 62, 114, 161–72
Organic Act (1868), 98, 197n9
organization: UC administrative, 47, 50, 51, 55–56, 59, 156, 159, 162–72, 206n10; UCSD structure, 31, 32. *See also* shared governance
outreach programs in K–12 public schools, ix, 49–50, 70–85, 158; accountability problem, 83–84; and educational disadvantage, ix, 75–76, 85, 195n11; funding, 78–85, 158, 186, 194n11; partnerships between schools and individual campuses, 76–84; Regents and, 79, 82–83, 87, 88, 176, 178, 179; school performance basis for, 76–79; Strategic Review Panel on UC Educational Outreach, 84; tests and, 129; UC history of, 75. *See also* Outreach Task Force (OTF)
Outreach Task Force (OTF), 70–79, 85, 129; Hart, 80–82; report, 69, 71, 79, 84, 178, 179, 195n11, 196n16
Owen, David, 135
Oxbridge model, 34–35

Pacific Gas and Electric Company, Clarke, 73
Packard, David, 100, 104
Pajaro Dunes conference, 112–13
Paramount Corporation, 21
Parker, James, 141
partnerships: K–12 schools with individual campuses, 76–84; UC-state budgetary, 62, 180, 181, 206n3. *See also* industry-university collaborations
patents: industry-university collaborations, 26–27, 106, 113–14; Japan, 103; Microsoft Corporation sued by UC for patent

infringement, 2184; rights, 26–27, 106; UC research, 26–27, 106, 178
Peck, Judy, xv
peer review: IUCRP, 109; NSF, 25–26, 28
Pelfrey, Bob, xv
Pelfrey, David, xv
Pelfrey, Matthew, xv
Peltason, Jack W., 11, 58; administrative organization, 51, 163, 171; and affirmative action, 5–11, 49, 93, 98, 99, 193n6; appointment as president, 12–13; chancellor at Irvine, 11; and patents, 113; Pelfrey work with, xiii; relations with Regents, 57; retirement as president, viii, 12
Penhoet, Ed, 108
Perry, Dorothy, 124–25, 130, 134
Peters, Darrilyn, xv
Peters, Paula, xv
Pierce's Disease Task Force, 180
Pister, Karl, vii–xi, xv; as Academic Senate Chair, 31–32, 79; Chancellor Emeritus (UC Santa Cruz), xi, 79; outreach leadership, 79, 82–83, 179; UC Berkeley, vii, 31–32, 79
Pittsburg High, Eligibility in Local Context (ELC), 95
Policy Analysis for California Education (PACE), 70
politics: California, 66; domestic partner benefits, 66–67; Republican, 49; of scarcity, 171; SP-1 demise, 86, 92; UC administration avoiding, 98–99, 197n12; Wilson presidential campaign, 4–5, 9, 48, 49, 66, 190n13. See also affirmative action; governors; labor relations; legislatures; protests; voters
Polkinghorn, Robert, 69
polygraph testing, defense laboratories, 143
predictive validity, SAT, 127–28, 132–33, 136–37
"Preparing for the Twenty-First Century," 179
presidency, UC, 157, 205n2, 207n32; authority of, ix, 59–60, 166; day-to-day responsibilities, 159; Dynes, 153, 184; Gilman, viii, 205n2; Hitch, xiii, 71; inauguration declined, 159, 160; internal constituencies (faculty, chancellors, Regents), 56–57; residence, 45, 165; role, xiv; symbolic aspect, 159–60, 165, 168, 170; Yudof, 163. See also Atkinson, Richard C.—UC presidency; Gardner, David P.; Kerr, Clark; Peltason, Jack W.; Saxon, David S.; Sproul, Robert Gordon; UC Office of President (UCOP)

President's Commission on Agriculture and Natural Resources, 179
President's Foreign Intelligence Advisory Board, 141
President's Retreat on UC's Relationships with Industry in Research and Technology Transfer (UCLA, January 1997), 113, 178
Press, Frank, 27–28
Princeton Review, 125
Princeton University, 118, 120, 159
Principal Leadership Institutes, 81–82, 84
Principles of Psychology (Atkinson), 21–22
Pringle, Curt, 45
Program Review Committee for Education, UC, 195n13
Project on Government Oversight, 204n16
Proposition 98, 70, 80
Proposition 187, 2, 4–5
Proposition 209, 85, 127; anti-affirmative action, 7, 52, 88, 190n10, 193n14; Clarke supporting, 73; diversity made more difficult by, 98; ELC and, 96–97; fairness, 125; minority enrollments after, 84; in RE-28, 176
protests: vs. anti-affirmative action, 10; Coalition to Defend Affirmative Action by Any Means Necessary, 87; defense laboratories, x, 150; RE-28, 91; San Diego, 33–34
Proxmire, William, 23–24, 28, 191n19
Prusiner, Stanley, 179
psychology: American, 17–18; Atkinson's most fundamental contribution, 21–22; and Atkinson's presidential style, 58; behaviorism, 17, 18; cognitive revolution, 17; experimental, viii, 18, 23, 34; mathematical, 19–23; neuroimagery research, 23; testing, 20, 117–20. See also Department of Psychology
psychometrics, 121
Public Administration Survey, 167
public employee unions, 67–68
Public School Accountability Act (1999), 80
publishing, digital, 157–58
Puente Program, 78
Pulaski, Art, 68
Pusser, Brian, 98–99, 190n12

QB3 (California Institute for Quantitative Biomedical Sciences), 110–11, 181
QUALCOMM, 106

Rabi, I. I., 26

race and ethnicity: admissions practices, 1–12, 14, 38, 95, 97, 98; ballot initiative Classification by Race, Ethnicity, Color, or National Origin (2003), 184; California's schoolchildren compared with voters, 70; Harvard enrollment, 119. *See also* affirmative action; Asians; diversity policy; immigrants; minorities; Proposition 209

radar, MIT/Harvard Radio Research Laboratory, 19, 101

radioactive waste, Advisory Group on Low-Level Radioactive Waste Disposal, 181

RAND report, minority students finding UC unwelcoming, 78

Rashevsky, Nicolas, 16–17

RCA, 110

RE-28, 89–92, 175–76, 182

reading, outreach programs, 80–81

Reading Professional Development Institutes, 81

Reagan, Ronald, 76–77

Reed, Patrick, 145, 153, 184

Regents. *See* Board of Regents

Regents of the University of California v. Bakke, 1–2, 9

regional college movement, 164

Reines, Frederick, 177

Republicans: governors, 49; Regents, 49

research: agricultural, 164; basic, 26, 30–31; California history, 180; defense laboratories, 150, 154; funding, 20, 24–27, 65, 102, 105–6, 110, 111, 187, 191n22; grant programs, 170; patents, 26–27, 106, 178; Pierce's Disease Task Force, 180; private, 105–6; UC expansion, vii. *See also* industry-university collaborations; research universities; science; technology

Research Applied to National Needs (RANN), 27

research universities, 100, 178; AAU membership, 323; federal funding, 102–3; knowledge value and applications, 106–7; marketplace role, 172; NRC rankings, 62; and technology sector, 26–27, 100–111; UC as collection of, 159, 161; UC history, 55; UCSD status among, 29, 36, 37. *See also* industry-university collaborations

"The Research University and the Development of High-Technology Centers in the United States" (Smilor, 2007), 100

retirement: Atkinson as president, 156, 160, 183, 185; UC system, 170

Revelle, Roger, 29–30

Richardson, Bill, 142–43, 203n3

Riesman, David, 16

The Rise of American Research Universities (Graham and Diamond), 178

Riverside: Citrus Experiment Station, 164, 165. *See also* UC Riverside

Robb, Agnes Roddy, 165

Romer, Paul, 107–8

Roosevelt, David P., Roosevelt College dedication (UCSD, 1995), 36*fig. 4*

Roosevelt, Franklin, 102

Roosevelt, Teddy, 100

Roper Center for Public Opinion Research, University of Connecticut, 41

Rowland, F. Sherwood, 177

Rudman, Warren, 141, 203n3

Russell, Richard, 196n16

Russia. *See* Soviet Union

Russian scientists, 140

Sacks, Peter, 135

Sacramento Bee, 12, 13, 55, 89–90

Sacramento State University, Institute for Education Reform, 80

salaries, 66; chancellors, 65; executive, 11, 12, 59, 162; faculty, 65, 186. *See also* compensation policies and practices; income

Salk Institute for Biological Studies, 100

Sandia National Laboratory, 204n20

San Diego, 33–34; Atkinson support in, 190n14; economy, 34, 37, 100–101, 104; individualism, 100; Regional Economic Development Corporation, 104; technology sector, 34, 37, 100–101, 103–6; unemployment rate (1980s), 104. *See also* Scripps Institution of Oceanography (SIO); UC San Diego (UCSD)

San Diego Union, 34

San Diego Union-Tribune, Roosevelt College dedication (1995), 36*fig. 4*

San Francisco. *See* UC San Francisco (UCSF)

San Francisco Chronicle, Atkinson appointment as UC president, 13*fig. 2*

Santa Barbara. *See* UC Santa Barbara

Santa Cruz. *See* UC Santa Cruz

SAT, 38–39, 76, 115, 120–38; *The Big Test* (Lemann), 135, 136; George W. Bush score, 117; "The Case for Not Scrapping the SAT" (Laird), 131; *The Case against the SAT* (Crouse and Trusheim), 123, 135; coaching effects, 125; critical-reading section, 136–37; and cumulative grade-point average (GPA) scores, 122; Gore score, 117; and graduation rates, 122; history, 119–20; McNealy score, 117; New, 134, 136–37; *None of the Above* (Owen), 135; predictive validity, 127–28, 132–33, 136–37; SAT I, ix, 89–91, 98, 116–17, 120–38, 157, 182, 183, 202n28; SAT II, ix, 120–33, 136–37, 202n28; SAT-R, ix, 134, 137–38; *Standardized Minds* (Sacks), 135; UC, 120–23

Saxon, David S., 58; administrative organization, 169; allocation of funds to campuses, 63; Atkinson as chancellor (UCSD), 29–32; Atkinson's restiveness during lengthy policy discussions, 58; Atkinson as successor (UC presidency), 35; and defense laboratories, 148, 150; endemic excellence, 207n33; inauguration declined by, 160; Pajaro Dunes conference, 112–13; Pelfrey work with, xiii; "Systemwide Leadership," 169

Scholastic Aptitude Test. *See* SAT

Schrag, Peter, xiv, 69

Schwarzenegger, Arnold, 59, 156

science: Atkinson post-presidential life, 160; big, 148; defense laboratories, 141, 143–44, 146, 155; federal funding, 24–27, 28, 102; MESA (Mathematics, Engineering, Science, Achievement), 78; UC Berkeley, 15–16; University of Chicago, 15–16. *See also* health sciences; National Academy of Sciences; National Science Foundation (NSF); research

Science at Its Best, Security at Its Worst (Rudman report), 141, 203n3

Science magazine, Atkinson assessment of computer-assisted instruction, 21

Science, the Endless Frontier (Vannevar Bush), 102, 103

Scientific American, 26

scientists: defense laboratories, x, 140–41, 146, 147, 155, 180; foreign, 140; industry-university collaborations, 199–200n30; Institute for Complex Adaptive Matter, 183; Nobel Laureates, x, 16, 146, 155, 177, 179, 180, 181; "star," 108, 199–200n30

Scripps, E. W., 101

Scripps Institution of Oceanography (SIO), San Diego, 29–30, 100, 101, 164, 165; Lerner, 110

security, defense laboratories, 139–44, 154

SEMATECH, 104

September 11 (2001), 132, 182

Serraino, Pierlugi, 55

shared governance, 31–32, 47, 50, 51–52; Atkinson presidency and, ix, 46–48, 60, 98; FCRSP and, 40; history, 55; RE-28 reaffirming, 182;

SP-1, 46–51, 87, 192–93n4; after SP-1, 98; SP-2, 48–51, 192–93n4

Shaw, Anne, xv

Shiffrin, Richard, 23

Silicon Valley, 102, 103, 104, 107

Simmons, Dan, 40–41, 193n6

Sinsheimer, Robert, 54, 112

60 Minutes, 9

Skinner, B. F., 17, 18

Smilor, Raymond, 100

Smithsonian Institution, Adams as secretary, 29

South Africa, divestment from businesses in, 11, 49, 99

Soviet Union: fall, 172; nuclear weapons, 140, 146–47. *See also* cold war

SP-1 (anti-affirmative action for admissions), viii, ix, 14, 38–53, 59, 68, 156, 173–74, 196n1; Academic Senate and, 38, 40, 42, 47, 50, 173, 193n8; admissions after, 60, 92–99, 125, 126, 127, 158; approved, 1, 9–10, 11, 48–52; ELC and, 96–97; implementation, 42–48, 51–52, 57–58, 156; *Molloy v. Regents, et al.*, 193–94n15; and outreach programs for minorities in K–12 public schools, 70–74, 76, 85, 158; Peltason and, 11, 49, 93, 98, 99; Pister vs., 79; rescinding, 40, 43, 47, 86–92, 90*fig. 5*, 91*fig. 6*, 157, 176, 182; shared governance and, 46–51, 87, 98, 192–93n4; Wilson and, 8–10, 11, 43–45, 48, 49, 58, 66, 79, 190n13, 193–94n15

SP-2 (anti-affirmative action for employment), viii, ix, 43, 174–75, 196n1; approved, 1, 10, 11, 48–52; *Molloy v. Regents, et al.*, 193–94n15; rescinding, 40, 43, 47, 87–90, 92, 176, 182; UCOP and, 98; Wilson and, 66, 190n13

Sporck, Charles, 104

Sproul, Robert Gordon, 159, 164–67, 205n2; administrative organization, 166–69, 170; and defense laboratories, 139, 146; "functional university," 166–67; one-university concept, x–xi, 114, 161–62, 164–69, 171

Stadtman, Verne, 165

Standardized Minds (Sacks), 135

"Standardized Tests and Access to American Universities" (Atkinson Atwell Lecture at ACE, February 2001), 115, 116–17, 126–31, 134–35, 182, 202n28

Stanford-Binet Intelligence Scales, 121

Stanford University: Applied Mathematics and Statistics Laboratory, 20; Atkinson, viii, x, 19–23, 22*fig. 3*, 101–2, 103, 121, 190n5; Business School dean McPherson, 104; Center for

Stanford University (*continued*)
Advanced Study in the Behavioral Sciences, 19; Consortium for Education Network Initiatives in California (CENIC), 178; Department of Psychology, 19, 20; Department of Statistics, 20; economist Paul Romer, 107; Institute for Mathematical Studies in the Social Sciences, 20–21, 22*fig. 3;* President Donald Kennedy, 112; President Gerhard Casper, 180; President Wallace Sterling, 101; quantitative approaches to the social sciences, 20; Lewis Termin in psychological testing, 20, 117–18; tuition rising, 35; UCSF Stanford Health Care, 178, 180, 181. *See also* Terman, Fred

"steeples of excellence" strategy, Terman's, 19, 101

Stever, Guyford, 23, 26

Strategic Review Panel on UC Educational Outreach, 84

Studley, Roger, 132

A Study of American Intelligence (Brigham), 118

Suppes, Patrick, 19, 20–21, 22*fig. 3,* 102

Supreme Court: California, 193n15; US, 1–2, 52, 125

"Systemwide Leadership" (Saxon), 169

Task Force on Alternative Futures for the Department of Energy National Laboratories, 154

Task Force on Undergraduate Admissions Criteria, 94, 96, 97

teacher education: outreach programs, 80–81. *See also* California state teachers' colleges

teaching assistants (TAs), collective bargaining, 68

technology: biotechnology, 108, 110, 112, 114; California, 62, 65, 108, 109–11, 158; copyright issues, 113; Japan, 103, 104; market incentives, 107–8; National Council on Science and Technology (CON ACYT), 178; New Growth Theory, 107–8; research universities and, 26–27, 100–111; San Diego, 34, 37, 100–101, 104; technology transfer, x, 26–27, 103, 105–6, 111, 113–14, 171, 182. *See also* computers; electronics industry; Internet; patents

Terman, Fred, viii, 19, 59; MIT, 19, 101; "steeples of excellence" strategy, 19–20, 101; study on engineering supply and demand (1960s), 199n17; university-industry collaboration, x, 37, 100, 101–2, 103, 106, 157

Terman, Lewis, IQ testing, 20, 117–18, 121

terrorism: 9/11 (2001), 132, 182; UC resources vs., 182

tests, standardized: achievement, 120, 121, 123, 127–31, 133–34, 137–38, 182, 183; ACT, Inc., 132, 134; admissions and, ix, 89–93, 97–98, 115–26, 128, 130–34, 136–38, 182, 183; analogies, 123, 124, 131, 134; aptitude, 115–23, 128–31, 136–37, 182; Atkinson and, 15–16, 115, 116–17, 121–23, 126–37, 157, 182, 202n28; Atkinson's Atwell Lecture "Standardized Tests and Access to American Universities" at ACE (February 2001), 115, 116–17, 126–31, 134–35, 182, 202n28; College Board, 116–27, 129, 130–37, 183; faculty and, 98, 116, 120, 124, 130–35, 137–38, 182, 202n28; fairness, 125–26, 129; Golden State examination, 122; and grades, 122–23, 127–28, 132–33, 136; IQ, 20, 117–20, 121, 123, 137; K–12 statewide, 72; minorities and, 90, 121–22, 128, 132–33; National Academy of Sciences's Board on Testing and Assessment (BOTA), 122, 123, 125; NRC and, 115; Public School Accountability Act (1999) mandating, 80; SP-1 and, 93, 97–98; Stanford-Binet Intelligence Scales, 121; teach-to-the-test mentality, 116. *See also* SAT

Thorndike, E. L., 17

Tidal Wave I, 60

Tidal Wave II, 60–61, 64, 65

Tien, Chang-lin, 9, 43

Tiger Teams, DOE, 151

Time, 117

Tomlinson-Keasey, Carol, 179, 180

Transition Team (1992), 170–71

Tri-Valley CAREs, 204n16

Trow, Martin, 86, 197n12, 207n32

Trusheim, Dale, 123, 135

two-tier system, admission, 87, 96, 171, 182

UC (systemwide), viii; administrative organization, 47, 50, 51, 55–56, 59, 156, 159, 162–72, 206n10; A-G requirements, 133; California's K–12 graduates, 70; California Studies Fellowship Program, 180; Commission on the Growth and Support of Graduate Education, 182; Commission on the Humanities, 180; Committee on Student Preparation, 195n13; Consortium for Education Network Initiatives in California (CENIC), 178; constitutional autonomy, 91–92, 98–99; decentralization, 159, 162–72; engineering programs, 105; Enron-Arthur Andersen lawsuit, 183; eScholarship Repository, 158; executive salaries, 11, 12, 59, 162; Extension, 157; flagship campuses, 158–59; "functional university," 166–67; holidays, 181, 183; Humanities Research Institute, 180; Institute for Labor and Employment, 181; "interrupted development," 169; K–12 outreach, ix, 71–85, 179; loyalty oath controversy, 99; Master of Advanced Study, 157, 180; MICRO, 109; Microsoft Corporation patent infringement suit, 184; National Council on Science and Technology (CONACYT) with Mexico, 178, 182; NRC ranking, 61–62; one-university concept, x–xi, 62, 114, 161–72; "of the people and for the people," viii; Program Review Committee for Education, 195n13; retirement system, 170; in *The Rise of American Research Universities* (Graham and Diamond), 178; SAT, 120–23. *See also* admissions; Board of Regents; faculty; UC budget; UC diversity policy; UC Office of President (UCOP)

UC Berkeley, 55, 165, 169; AAU membership, 33, 169; Agricultural Genomics institute, 181; applications, 3, 9; Bay Area Writing Project, 80; Berdahl chancellorship, 131, 178; Bowker chancellorship, 191n10; budget, 63, 64, 164; chancellorship established, 167; CITRIS, 111, 181, 182; comprehensive review, 96; flagship campus, 158; Garcia as education dean, 121–22; Hayashi, 127; Heyman chancellorship, 104, 112; Heyns chancellorship, 38, 52; Kerr chancellorship, 167, 207n32; Laird as admissions director, 131; MESA launched at, 78; minorities admissions, 39, 98; NRC ranking, 36, 61, 177; outreach programs, 78, 80, 81–82; Pelfrey, xiii; Pister, vii, 31–32, 79; QB3, 111, 181; School of Education, 80; science, 15–16; Sproul presidency, 164, 165. *See also* Lawrence Berkeley National Laboratory (LBNL)

UC budget, 187; allocation of funds to campuses, 63–65, 177–78; Atkinson presidency and, 60–65, 156, 158, 159, 177–78; Berkeley, 63, 64, 164; and collective bargaining, 68; contributions from alumni and friends, 179, 187; decentralization and, 159, 162, 167; downturn (1980s), 30, 35; enrollments and, 35, 63–64, 158; fee increases, 3, 184; indirect cost funds to campuses, 63, 64–65, 177–78; and "interrupted development" of campuses, 169;

licensing revenue, 114; Opportunity Funds, 65; outreach, 79–80, 82; Peltason and, 7; politics of scarcity, 171; Regents' divisions over, 13–14; SP-1 inspiring legislative threats to, 39–40, 89, 92; Sproul era (1948), 167; UCOP, 2, 62–63, 163, 170; UCSD, 32, 35; winter admissions and cuts in (2003), 184. *See also* California funding of UC budget; compensation policies and practices

UC Davis, 164, 165; AAU membership, 159, 169, 178; Agricultural Genomics institute, 181; allocation of enrollment funds to, 64; *Bakke* case, 1–2, 9; CITRIS, 111, 181, 182; Cook case, 4; indirect cost funds, 63; medical school, 1, 5; Simmons, 40, 41; Vanderhoef chancellorship, 55, 163

UC Digital Library, 157, 179

UC diversity policy, 83, 158; Atkinson, 61, 86, 94, 158, 159, 1170; BOARS and, 93–95; California legislature, 7, 83, 93–94, 98, 197n9; multicampus, 159, 170; outreach programs and, 73, 74, 85, 88, 158; RE-28, 182; Regents, 7, 88, 173, 174, 175–76; SP-1 and, 39, 74, 87, 93, 97–98, 158, 174; UCLA School of Law, 39

UC Engineering Initiative, 179

UC Flood and Emergency Resource Task Force, 178

UC Irvine, 169; AAU membership, 159, 169, 178; admission policies, 9; allocation of enrollment funds to, 64; Calit2, 111, 181; Cicerone chancellorship, 179; indirect cost funds, 63; Peltason chancellorship, 11; Systems Biology institute, 181

UCLA, 165, 169, 205n1; AAU membership, 33, 169; All-University Conference on Teaching and Learning Technologies (March 1997), 178; applications, 3, 9; Atkinson, 19, 30; budget, 63, 64; Carnesale chancellorship, 178; chancellorship established at, 167; CNSI, 111, 181, 182; flagship campus, 158; Kerr inaugural remarks (1958), 167; minorities admissions, 39, 98; Murphy chancellorship, 167–68; NRC ranking, 36, 177; opening (1932), 161; outreach programs, 81–82; President's Retreat on UC's Relationships with Industry in Research and Technology Transfer (January 1997), 113, 178; School of Law admissions policies, 39; Sproul presidency, 161, 164, 165

UC Merced: academic planning, 179; Atkinson presidency and, xiv, 157, 179; CITRIS, 111, 181, 182; funding, 65, 183, 195n11; opening,

UC Merced (*continued*)
184; site selection, 60–61; Tomlinson-Keasey positions, 179, 180, 183
UC MEXUS, 182
UC Nuclear Weapons Labs Conversion Project, 204n16
UC Office of President (UCOP): administrative organization, 55–56, 162–64, 168–72, 206nn10,11; allocation of funds to campuses, 63–65, 177–78; and anti-affirmative action, 43, 98; benefits for all retired faculty and staff, 170; budget, 2, 62–63, 163, 170–71; bureaucracy, 55, 162–63; crisis-ridden and disorderly, 59; day-to-day running, 59; decentralization and, 167–70; and defense laboratories, 149, 150, 152, 153; Early Academic Outreach Program (EAOP), 78; "earned delegation," 171; and enrollment declines (1980s), 35; executive compensation debacle, 2, 11, 59, 162; Geiser, 127; industry-university collaborations, 113; Kaiser Center, 55; leaking speech drafts, 116; Opportunity Funds, 65; overhead/indirect costs, 63; and patents, 113; Pelfrey, viii, xiii, xv; protests, x; relocating to 1111 Franklin Street, Oakland, 180; role, 98–99; school improvement outreach programs, 76–78, 81; selective centralization, 171. *See also* presidency, UC
UC President's Council on the National Laboratories, 143, 145, 152
UC Riverside: Agricultural Genomics institute, 181; Citrus Experiment Station, 164, 165; Cordova chancellorship, 183; "interrupted development," 169; Latinos, 122; NRC ranking, 62
UC San Diego (UCSD), 29–30, 101, 169; AAU membership, 33, 169; allocation of enrollment funds to, 64; Atkinson Hall, 160; Atkinson post-presidential life, 160; Atkinson successor, 44; Calit2, 111, 160, 181; Center for Magnetic Recording Research, 105; Center for Molecular Genetics, 105; Center for Wireless Communications, 105–6; charter middle and high school, 81; comprehensive review, 96; Cook case, 4; Department of Psychology, 34; Dynes chancellorship, 177; enrollments, 35, 37; Extension, 100, 104–5; faculty-chancellor relations, 31–32; flags, 34; general campus designation (1960), 29; indirect cost funds, 63; industry collaboration,

x, 101, 103–6, 111, 157; Kerr visit, 31–32; law school attempts, 37; Library Walk, 33; Lytle, 79; McElroy chancellorship, 30–31, 32, 34, 37; McGill chancellorship, 30, 33–34; medical school, 4; neurosciences ranking, 36; NRC ranking, 36, 61–62, 177; oceanography ranking, 36; one-year student retention rate, 34; organizational structure, 31, 32; physical planning, 32–33; Price Center, 32–33; and San Diego high-technology sector, 34, 37, 100–101, 103–6; School of Engineering, 105; Skaggs School of Pharmacy and Pharmaceutical Sciences, 183; status among research universities, 29, 36, 37; tree removal, 33. *See also* Atkinson, Richard C.—UCSD chancellorship
UC San Francisco (UCSF), 5–6, 164, 165; Bishop chancellorship, 179; Debas chancellorship, 178; dental hygiene program, 124; indirect cost funds, 63; Jendresen, 150; Mission Bay site, 178; QB3, 111, 181; RE-28 protests, 91; UCSF Stanford Health Care, 178, 180, 181
UC Santa Barbara, 164; AAU membership, 169; BOARS conference (November 2001), 132; CNSI, 111, 181, 182; Donald Bren School of Environmental Science and Management, 179; "interrupted development," 169; *Molloy v. Regents, et al.*, 193–94n15; NRC ranking, 62; School of Environmental Studies, 179; Yang chancellorship, 177
UC Santa Cruz, 34, 169; CITRIS, 111, 181, 182; Greenwood chancellorship, 177; indirect cost funds, 63; Latinos, 122; NRC ranking, 62; Pister as Chancellor Emeritus, xi, 79; QB3, 111, 181; Sinsheimer chancellorship, 54, 112; undergraduate enrollments (late 1990s and early 2000s), 64
UCSD. *See* UC San Diego
UC Washington Center, 179, 183
unemployment rate, California, 2
unionization, UC employees, 67–68
United Auto Workers (UAW), 68, 104
United Farm Workers, 183
United Kingdom, academic and commercial exchange between California and, 180
United States. *See* US
University of California. *See* UC
University of Chicago: Adams as provost, 29; Atkinson, viii, 15–18, 101, 117, 121; core curriculum, 35; Great Books curriculum, 16; liberal

education, 16; Observation, Interpretation, and Integration class, 16; science, 15–16; and tests, 117, 121; UCSD faculty from, 30
University of Connecticut, Roper Center for Public Opinion Research, 41
University of Delaware, 123
University Farm, Davis, 164, 165
University of Georgia, 137
University of Michigan, 135, 159
University of Southern California: Atkinson interviewing for presidency of, 29; Consortium for Education Network Initiatives in California (CENIC), 178; rising tuition, 35
University of Texas, the Top Ten Percent Program, 94–95
urban crisis program, 71
US Army: Atkinson, 18; IQ tests, 118–19
US Congress: Atomic Energy Commission, 146; and defense laboratories, x, 139–40, 142, 143, 145, 148, 150, 151, 154, 155, 184; and DOE, 154; House Subcommittee on Oversight and Investigations, 139, 155, 184; National Academy of Sciences established by (1863), 160; and NSF, 24–26, 28, 198n6; Senate Subcommittee on Health and Scientific Research, 26
US Department of Energy (DOE), x, 139–44, 204n20; Advisory Committee on the University's Relations with the Department of Energy Laboratories, 139; contracts, x, 145–47, 151–54, 178, 182, 203n11, 205n27; defense laboratories, 134–54, 178; ES&H (environmental safety and health), 151; mutuality with UC, 147, 152–53; National Nuclear Security Administration (NNSA), 203n3; Obama administration, 155; Regents' Committee on Oversight, 152, 203n11; Rudman report, 141, 203n3; Secretary Bill Richardson, 142–43, 203n3; Secretary James Watkins, 146, 150–51; Secretary Spencer Abraham, 145–46; Tiger Teams, 151; undersecretary Linton Brooks, 145–46
The Uses of the University (Kerr), xiv
US Information Agency, 27
US Justice Department, Bush's, 67
US Naval Academy Foundation, 191n5
US Office of Education, 20–21
US Supreme Court, 1–2, 52, 125

Vanderhoef, Larry, 55, 163
Vannevar Bush Award, Atkinson, 184

Veteran's Day (November 11), official UC holiday, 181
Vietnam era, 33–34, 148
"vision of the University in the future," 1, 14
voters, California: vs. ballot initiative Classification by Race, Ethnicity, Color, or National Origin (2003), 184; Proposition 209 misunderstandings, 193n14; race and ethnicity, 70

Walsh, Sean, 44
Walshok, Mary, 100, 104–5
Washington, DC, UC Washington Center, 179, 183
Washington Group International, 153
Washington Post, 28; Broder, 16; Graham, 37
Watkins, Dean, 203n11
Watkins, James, 146, 150–51
Watson, J. B., 17
Watson, James, 16
Waugh, N. C., 23
Widaman, Keith, 125
Wilson, Charles, 178
Wilson, Pete, 10*fig. 1*; anti-affirmative action, 2–11, 43–45, 48, 49, 58, 66, 79, 173, 174, 190n13, 193–94n15; anti-domestic partner benefits, 66–67; presidential campaign, 4–5, 9, 48, 49, 66, 190n13; UC budget, 62, 65, 79
"Winning Technologies: A New Industrial Strategy for California and the Nation" (CCII), 104
World War I, aptitude testing, 117–18
World War II: atomic bomb, 141, 146; Vannevar Bush as president's science advisor, 102; Japan, 103; Lawrence Berkeley National Laboratory (LBNL), 203n12; Fred Terman, 19, 101; UCSD Extension, 105
writing: Atkinson, 16; outreach programs, 80; tests, 123, 131, 134, 136–37

Xerox, 110

Yale University, 120
Yang, Henry, 177
Year of the Monkey (McGill), 33–34
Yoo, John, 67
Yudof, Mark, 163

Zinner, Paul, 148–49, 150
Zucker, Lynne G., 199–200n30

TEXT
10/12.5 Minion Pro
DISPLAY
Minion Pro
COMPOSITOR
BookComp, Inc.
INDEXER
Barbara Roos
PRINTER AND BINDER
IBT Global